EMPLOYMENT AND OPPORTUNITY

By the same author
SOCIOLOGY AND SOCIAL RESEARCH
MOBILITY AND CHANGE IN MODERN SOCIETY

Employment and Opportunity

Geoff Payne
Dean, Faculty of Social Science
Plymouth Polytechnic

© Geoff Payne 1987

All rights reserved. No reproduction, copy or transmission
of this publication may be made without written permission.

No paragraph of this publication may be reproduced, copied
or transmitted save with written permission or in accordance
with the provisions of the Copyright Act 1956 (as amended).

Any person who does any unauthorised act in relation to
this publication may be liable to criminal prosecution and
civil claims for damages.

First published 1987

Published by
THE MACMILLAN PRESS LTD
Houndmills, Basingstoke, Hampshire RG21 2XS
and London
Companies and representatives
throughout the world

Printed in Hong Kong

British Library Cataloguing in Publication Data
Payne, Geoff
Employment and opportunity.
1. Social mobility—Great Britain
I. Title
331.12'7941   HD5717.5.G7
ISBN 0-333-41827-1 (hardcover)
ISBN 0-333-41828-X (paperback)

To Evan

Contents

List of Figures		viii
List of Tables		ix
Preface		xi
1	Occupations and Mobility	1
2	The Historical and Social Context of Mobility	8
3	The Occupational Structure	35
4	Occupational Fluidity and Class Structure	60
5	Trends in Occupational Mobility	91
6	Education and Mobility	122
7	Careers, Cohorts and Classes	155
8	Mobility and Social Class	189
Appendix: Methodological Details		193
Notes		198
Bibliography		199
Author Index		206
Subject Index		208

List of Figures

2.1	Population per 10 km square: a bird's eye view	13
3.1	Changes in highly skilled non-farm occupations, 1921–71	40
3.2	Changes in low-skilled non-farm occupations, 1921–71	44
3.3	Changes in intermediate-skilled non-farm occupations, 1921–71	49
3.4	Changes in farm occupations in Scotland, 1921–71	52
4.1	Distribution of origins and destination to scale	64
5.1	Diagrammatic representation of factors in changing mobility rates	92
5.2	Five-year moving averages for non-manual employment and mobility on first entry to labour market	95
5.3	Five-year moving averages for non-manual employment and mobility, ten years after entry to labour market	97
5.4	Percentage sample in each of the four classes	102
5.5	Percentage of each non-manual class recruited from manual origins	104
5.6	Percentage of total upward mobility distributed among four classes	106
5.7	Mobility factors	107
5.8	Proportions of upward mobility in industrial sectors	108
6.1	Diagrammatic representation of education and occupations	135
7.1	Direct and indirect entry to non-manual work	159
7.2	Moving averages for five-year cohorts: proportions entering skilled and less skilled manual first jobs	173
7.3	Moving averages for five-year cohorts: career mobility from skilled manual first job	174
7.4	Moving averages for five-year cohorts: career mobility from semi-skilled or unskilled manual first jobs	176
7.5	Moving averages for five-year cohorts: career mobility from lower range non-manual first jobs	177
7.6	Moving averages for five-year cohorts: career mobility from skilled manual first job	178

List of Tables

2.1	Performance of four British industries	19
2.2	A comparison of the industrial bases of male employment in Scotland and England and Wales, 1921 and 1971	26
2.3	Industrial base, Scotland 1921, 1951, 1961, 1971 (excluding out of work) – male jobs	27
2.4	Main sectoral changes	28
3.1	Highly skilled non-farm workers (SEG 1–5) in Scotland, by sex	39
3.2	Non-farm manual workers (SEGs 7, 9, 10 and 11) in Scotland, by sex	43
3.3	Intermediate non-farm workers (SEGs 6, 8 and 12) in Scotland, by sex	48
3.4	Farm occupations (SEGs 13, 14 and 15) in Scotland, by sex	51
3.5	Shift/share analysis of occupational change: Scottish males, 1961–71	54
3.6	Deviations between observed and expected frequencies in Scottish SEGs	56
4.1	Intergenerational male mobility: numbers and percentage inflow	65
4.2	Proportions of mobility associated with classes	66
4.3	Intergenerational outflow mobility	72
5.1	Sectoral share of upward mobility, 1930–9 and 1960–9	117
5.2	Intra-sectoral changes, 1930–9 and 1960–9	119
6.1	Type of secondary schooling	129
6.2	Type of secondary schooling and social mobility of men born into UMC families	130
6.3	Destination of those with UMC origins by educational success	131
6.4	Type of secondary schooling: inflows	132
6.5	Inflow to UMC by level of educational qualifications	133
6.6	Types of schooling of elite groups in various studies	139
6.7	Proportion of upmobiles: men intergenerationally mobile from manual origins to non-manual destinations who had 'high qualifications'	144
6.8	Proportions of mobile groups with 'high qualifications'	145

6.9	Percentage correct predictions of association between qualifications and occupational status on the basis of the tightening link hypothesis	147
6.10	Inter-industry variations in prediction rate (%) of the tightening link thesis	149
6.11	Inter-industry variation in prediction rate of the tightening link	150
7.1	Goldthorpe's data on counterbalance: outflow percentages	157
7.2	Direct and indirect entry to manual and non-manual classes	159
7.3	Direct and indirect entry to non-manual occupations in four cohorts	160
7.4	Percentage gross mobility/immobility, non-manual occupational destinations	162
7.5	Entry to non-manual employment by origin class: five industrial sectors	166
7.6	Access to non-manual occupations by cohort, sector and origin class	168
7.7	Mobility between first and present job for adult males born 1909–48	184
7.8	Number of previous jobs by current industrial sector	185
A.1	The Scottish Mobility Study class schema	195

Preface

This book draws together many of the ideas and empirical findings of the Scottish Mobility Study. It would be wrong to say that all the fruits of years of research can be neatly integrated into a single tidy unit, but at least the elements now have some semblance of order. The present work can be seen as a case study of mobility analysis in an example of modern society, or as an account of one aspect of life in Scotland. If the former, then the distinctive feature of the analysis at its emphasis on the occupational and industrial processes that create mobility in any society. If the latter is preferred, the book goes towards filling a substantial gap in the sociology of British society.

Although concerned with concepts and theories, the contents of this book are predominantly empirical. Every attempt has been made to present the data as simply and clearly as possible, and the tables, percentages and graphs are interspersed with more general discussion. The main theoretical issues are not, however, developed here: a much fuller treatment is available in a companion volume, *Mobility and Change in Modern Society* (Payne, 1986).

In that other book, I thanked a number of colleagues and friends for their help over the years. There is no harm in repeating my debt to Mick Carter, who compensated for any lack of specialist interest in the technicalities of mobility, with a fierce loyalty to the project and a complete honesty – often not appreciated by all those with whom we had to deal – about professional standards of research. I also received similar support from his successor at Aberdeen, Robert Moore. My colleagues during the core work on the study, Catherine Robertson and Graeme Ford, retained their temper and enthusiasm throughout. Graeme's rigorous approach to any idea or task stood us in good stead: he was the sternest critic of any new writing I produced, and no Research Director could ask for more from a research assistant. In the later stages of my research, my wife Judy took over most of the computer runs for the analysis: her efforts in sustaining my labours are as important as her academic contribution (marked by our several co-authored papers). Richard Brown was another key source of encouragement.

I have drawn material from a number of articles and conference papers to construct the present work. Most have been rewritten, but there are overlaps with the following: Chapter 3 appeared in *Socio-

logical Review vol. 25, no.1; part of Chapter 4 first appeared in the *Scottish Journal of Sociology* vol. 1, no. 1; the main trend analysis in Chapter 5 was reported in the *British Journal of Sociology*, vol. 34, no. 1; the main ideas for the education section appeared as *SIP Occasional Paper No. 8*; and the latter part of Chapter 7 was first published in *Scotland: The Real Divide*. I am grateful to the respective editors and publishers for permission to use this material.

In preparing both these earlier drafts and the manuscript for this book, I have been extremely fortunate in the support I have received from my office staff. In their various ways, Mae Lowe, Jane Doughty, Dawn Cole, Janet Berthon and Carol Vincent have eased my administrative load and typed with speed and accuracy. How they retained their patience and good humour I do not know, and I continue to marvel at their resilience.

The Scottish Mobility Study was financed by a grant from the SSRC. This book was written during a period of sabbatical leave from Plymouth Polytechnic, spent at the Research Centre for the Social Sciences, Edinburgh University. I am grateful to both my employers and my host for their contributions. Finally, I wish to record my thanks to all the many others who contributed information, collected and processed it, or have since talked mobility to me. Their help was essential to the project, although, of course, any defects in the final product are my own responsibility.

GEOFF PAYNE

1 Occupations and Mobility

There are two main types of discussion about social mobility. One is of a completely non-academic kind, often consisting of questions about 'getting on in life'. What are my chances of getting such and such a job, or even any job? What qualifications will I, or my child, need? If I take this job, where will I be in ten year's time? It is like a fascinating, real life, soap opera in which we all take part and could be called 'Getting On', or indeed, 'Room at the Top'.

The other kind of discussion is based in academic sociology. Here the questions are more typically posed in terms of open or closed social structures, and inflows and outflows between social classes. The answers come in the form of indices and models. The discussion is more technical, but basically it is about the same issues.

The key word here is *basically*, because mobility analysts have moved from the simpler questions towards seeing mobility centrally in terms of social classes. Thus social mobility is usually presented as movement from a family background, defined as parental class, to a later class destination in adult life. Social mobility is often referred to as class mobility, and the widest use of results from mobility studies has been by writers on the contemporary class system. This reflects the central interest of British sociology, the problem of structured social inequality. It is mainstream sociology's concern with class that has been the driving force behind post-war research into mobility.

As with mainstream sociology, there has also been an emphasis on theoretical development. Unlike the non-academic discussions, mobility has increasingly been treated as an abstract process, at one removed from the ordinary world. Because social class is a theoretical concept, the movements reported are between abstract origins and destinations, detached from the concrete setting of a unique historical period. To take two simple examples, the Depression and the Second World War must have changed the lives of people living through the 1930s and 1940s, but they feature little in reports of mobility research. Millions experienced unemployment, or during the war women were brought into the labour market when men were conscripted into the armed forces. Yet accounts of social mobility take little notice of such occurrences. It is true that the mobility rates of cohorts are compared, and that the debate about educational qualifications as a mobility mechanism refers to changes in the various Education Acts. But there has been little attempt to place these changes in a proper historical context. What is needed is a view of mobility which relates the various flows in any period to the wider set of social changes that were going on at the same time. There is nothing wrong in an interest in class mobility, but class mobility does not exist in isolation from every day events (see Payne, 1986).

Indeed, what we call class mobility is operationalised as movements between occupational origins and destinations. It may be a movement from being a child of a manual worker to becoming a non-manual worker oneself, or from being a child of a semi-skilled employee to becoming a professional. A range of occupational groupings (or 'classes') is available to us. Despite the convention of writing about *social* mobility between *classes*, we are in fact talking about occupational mobility which is reconceptualised as class movements.

In other words, if we want to understand why class mobility rates change, one of the first questions to be asked is how do people get their *jobs*? This immediately puts mobility analysis in touch with the sociology of economic life. Labour markets, unemployment, participation rates, credentialism, the growth of white collar employment, the proletarianisation of skilled labour, the gender segregation of occupations, the decay of traditional industries, the occupational character of advanced capitalism now become the essential parts of any explanation of mobility. Before we can provide a satisfactory account of class mobility – which remains an essential task – we have to take the metaphor of mobility more literally and examine the patterns of, and the reasons for, occupational movements.

This is in practice no easy matter, but it does provide a focus for our earlier observation that mobility research needs a proper historical grounding. In particular, it needs a grounding in the history of occupational and industrial change. For that reason this study is of mobility in Scotland since the First World War. We would expect mobility to be similar to that reported for England and Wales, and indeed much of Europe, because these are all countries with similar forms of capitalism and a shared recent history. However, we would not expect precisely the *same* patterns of mobility because Scotland has not shared an identical history. Its separate culture and historically subordinate relationship to England mean that its employment opportunities have been distinctive. It is therefore worth studying Scotland, on the one hand, as an example of an advanced capitalist society and, on the other hand, as a unique setting, of interest in its own right. Given the relative lack of basic sociological accounts of Scotland, the latter is not unimportant.

At the same time, this study is a conscious attempt to recover two kinds of lost ground. First, it is seeking to demonstrate that, not only is mobility better understood by introducing a specifically occupational dimension, but that there are more fruitful points of contact between mobility research and general sociology than have been realised to date. Mobility needs to escape from its ghetto of social class analysis, whilst still retaining its roots. Second, despite a heavy reliance on quantitative data and use of sociological theory, we are going back to those non-academic questions about 'getting on in life' and 'getting a good job'.

Central to an answer to such questions is the problem of the evolution of occupational structures. Put at its most simple, in modern society there is an increasing proportion of white collar ones. This creates new opportunities for both upward mobility and the 'inheritance' of non-manual employment by the children of non-manual workers. Mobility rates are therefore seen as directly related to the way in which demand for labour in a society changes over time. While it is a significant step to explain mobility in terms of occupational change, and this is not without its problems, it is also necessary to ask what brings about this increase in the proportion of white collar jobs? We can draw eclectically on two main currents of sociological theorising about contemporary society for an answer. For convenience, these can be called the Marxist tradition, and the post-industrial society tradition (a fuller account of these arguments can be found in Payne, 1986).

For our particular purposes, the key element within Marxist writing is the need of advanced capitalism to develop and organise its elaborate commercial transactions and its state apparatus. While it can be argued that Marxist accounts of the scale of the new occupations thus created, and their role in the class struggle, are less than satisfactory, we do at least have the germ of an understanding of occupational transition. Furthermore, we also have reasons for its occurrence which are historical and based in the human motives of power and profit and are so evident in our personal experience of the everyday world. Despite the confusion of the internal disputes between post-Marxists, the political future of these new occupational groups is crucial in explaining current and future social developments.

It is precisely this historical, human and political edge that is lacking in much of the theoretical work on post-industrial society. What the latter offers instead is a more advanced description of occupational and industrial change, with technological innovations singled out as the key mechanism. In dealing with the detail of change, the notion of two opposing classes disappears, but it is not replaced by alternative credible models of either political processes or human action. The *deus ex machina* is a machine.

Two alternative explanations are available: on the one hand, the Marxist view sees the conditions of production under monopoly capitalism as the root cause, while on the other, the theory of industrial society attributes occupational transition to new technologies and the logic of industrialism. The former view also tends to play down the significance of this structural change for class relations, whereas the latter view places the new middle classes at the centre of the stage.

Much of Marxist writing on mobility and occupational change is concentrated around two problems, the nature of the 'new middle class', and the deskilling of the labour process. Despite recent claims to the contrary, Marx wrote very little on the new middle class or mobility, nor did he see its importance. This is not surprising, because he also failed to account adequately for the occupational strata that lie between the bourgeoisie and manual labourers. Recent debates (for example, the writings of Poulantzas, Hunt and Wright) are reluctant testimony to the fact that while Marx recognised the existence of the growing middle strata or 'dritte personen' he afforded them little attention. None the less, it is possible to identify within the organisation of monopoly capitalism factors that generate new occupational roles: the banking system and competitive exploitation of science for profit maximisation are two examples.

The second theme in Marxist accounts of the labour process is the degradation of skills and the proletarianisation of marginal labour. Although such views have recently come under attack, a further test of such models is to examine flows of recruitment between occupational classes with similar skill levels. Deskilling and proletarianisation are important for accounts of mobility because they propose that the genuine opportunities for mobility are increasingly restricted. In contrast, theories of industrial society explicitly identify the upgrading of skill levels, that bring about increases in social mobility, as core elememts of advanced industrialisation. Because specialist abstract knowledge is central to the technology on which modern or post-industrial societies depend, new occupational roles are needed to acquire, apply, and co-ordinate that knowledge. The new middle classes that result are seen to be sufficiently numerous and influential to warrant a revision of traditional class theory.

While some writers suggest that class conflict is replaced by a new social order, others regard class conflict as substantially modified by the existence of the new classes. It is the latter view that the present author finds more plausible, and the professional/managerial class is singled out as requiring particular attention in the empirical analysis. Not least, the relationship between occupational achievement and educational qualifications is identified as an important factor in recruitment in this class. Following Giddens and Parkin, credentialism and mobility are seen as central to an understanding of this class, although perhaps such an 'understanding' has yet to be achieved.

Three main themes from the theory of industrial society can be regarded as particularly relevant to mobility research. The first is the idea of sectoral shift of employment from primary production and manufacture into service industries. This creates new kinds of occupations and reduces the level of employment in older types of occupation. Sectoral shift means occupational transition and therefore analysis by industrial sector is one of the main tools to be used in the investigation of mobility rates. Second, writers on modernisation and convergence have also claimed that mobility rates increase in response to occupational transition. Data from the 1975 Scottish Mobility Study are used to explore this idea for the period since the First World War. Finally, the idea of labour markets and their segmentation can be used to explicate certain assumptions about mobility processes and in turn mobility rates are proposed as possible means of identifying labour market boundaries.

Each of the two basic theoretical perspectives provides the necessary framework in which to explain the occupational transition effect. Their significance for the present study is that they offer a series of conceptual reference points so that mobility can be attached to other sociological work in addition to its conventional siting in stratification theory, and can guide the historical account which is presented in Chapter 2.

None the less, the structure of the present mobility analysis is still based on the conventional questions of mobility research. How much movement is there between classes, such as the manual and non-manual classes, in the course of one generation? Is mobility increasing or decreasing? What effects do qualifications have on chances of mobility? How much mobility takes place within a person's career?

One further point of conventionality is, sadly, also followed. This is a study of males, with very little said about female mobility. The reasons for this can be found elsewhere, and some information from the Scottish Mobility Study on married women is available (see Payne *et al.*, 1980, 1983a; Chapman, 1984). In general, male and female mobility should be analysed separately, because the genders experience such widely different lives, not least in a gender segregated labour market. This book is not a complete statement about mobility because it deals only with the male labour force. There is no alternative to this at present, but no doubt in due course another generation of mobility studies will remedy this weakness, which is shared by almost all such studies of its time.

That said, the present study marks a new beginning in another way. Partly because it is a study of occupational mobility, it tends to draw attention to how *much* mobility there is, rather than how *little*. Largely this is a matter of style of commentary: earlier writers who were only concerned with class mobility tended to dwell on the low levels of upward movement, in order to show how closed British society is. They did not suppress evidence but rather highlighted those parts of it which were most relevant for their interests, both in their narrative and in the choice of indices. But because here the emphasis is on *occupational* movements, there is less of an ideological straight jacket. If one does indeed find a great deal of occupational movement, at one level it is less threatening because it is not class movement. However, such a finding must then be incorporated into our thinking about class: if our schema is too rigid it must be modified to take account of the empirical evidence.

To illustrate this point we can consider Goldthorpe's finding of an inter-generational upward mobility rate across seven occupational classes of 43 per cent – i.e. 43 in every 100 men in the population have been upwardly mobile (see table 2.1, Goldthorpe 1980a, p. 41). The remaining 57 will themselves have children (or realistically about 80 per cent of them will) which gives 46 children. If the 43 per cent upward mobility rate applies to these 46, 20 will be upwardly mobile. So on the basis of *family* experience – and here we get back to our common-sense discussions of mobility – 63 in every 100 people will either have been mobile themselves or had mobile children. Only about one-third of families will not have experienced upward mobility, and some of that one-third are already so high in the class hierarchy that there is really nowhere higher to which to be mobile.

Such an emphasis points to a society with a relatively high level of occupational fluidity. It is certainly a level of fluidity that as sociologists we need to take account of in our theories. That is not to say that Britain is an open society. As we shall see in our analysis, family background is still a major influence on occupational destinations, and indeed in some respects, an increasing one. The moral outrage that informs so much of British writing on the inequalities of class and mobility is certainly justified. However, that moral outrage must not blind us as social scientists to the high rates of occupational fluidity that typify modern society. If nothing else, by concentrating on that occupational dimension we can put the fluidity in perspective.

The first step in making sense of the occupational dimension is to consider how the industrial and occupational character of our chosen society has developed. The economic and social history of Scotland is a complex one, with the past 200 years seeing marked changes in fortunes, It will not be possible to do more than outline these changes as a basis for a more detailed treatment (in Chapter 3) of occupational transition. However, these two chapters will provide the framework on which to consider not just how much mobility occurs, and how rates of mobility have varied in the course of this century, but *why* and *when* these changes have taken place and what this tells us about the nature of modern society.

2 The Historical and Social Context of Mobility

The first step in coming to terms with occupational mobility is to set these movements in a historical and social framework. On the one hand, this involves a concern with the unique situation of Scotland, while on the other, the theories of society already discussed suggest key processes requiring attention as typifying capitalist or industrial society. For example, much of Scotland's particular development can be attributed to her patterns of capital accumulation and transfer, and ownership of production, together with the introduction of new technologies and changes in the public administration of the country. How do these affect mobility?

The task of situating mobility in a wider context is not without difficulties. In the first place, we need to consider why 'Scotland' is a suitable unit of analysis. The reason depends less on seeing Scotland as a nation-state than on seeing the country comprises an interesting set of social processes which cannot be explained without some reference to Scotland's discrete existence within a wider web of connections. There are several facets to Scotland's discrete existence. It has a distinct physical area, with a very sparsely populated and geographically extensive southern border country, so that it is both distant and separate from England. It is an administrative unit, with separate laws and state powers operating within its boundaries. Third, it can be claimed that it possesses a national culture, which exists not so much in the artificial symbols of kilts, haggis and highland games, as in the shared interests in the mundane events of life north of the border. Finally, since so much of 'British' sociology stops short of that border, it can be claimed that *de facto*, sociology has defined Scotland as something different, if only in the negative sense of not including the country in its actual studies. That is to say, English sociologists have on the whole carried out no empirical research in Scotland, despite in practice going on to describe 'British' society, thus implying (but without any evidence) that Scotland is just the same as England. (See, for example, Westergaard and Resler. 1977; Butterworth and Weir, 1984; and to a lesser extent Noble, 1980.)

This negative approach to Scotland's separate existence actually compounds a second difficulty, that of relating sample survey data to other kinds of social science information. Not only is information often not available on Scotland as a distinct from Britain, but what is known about related social processes (from, say, the Census or economic histories) covers a variety of periods, a range of selected phenomena and multitude of classifications and definitions. Integration and comparison is therefore at times not possible.

A further difficulty is that despite the small amount of sociological research on Scotland, the field is already disputed by competing schools. These divisions are not just between theorists of capitalist society and theorists of industrial society (e.g. Dickson, 1980, pp. 9–10) but between those who variously stress the separateness of Scotland or her dependence on England, the place of Scotland in the world system or her distinctive cultural development, the uniqueness of Scotland or her similarity to other types of society. Kendrick and McCrone (1981, p. 10) have recently suggested that three sorts of mechanisms must all be examined: those dealing with the international division of labour and external relationships; those dealing with the processes common to all societies of similar types, and those specific to Scotland herself. They argue that most accounts concentrate too much either on the last of these, so exaggerating differences, or on the particular relationship with England, so distorting the picture into one dominated by rigid notions of dependency. The former (and for us less significant) error lies in histories of Scottish culture and her people, particularly debates in Marxism about the role of indigenous ruling classes. The latter error is to be found in the writings on national identity by such commentators as Nairn (1977) and Hechter (1975).

Thus, for example, Hechter's explanation of Scotland's development attaches more weight to her political domination by England than to events within Scotland. His list of 'possible' features of dominance is all-embracing: economic, legal, political, military, religious and 'other cultural forms', although he admits that 'there does not seem to be a general consensus' on what is to be included (1975, p. 33). There is no need to dwell on the details of his case here (see Page, 1978; Rallings and Lee, 1980): his theoretical framework, like Bryden (1979) and Buchanan (1968), represents an overambitious attempt to transfer a core/periphery model from one context to another, inappropriate one.

Nairn takes a broader view, regarding nationalism as a response by a less developed nation to the impact of more advanced capitalism, i.e. by the uneven development of world capitalism. In concentrating on the global scale, he needs to treat Scotland as both over and underdeveloped. Neither view squares with the fact that Scotland was part of the world's first industrial revolution (Kendrick et al., 1983, p. 3).

While Kendrick and the Social Structure of Modern Scotland Project team at Edinburgh University are correct to criticise both ethnocentric and excessively externalist theories, their own position attaches an unusually high importance to the lack of difference between contemporary Scotland and England. By concentrating on the similarities between Scotland and other industrial societies the reader may underestimate the extent to which Scotland does have a separate cultural and historical existence. For Scots in particular there is a framework of institutions and identities that is integral to their daily lives, and this has to be taken into account together with the external linkages and the similarities between societies. In order to establish this balance, the review of Scottish history that follows starts with some of the contemporary differences between Scotland and England, before going on to consider how, among other things, world markets, political control and international flows of capital shaped the economic conditions of twentieth-century Scottish society.

CONTEMPORARY SCOTLAND

It is in itself interesting that it should be necessary to say something about Scottish society for an English audience. While the political debate over devolution in the 1970s went a long way to acquaint the English public with some of the more obvious differences, there had been little sociological analysis of Scotland (the first chair of Sociology was not established in Scotland until 1968). A need still exists to differentiate between the popular image and a systematic analysis of Scottish life, namely life in a society highly concentrated, long urbanised and essentially industrial. The culture of Scotland is not dependent on language, unlike Wales: less than 2 per cent speak Gaelic. Rather, regional dialect helps to reinforce a worldview created by Scottish institutions, despite a relatively limited literary and musical culture. (See, for example, Paton, 1968, pp. 215–21; Kellas, 1968, pp. 6–9; and Hanham, 1969, pp. 44–6, 147–50.)

What is being argued here is that a separateness based on major institutional forms is more important than the relatively superficial customary or cultural signs. The totality of such institutional differences from England justifies treating Scotland as something more than just a *region* of Britain: in contrast, Wales for all its cultural distinctiveness, is *institutionally* more akin to England and regional status. We cannot assume *a priori* that what we know as sociologists about England (e.g. the basic studies in the 1950s and 1960s of community life, education, religion, etc.) also applies to Scotland, for there has been very little sociological study of Scotland (Anderson, 1974; and Kent, 1980):

> as yet there is relatively little empirical material which would, for example, make possible comparative studies between Scotland and England and Wales. In short the sociography of Scotland is weak and needs to be developed. (Anderson 1974, p. 1)

Despite the appearance in 1977 of the *Scottish Journal of Sociology*, Parsler (1980, p. vii) could still identify the same gap in 1980. The present chapter can be seen as a contribution, albeit a brief one, towards identifying and filling this gap.

The list of separate Scottish institutions is an extensive one. Radio and television production centres, both BBC and ITV, regional programming, Scottish editions of the *Mail* and *Express* together with five major indigenous daily papers and two Sunday papers provide an introspective involvement in the country's own doings. Education, religion, legal/judicial and local political systems were not fully integrated under the terms of the Act of Union. The education system does not share England's structure, selectivity, subject specialisation, lack of practical orientation or final qualifications (Ford *et al.*, 1975). The churches have much higher membership, with Catholicism and Presbyterianism both playing a more important part (Highet, 1960). The law is based on Roman law, and requires separate Acts of Parliament (which are often not forthcoming) to bring about changes. Although for some periods the administration was run from London, increasingly affairs have been concentrated in Edinburgh (Public Health, Registration, Public Works, Police and Prisons, Trading Standards, Education, Transport, and parts of Manufacturing, Fisheries, Taxation and Local Government (HMSO, 1970)). By the mid sixties there were 55 000 civil servants in Scotland dealing with the local problems (Kellas, 1968, pp. 150 and 120–55; Hanham, 1969, pp. 50–63).

In addition, there are separate employees and employers organisations, separate trade associations, banks, charities and political parties. In October 1974, almost a third of Scots voted for a party not contesting any seat in England and Wales, and Budge and Urwin (1966) have argued that separate voting traditions even for the main parties operate in Scotland. Scotland may not be a classic nation-state but together these various elements form a pattern of distinctiveness nowhere matched by any mere region of England or Wales (for further details, see Payne *et al.*, 1975). The cumulative effects have prompted one commentator opposed to Scottish separatism to admit that Scotland demonstrates 'a unity and cohesion of its own' (Cairncross, 1954, p. 1).

One other type of difference is the physical disposition of the population. At the beginning of the century over 74 per cent of the population was classified by the Registrar-General as 'urban' and by 1931 this figure had risen to 81 per cent (HMSO 1951a; 1966, pp. 182–3). In fact this means that around 65 per cent of Scots lived in towns of over 20 000 populations. This is a low definition of 'urban', but the 1971 figures for population density – which are not radically different from the earlier part of the century – confirm Scotland's centralised nature. The average urban density was 3007 persons per square kilometre (compared with 1755 in England and Wales): the rural density was 20, compared with 85 (Morton, 1975, p. 800).

> Four-fifths of the Scottish people live in the highly urban central lowlands – in the planning regions around Glasgow, Stirling–Falkirk, Edinburgh and Dundee. About a tenth live in Aberdeen and its hinterland. The vast areas covered by the Highlands, South Western and border regions contain the remaining tenth.

> This concentration and the isolation effect of the sparsely populated Border countries, is clearly visible in Figure 2.1. In the Highlands, with its population of 283 000 in an area of 14 500 square miles, the average density is less than 20 to the square mile while that for the rest of the UK is 95, and for central Scotland is 910. Although the highlands consist of 20 per cent in the UK land area.

> Two-fifths of the population live in settlements of less than 1,000 people and a further one-fifth live on crofts . . . For the provision of education, transport and public services in general, the sheer physical extent of inhabited country presents a difference of degree so great as to constitute a difference of kind. (MacKay 1973, p. 21)

Figure 2.1 Population per 10 km square: a bird's eye view

There is a column for each national grid 10 km square (an area of 100 sq km) and the height of the column is proportional to the number of people in that area. Britain is seen from over the North Sea (the view is orientated along a line 20° east of north), but there is no perspective in the diagram (the projection used is orthographic) and so the same numbers of people are shown as the same height of column everywhere on the diagram.
(Absolute numbers: number of people per 10 kilometre square.)
SOURCE: HMSO, 1980, pp. 22–3.

The Highlands are also characterised by concentrations of land ownerships: half of its 6.5 million acres are owned by 140 individuals or firms (McEwan, 1975, p. 236). Thus the Highlands is, in a social sense, a small, separate region of Scotland that has different characteristics from the rest of the country; while it needs special attention, there is a danger of it distorting one's perception of Scotland, precisely because of its physical scale and the extent of its problems as a declining area increasingly dependent on tourism. In fact, most Scots are willing to collude with the English whose holidays in the Highlands (and conference trips to the north) and whose reading of nineteenth-century literature, lead to a romantic image which misses the basic truth: the main bulk of Scottish life is essentially urbanised and industrial and has been for the whole of this century.

THE EMERGENCE OF MODERN SCOTLAND: 1700–1918

Contemporary Scotland developed out of a long and complex history, during which the country became increasingly involved in outside forces. A convenient starting point is around 1700, at which time Scotland, despite a strategic location on trading routes, was still a poor agricultural society, exporting a few basic raw materials (Lythe, 1960, pp. 233–46). Still largely feudal with strongly independent burghs, difficult geographical conditions, weak government and protectionist trade restrictions abroad hindered economic growth of the kind beginning on the Continent and in England:

> The tragic dilemma of the years around 1700 was that the old economy was already moribund because it could not work without complete separation from England and the new economy must fail because it could not work without complete integration; as the existing Union of Crowns provided neither, the nation was rapidly heading for commercial disaster. (Smout, 1963, 278)

The Act of Union in 1707 provided the beginnings of a solution, and integration into the English sphere of economic influence rapidly followed.

The Act of Union dealt not just with political links to the British state but also with fiscal and trade matters – codifying taxes and standardising navigation privileges together with weights and measures (Lenman, 1977, pp. 58–60). Further measures to extend English control inevitably followed the Jacobite rising. The long process of economic integration had begun, setting up a 'unique blend of economic experiences which shaped the political and social habits of its people' (Lenman, 1977, p. 7).

The integration of the Scottish economy during the late eighteenth and early nineteenth centuries worked in a number of ways to stimulate a precocious industrialisation. Markets in the Americas, from geographically advantaged west coast ports, were newly available and were followed by those in China and India: manufactures could flow out, raw materials flow in (Harvie, 1977, pp. 106–7). The failure of the '45' resulted in a more powerful, homogeneous, and less traditional elite based in the Lowlands, which was not slow to exploit such opportunities. It also resulted in improved internal communications for reasons of military security, and in a ready supply of cheap labour from the Highlands, later augmented through connections with Ireland (Lenman, 1977, pp. 101–6).

The supply of cheap labour, combined with traditional activities like linen-making and cattle breeding, was the basis of Scotland's economy until the second half of the eighteenth century (Lenman, 1977, p. 87). The country, particularly the west, was dependent on English capital and imported technology, but the opening of colonial trading in tobacco marked a new turning point, providing not only a source of capital but also a network of contacts and associated trading connections (Slaven, 1975, p. 24). Capital from tobacco reinforced the linen trade, and in turn provided the appropriate setting for the new cotton trade: the same merchants and manufacturers were involved in all three (Lenman, 1977, p. 117; Slaven, 1975, p. 90). The same period saw the foundation of the banking system (Campbell, 1965, pp. 135–51).

Cotton, wool and later jute textile manufacturing showed the first signs of use of inanimate power sources and factory production, together with the associated chemical industry. By the last quarter of the century Glasgow was the premier linen town in Britain, with the power loom and the help of English capital prompting a rapid growth in cotton from the turn of the century to 1830. At the same time, the primitive road system was substantially upgraded, to be followed by the railways which like England were major foci for capital and employment, although, of course, concentrated in the Lowlands. The railways stimulated the iron industry, which expanded to the extent that by the middle of the nineteenth century 90 per cent of Britain's iron exports came from lowland Scotland. The population was 1.6 million in 1801, 2.9 million in 1851, and 3.4 million by 1871: most of that growth was concentrated in West Central Scotland (Lenman, 1977, p. 103; Campbell, 1965, p. 178). The same part of the country saw a second wave of new banks, with largely Scottish directors (Scott and Hughes, 1980, pp. 20-5). Scottish capital was by now largely self-sustaining and could draw its technology from home and abroad.

Well before the middle of the century, a combination of world trade factors (not least the growth of Empire markets) and new technologies meant that shipbuilding, iron and coal had taken over as the major sectors of growth, with 60 per cent of British steam tonnage launched on the Clyde. Further development of the steam engine – particularly in their railway and marine applications – followed, so that half or more of the British shipbuilding labour force was employed in Scotland, and Glasgow was the biggest world centre of locomotive exports well into the twentieth century (Lenman, 1977, p. 173). Steel-making developed rather late, in the 1880s, partly due to Scotland's iron ore having an unsuitably high phosphorous content, but also due to this ready market for cheap pig iron. There was no shortage of technological information: traditional links with continental Europe made Scotland a fruitful place for generating new developments in production originating in England.

This was aided by Scotland's advanced education system. In 1868, 1 in 40 Scots attended a secondary school; in England only 1 in every 1300. Similarly 1 in 1000 Scots attended university compared with 1 Englishman in 5800 (Wade 1939, pp. 25-33). What is more, the Scottish system paid more attention to 'practical' knowledge than did its English counterpart.

It would not be an exaggeration to say that Scotland shared with England almost all the conditions which promoted the Industrial Revolution south of the border (Hanham. 1969, p. 23), together with several additional advantages of her own. Up to the outbreak of the First World War, Scotland was every bit as 'advanced' as any part of Britain outside London.

Yet in less than a decade Scotland was showing clear signs of economic distress, and was soon to suffer all the woes of the English economy to an even greater extent. The last sixty years, the lifetimes of the older men in the Scottish Mobility Study and sample, have seen Scotland slip further behind England on almost every indicator of economic success. Why did such a dramatic turnabout occur?

THE DECLINE OF MODERN SCOTLAND: THE TWENTIETH CENTURY

Central to this decline was the use of Scottish capital. The initial surpluses from trade and textiles had gone into indigenous development such as the railways constructed in the 1840s, shipbuilding and iron smelting. However, in the wake of international trade, from the latter half of the nineteenth century the profits of Scottish industrialisation were reinvested not in Scotland but abroad. Investment from Edinburgh and Dundee in American railways, real estate, mining and ranching, from Aberdeen and Dundee in railways and commercial agriculture in the Indian subcontinent, from Edinburgh and Aberdeen in Australia and New Zealand, and from Dundee in South America, was channelled through the comparatively well-developed and effective Scottish banks and investment trusts, As a contemporary commentator remarked,

> whether this vast exportation of our surplus wealth be wise or unwise, Scotland is to a large extent responsible for it. In proportion to her size and the number of her population, she furnishes far more of it than either of the sister kingdoms . . . Scotland revels in foreign investment. (*Blackwoods Magazine*, Oct. 1884, quoted in Jackson, 1968, p. 297)

Lenman, who is no critic of what he regards as a natural feature of 'mature economies', estimates that 'Scottish foreign investments may have risen from £60 million in 1870 to as much as £500 million in 1914' (Lenman, 1977, p. 193).

Although a parallel process was taking place in English capital (Hobsbawm, 1969, pp. 188–92), it was more pronounced in Scotland. Nor was it an unreasonable policy of self-interest by the Scottish capitalist class: their home production was yielding a good return (allowing for trade cycles) but could not be indefinitely expanded in the home market, whereas an expanded overseas market offered new growth potential. The very success of Scottish industry was a disincentive to further investment. Furthermore, land, railways and mining were sectors with which Scottish investors were familiar, and which offered high returns with relatively low risks. They were therefore more attractive than investment in new industrial technologies at home. Apart from the steel industry, which attracted new funds in the face of problems with iron ore supplies, and some developments in marine propulsion (i.e. the turbine), little new industry was established in Scotland in the sixty-year period following 1880. Two exceptions were the Singer sewing machine factory in Clydebank (1884) and some generally unsuccessful small motor vehicle companies in the first two decades of the twentieth century. As Hobsbawm (1969, p. 188) has observed:

> to change from an old and obsolescent pattern to a new one was both expensive and difficult: it involved the scrapping of old investments still capable of yielding good profits . . . (in favour of) new investments of even greater initial cost; for as a general rule newer technology is more expensive technology.

The result was a Scottish economy that was undercapitalised, narrowly based on the old staple industries of textiles, shipbuilding, iron, steel and coal, and largely dependent on international trade. In as far as there was a home market, it chiefly consisted of a few main industries interdependent on each other; coal and steel being largely geared to shipbuilding (see Slaven's (1975) account of the failure of the West of Scotland coal industry due to the coincident decline of its two markets, steel and shipping at home and international competition abroad). The low wages of the labour force that had for so long helped the competitiveness of Scottish industry, meant that there was little home market for consumer goods or new housing. It was these latter markets which led the slow recovery of the inter-war years in England when, after the First World War, the rise of new nations in international trade, and finally the Great Slump, had destroyed the foundation of the old industrial order.

In other words, many of the defects of the English economy were to be found in accentuated form in Scotland. Almost immediately after the end of the Great War, production began to fall and labour was laid off. There were few alternative sources of work because what distinguished the Scottish economy was its concentration in the heavy industrial sector. These 'old staples' suffered wherever they were located in Britain, but the consequences were worse in Scotland. Most of the staples experienced absolute falls in employment, while cotton and shipbuilding suffered absolute falls in trade between 1920 and 1937. With most relying on exports for nearly half their markets, all saw relative falls in share of trade and proportion of the labour force employed during the period 1913 to 1937 as the staples' share of a static world trade fell from 14 per cent to 9.8 per cent by value (Glynn and

Oxborrow, 1976, pp. 89–90). Table 2.1 shows the decline in four major industries:

Table 2.1 Performance of four British industries

Industry	1912–13	1938
Shipping	12m tons	less than 11m tons
Shipbuilding	almost 1m tons	less than 0.5 tons
Cotton – production	8000m sq yards	3000m sq yards
– export	7000m sq yards	1500m sq yards
Coal	287m tons	227m tons

SOURCE: Adapted from Hobsbawm, 1969, p. 207.

At the low point of the Depression in 1931–2, unemployment among miners reached 34.5 per cent, among pig iron workers 43.8 per cent, among steelworkers 47.9 per cent, and among shipyard workers 62 per cent. 'Central Scotland resisted even the modest recovery of the later 1930s' (Glynn and Oxborrow, 1976, pp. 208–9), not least because more even than other parts of Scotland its industries were interdependent (McCrone, 1980). The likelihood of son following father into the same job was perforce reduced.

Elsewhere in Britain, and particularly in the Midlands and South East of England, the rigours of the Depression were palliated by the development of new products in high technology industries. The interwar period saw the introduction of the small electric motor, resulting in more flexible factory layouts, and a new complex of machine tools and engineering techniques. The internal combustion engine, artificial yarns (rayon), plastics (bakelite, casein, celluloid) and radio were all older inventions which went into industrial production. Other innovations included new steel alloys, paper based on wood pulp, and organic chemistry. While older industries changed their products, printing, furniture, leather goods and the construction industry began to gear up for a consumer market. The press, the vacuum cleaner, electric irons, cosmetics, the cinema, electric light, the department store are creations of the twenties and thirties (Glynn and Oxborrow, 1976; Hobsbawm, 1969, pp. 218–9). In contrast, Harvie's account (1977, pp. 168–74) of the decline of the old staple industries in Scotland, both before and after the Second World War is a depressing tale.

Comparatively little of this penetrated north of the Border until well after the Second World War. Even new ventures, such as the Argyll

Motor Company, failed due to lack of a local market and undercapitalisation (Slaven 1975, p. 200). Scottish capital was dedicated elsewhere (with dividends severely reduced) while the absence of local consumer demand and the additional problems of transport motivated English capitalists to invest south of the Trent, let alone the Border. Scotland remained trapped in her dependence on older industries that could no longer support her until newer forms of engineering began to be established from around 1950 (Lenman 1977, p. 204).

A rival interpretation has recently been advanced by Kendrick *et al.* (1983, p. 20) who argue that:

> In terms of the pattern of industrial employment the most striking aspect of the Scottish distribution has been its similarity to that of Britain as a whole. Contrary to conventional wisdom, Scotland as a whole ranks among the least specialised regions of Britain, and in many respects, its industrial structure is the most diversified of them all.

This radically different conclusion is based on examining positive percentage differences (PPDs), i.e. a measure of where Britain exceeds Scotland, for two time series scores: those for industrial sectors (Lee, 1979) and socio-economic groups (Payne, 1977a). While the authors present a great deal of interesting material, particularly on sub-regional variations (see also Kendrick *et al.*, 1982b), their conclusions are closely tied to the way in which they use the PPD calculations. Thus their main evidence relates to *male and female* employment *within manufacturing*, in a comparison of *Britain and Scotland*, whereas much of the present study is concerned with *male* employment across *all* sectors in a comparison of *Scotland with England and Wales*. Second, the PPD is a reasonable indicator of overall differences, but obviously does not indicate where *within* a set of variations the chief source of difference lies.

For example, if we consider 1851 and 1911, Scotland had PPDs of 12.3 and 10.3 with Britain as a whole (Kendrick *et al.*, 1983, pp. 7, 22). That means that there was a growing similarity between the two countries, but the nature of that similarity (or difference) was very different across the two time points. In 1851, the bulk of the differences lay in Scotland's overcommitment to textiles (44.4 per cent to 32.2 per cent): if we remove that industry, and recalculate the percentages for the remaining industries, the new PPD is 6.2 not 12.3. In other words, apart from textiles, the two areas were not greatly dissimilar on this measure, with no contribution to the PPD from shipbuilding, the metal trades, or mining because these have excesses in *Scotland*, rather than excesses in Britain (the PPD could, of course, be calculated in reverse so that these sectors would show up directly as contributions to the Scottish PPD).

In contrast, the 1911 distribution shows textiles much more in line, 19.3 per cent in Scotland and 18.1 per cent in Britain, so removing the textile sector would not change the other percentages and therefore the PPD very much. The PPD of 10.3 must be produced by other variations, so that while the textile factor produces a closer similarity, that one factor masks a number of other changes. For example, mining, metals and shipbuilding comprised 38.8 per cent of Scotland's manufacturing employment in 1911, as against 30 per cent in Britain. Sixty years before the respective figures were 18.1 per cent and 19.4 per cent.

This argument refers to manufacturing, not to other sectors, but we can extend this by using Kendrick *et al.*'s table 6 (1983, p. 27). This shows that manufacturing for 1911 (old series) provided 52.6 per cent of Scottish employment, and 47.8 per cent of Britain's employment. Mining, metals and shipbuilding therefore catered for 20.4 per cent of all Scottish employment, compared with 14.3 per cent in Britain as whole. Of course, that 14.3 per cent or 2.5 million workers owed a lot to Scotland; 0.4 million or over 2 of the 14.3 percentage points.

Although the methodology used by Kendrick *et al.* does not therefore reveal all aspects of Anglo-Scottish differences, one can none the less accept their first conclusion (1983, p. 9–10) that at the turn of the century, Scotland was uniquely well placed to exploit the Empire markets. Where one would wish to differ is in their analysis of the period after the First World War, when they underestimate the extent to which Scotland remained tied to the old staples until recent times. It would be wrong, however, to overemphasise the alternative view. In the first place, as their data show, the under-representative proportions of service employment begin to disappear during this century, and most of the broad brush changes move in parallel (1983, p. 27). Second, even though there was disproportionate dependence on increasingly non-viable old staple industries, there were considerable changes taking place even in – or even arguably because of – the Depression.

First, as implied above, even existing industries introduced new processes, such as the new manganese steel alloys in steel-making, and changes in hull design in shipbuilding. These, combined with labour lay-offs, ensured that productivity was actually increased: in fact 'productivity increases were greatest in the primary and secondary sectors of the economy . . . Some of the old staple industries made remarkable increases in productivity' (Glynn and Oxborrow, 1976, pp. 91–2). Changes in product and production processes mean changes in the type and amount of labour required.

Second, the economy experienced a drastic concentration of ownership and control. The pre-war economy, outside heavy engineering had been

> wedded to the small or medium sized, highly specialized family-operated and family financed, and competitive firm . . . in 1914 Britain was perhaps the least concentrated of the great industrial economies, and in 1939 one of the most. (Hobsbawm, 1969, p. 214).

By that latter year, Pollard (1972, p. 168) could observe that 'as a feature of industrial and commercial organisation, free competition has nearly disappeared from the British scene'. The combination of new technology with capital concentration resulted in new giant combines: of the top twenty firms in 1965, nineteen were twentieth-century creations. Shell, BATs, Imperial Tobacco, and Courtaulds have Edwardian origins; ICI, AEI, Ford, Bowater, and GKN started between the wars, a period which also saw the emergence of major banking and insurance groups. Hobsbawm (1969, p. 17) argues that

> the economic concentration which took place between the wars cannot be primarily justified on grounds of efficiency and progress. It was overwhelmingly restrictive, defensive, and protective. It was a blind response to depression, which aimed at maintaining profits high by eliminating competition, or at accumulating great clusters of miscellaneous capital which were in no sense productively more rational than their original individual components, but which provided financiers with investments for surplus capital or with profits of company promotion. Britain became a non-competing country at home as well as abroad.

These changes received active backing from the government (Stevenson, 1977, pp. 19–21).

The occupational implications of these changes are considerable. At first between the wars and then after the Second World War, large organisations required bureaucratic systems of operation: face to face communication was replaced by written records, vastly expanding the army of white collar workers. At the same time, economies of scale permitted greater specialisation, so that new specialisms developed out of increased division of labour. As the theory of industrial society suggests, the owner no longer manages, the manager no longer buys, or does the accounts, or hires and fires, or watches over the test bench or laboratory. The age of the professional expert is born. Large organisations also have greater capital resources, so that investment in new, more expensive technologies is at least in principle much easier to achieve. This again promotes occupational change either by creating new skills (the new machining techniques referred to above) or by deskilling manual tasks (as in large-scale furniture-making).

The third major industrial change which dates from this period is the growth of a governmental apparatus to cope with greater state intervention in regulation, taxation, and the provision of welfare services. Government controls during the First World War had acquainted the country with the possibilities for intervention. Commissions on the collapsing coal and shipbuilding industries advocated concentration and reduction in capacity, which was achieved in the second case. The Special Areas and Special Areas Amendment Acts also empowered regional development programmes to the 1930s even if their impact until the 1940s and 1950s was not great (see Slaven, 1975). Following the Second World War, Scotland as part of Britain saw the nationalisation of the power, rail, and iron and steel industries, the establishment of a National Health Service, expanded unemployment benefit provision, increased council house building, a new towns policy, a change in educational provision and greater local and national government administrative involvement in planning and regional development (see Harvie, 1977, pp. 196–70). These new ventures, together with a leisure industry based on shorter working hours and greater affluence, constitute an entirely new service sector, with new kinds of occupations. Thus the old occupational structure, tied to the old staple industries, was modified not just by their economic decline, but by the growth of whole new enterprises requiring a different workforce. Employment dependent on the old staples thus was in *relative* decline, whatever their *absolute* fate at the hands of market forces.

It is important to balance these general trends against the actual experiences of Scotland. Nationalisation, for example, did not result in the central offices of the new organisations being located in Glasgow or Edinburgh (LMS and LNER became ultimately the London based

British Rail), while Shell's research and development sections are not based in Grangemouth along with its refinery. When Brunner-Mond, United Alkali and Nobles became ICI, control and occupations of control went to England. The 'branch plant' syndrome may provide a route for Scots to high status occupations, but it is a high road that leads to England. The Scottish occupational structure is modified by concentration of capital and technological development, but because of the metropolitan pull of South-East England, less so than the theory of industrial society might suggest.

Nor does the branch plant syndrome extend merely to the control of Scottish capital by the English. From the late 1930s it has been government policy to move 'work to the workers'. Slaven (1975) identifies sixteen new Scottish factories for external companies resulting from state intervention by 1940, and the establishment of new towns (Cumbernauld, Glenrothes, etc), and a vigorous campaign following the publication of the Toothill Report (1961) saw an influx of international – and particularly American – capital. Ten American firms set up plants during the 1940s, and the total was over forty by 1960. By 1973, the number had reached 148, employing 15 per cent of Scotland's manufacturing labour force, and almost a third of new jobs created post-war (Harvie, 1977). Firn (1975) and Scott and Hughes (1975) have also documented this shift in control of Scottish industry away from the indigenous capitalist class. Scottish capital is now doubly internationalised; the export of capital at the end of the last century has been matched by the import of capital in the middle of the twentieth century.

The introduction of foreign capital under government schemes helped to build up light and electrical engineering during the 1950s and 1960s, and went some way to lay the basis for localised developments in electronics in the 1970s. It has not, however, been without problems. Firms like National Cash Register in Dundee, or Singer in Clydebank, provided largely female employment so that male unemployment is not 'solved'. Nor are the long term prospects assured. In the face of recession, branch plants are vulnerable to closure decisions taken elsewhere: NCR, Timex, Singer and Monsanto are but a few of the major companies which have developed subsidiaries on the basis of fiscal inducements, only to close down their Scottish operations while maintaining their original operations intact when world trade contracted in the 1970s. The new plants provided only a limited range of occupations (management was almost always introduced from outside Scotland) for only a limited period. American firms with a combined

Scottish labour force of over 87 000 hired only around fifty Scottish graduates a year in the late 1960s (Hargreave, 1971, p. 32). This does not form the basis for careers or life strategies.

To some extent, the same use of foreign investment was also made in England, in areas like the North East, and in South Wales. However, the large English-based combines were able to operate in a larger market and the greater diversity of the English economy cushioned many of the upheavals. The Scottish economy remained less diversified for much longer and its industrial history over the last sixty years has constrained employment opportunities, so giving the Scots a distinctive set of mobility life-chances if they wish to work and live in their own country.

INDUSTRIAL EMPLOYMENT

This can be seen by contrasting industrial employment between Scotland and England (where developments happened 'faster') and between the Census years of 1921 and 1971 which bracket the life experience of the men in the Scottish sample. Fourteen per cent of Scotland's workforce was directly employed in 1921 in shipbuilding and iron and steel production, with a further proportion in allied trades, which was serving the needs of these two groups. The rest of the economy was relatively undiversified.

As Table 2.2 shows, more Scots worked in primary industry (including mining) than in England and Wales (23 per cent to 19 per cent) and fewer in general manufacture, other engineering trades, distribution and commerce, public administration and defence, and miscellaneous services. The service and distribution sectors are also noticeably different: in Scotland, these were just under 25 per cent of all male jobs: but in England and Wales they made up 32 per cent. At the start of the contemporary period then, the two economies were structurally different, although each area was contributing economic functions to the other (see also Jones, 1977, pp. 402–3).

By 1971, the national differences had changed. Primary industry had shrunk to less than 7 per cent, and showed only a small excess over the England and Wales figure. General engineering was now more important in Scotland, while ships and metals had virtually disappeared. Although services and distribution still provided more employment south of the Border, the difference had decreased to only a couple of percentage points. The two countries had become

Table 2.2 A comparison of the industrial bases on male employment in Scotland and England and Wales, 1921 and 1971

	1921		1971	
	Scotland	England & Wales	Scotland	England & Wales
Agriculture, Fishing	12.1	8.9	5.7	3.3
Mining, Quarrying	11.5	10.1	2.6	2.5
Shipbuilding, Iron and Steel	14.1	5.4	6.1	3.4
Other engineering	8.6	10.5	13.7	11.2
Textiles, Clothing	5.3	7.1	3.0	3.2
Food, Drink, Tobacco	3.2	3.2	4.4	2.8
Other Manufacture	6.5	7.5	8.4	17.5
Building	4.3	5.9	12.3	10.3
Transport	9.7	9.6	8.7	8.6
Distribution, Commerce	12.1	14.0	13.1	15.0
Misc. service	3.6	7.8	6.5	7.2
Professional services	2.3	2.3	7.2	6.9
Admin. and Defence	6.4	8.1	7.9	7.4
Other	0.1	0.1	0.3	0.6
	n= 1 521 337	n= 12 127 118	n= 1 350 100	n= 13 681 450

modernised, and in that respect more alike (see also Kendrick et al., 1983).

This process of change since 1921 has not been a simple or uniform one. Agriculture and fishing have dropped from just under 184 000 jobs to 76 800; mining from 175 000 to 35 620; shipbuilding and steel (currently under further review) from 214 500 to 82 800. In 1921, these three sectors had over 38 per cent of Scottish jobs. By 1931, at a time of massive unemployment, only agriculture and fishing was holding its position while the other two industries had contracted to about 75 per cent of their previous size. By 1951, all three were in decline and this has continued to the present; it has steepened slightly between 1961 and 1971. At the latter census, only 14.4 per cent of male Scots were working in the three industries which had formerly provided 38 per cent of the jobs. Any career structures or life plans based on the organisations in these industries would have required major reorientation.

The other industries of Scotland show a more mixed pattern. Transport has fluctuated narrowly around the 10 per cent mark, which is not unlike England and Wales, while textiles and related trades have declined consistently from 5.3 per cent to 3.0 per cent. Only building and professional services show a consistent increase, with both being nearly three times as important in 1971 than in 1921.

Although these clear trends are more appealing, the remaining industries are of interest in a different way. 'Other engineering', food, 'other manufactures', administration and defence, distribution, and miscellaneous services all show variations over the period. The census

Table 2.3 Industrial base, Scotland 1921, 1951, 1961, and 1971 (excluding out of work) – male jobs

	1921	1931	1951	1961	1971
Agriculture, Fishing	12.1	13.1	9.6	7.8	5.7
Mining, Quarrying	11.5	8.6	6.4	5.6	2.6
Shipbuilding, Iron and Steel	14.1	6.3	8.6	7.8	6.1
Other engineering	8.6	6.8	12.4	11.4	13.7
Textiles, Clothing	5.3	4.7	4.0	3.2	3.0
Food, Drink, Tobacco	3.2	3.5	3.9	3.3	4.4
Other Manufacture	6.5	7.6	8.4	7.9	8.4
Building	4.3	6.4	9.5	11.0	12.3
Transport	9.7	11.2	10.0	9.9	8.7
Distribution, Commerce	12.1	16.8	12.3	14.1	13.1
Misc. services	3.6	5.5	3.7	5.9	6.5
Professional services	2.3	3.9	4.1	5.3	7.2
Admin. and Defence	6.4	5.4	7.0	6.4	7.9
Other	0.1	0.2	0.1	0.4	0.3
n=	1 121 337	1 253 403*	1 526 754	1 504 210	1 350 100

*SOURCE: 1951 Census reports, table L, p. XXIX adjusted totals, except for Shipbuilding and Iron and Steel, which are not available in this form, and are therefore unadjusted. In the 1931 Census 65 788 men 'in' these industries were jobless, and only 80 188 were in work – an industry unemployment rate of over 45 per cent.

28   *Employment and Opportunity*

of 1961 seems to mark a relative and absolute fall-back on steady growth, and while 1971 had in the case of the first four of these industries shown a recovery of their growth, the inter-censal contraction and expansion has been between 12 000 and 25 000 jobs in each industry. Distribution and miscellaneous services have troughs in 1951 and the former a compensating peak in 1961. This may be an elaborate way of saying what should be obvious: a modern industrial society not only goes through booms and depressions, and changes in its structural balance, but that its various sectors display trends of expansion and contraction at varying rates.

Although there are no very clear patterns, there is an interesting underlying current of change which can be detected by calculating percentage differences between censuses. The largest difference (in PPD terms) is between 1921 and 1931: as Table 2.3 deals with those actually in work, this is not surprising, because as argued earlier unemployment was differentially associated with various industries. Next in magnitude comes the twenty-year gap between 1931 and 1951, but if this is averaged out by dividing it by two, the mean decadel rate of change is half that of the 1920s, and what is more, about the same for the 1950s, i.e. about seven percentage points. Finally, between 1961 and 1971, the pace of change increases to a PPD of over ten. A similar conclusion is drawn by Kendrick *et al.* (1983, p. 12).

But as we have just seen, these PPDs are made up of a range of sectoral changes. The main changes can be listed as follows:
This shows that both new employment opportunities, and reduced opportunities in other fields, varied, so that men starting work at different periods would have different experiences. Not least, the opportunity structure typical of the earlier years, in heavy industry and

Table 2.4   Main sectoral changes

Census period	Increases	Decreases
1921–31	Distribution and Commerce	Shipbuilding, Metals, Mining
1931–51	Building, other Engineering	Distribution and Commerce, Agriculture
1951–61	Building, Services	Agriculture
1961–71	Building, Service other Engineering	Agriculture, Mining Shipbuilding

agriculture, is replaced, and services become a feature, particularly in the 1960s when the rate of change increased.

Lesser and Silvey (1950, pp. 173–4) have argued that the inter-war period was marked by several kinds of industrial decline. Not only were the old staples in decline – as they were elsewhere in Britain – but of equal importance was the failure of the 'expanding manufacturing industries' to expand as rapidly as in the South. This they attribute largely to product failure, i.e. a failure to produce the right kinds of goods for available markets. Product failure was compounded by 'contagion': particularly in an economy dependent on a small range of industries, poor performance by even one large firm depresses local demand, dragging down both those trades servicing the key firm, and those not directly connected but reliant on the local market. Lesser and Silvey, and Jones (1977) talking about 1971, also make the point that within industrial classifications are contained considerable variation of product and organisation: for example, the Scottish iron and steel industry relied on older labour-intensive production methods to produce relatively old-fashioned alloys, and the branch plant syndrome referred to above means that Scottish plant employed more workers and fewer managers than did equivalent factories in England. Jones appears to give these technologies and organisational factors a larger part to play in sectoral composition. Having examined the 1971 Census, socio-economic and industrial order data using shift-share analysis to identify *between* industrial sector, and use of occupations *within* sector, differences, he concludes that, 'Scotland's relative excess of "undesirable" jobs has been, in the recent past, due as much to the internal structure of her industries as to the industrial distribution of the labour force' (Jones, 1977, p. 405). Kendrick *et al.* (1982b, 1983) adopt a similar position, but do not advance an explanation as to why the occupational structures differ if it is not due to industrial composition. Their analysis deals with the period 1961 to 1971 in some detail (1982b, pp. 95–132) leading to the conclusion that for this particular decade, while professional and scientific services (notably Health and Education) were a very important industrial factor, and one can discern the beginning of new technological innovation that was to follow:

> For the non-manual groups it is safe to say that the occupational component of change predominated . . . for male manual workers, industrial change tended to be the main factor although the effect of occupational change was almost as great. (1982b, p. 95)

Although the Kendrick *et al.* analysis may appear to emphasise the occupational rather than the sectoral, it would be wrong to attach too much weight to this. First, their evidence by no means dismisses the sectoral effect, and second, as we have seen, the 1960s differ from earlier decades. One cannot extrapolate from one to the other. A third factor to be borne in mind is that the occupational effects *and* the industrial effects are products of particular historical processes which have operated differentially in the two countries, not least because of their close proximity and mutually interacting histories. There remain two other aspects of those histories which might arguably affect mobility which can best be dealt with here, before exploring occupational change in more depth in the next chapter.

UNEMPLOYMENT AND MIGRATION

The two outstanding issues are unemployment and emigration, both of which can be seen as outcomes of limited occupational opportunity. Unemployment rates for Scotland are consistently higher than those in Britain as a whole, and even by current standards, exceptionally high in the years 1923 (the first year of reliable figures) to 1939 during which time the rate was never less than double figures, with a peak in 1932 when one in every four Scots was out of a job. Since the Second World War, Scottish unemployment has run at twice the British average. In general, the difference in rates is greatest in 'good times': only in 'bad times' does the rest of the British economy begin to approach Scottish rates. Thus the *lowest* post-war Scottish rate (2.4 per cent, 1955) is only matched by the two highest years for Britain as a whole (2.5 per cent, 1963 and 2.4 per cent, 1967). The most recent figures show no change in this relationship (see Kellas, 1968, p. 243; and HMSO, 1971c, tables 165, 166).

Unemployment in Scotland would have been even higher, had not emigration taken place on a large scale. In as far as there was a government policy to tackle this situation after the First World War, it consisted of the hopes of the Cabinet that a simple outflow of population, particularly to Canada and Australia, would solve the problem. Until the changes of policy brought about by the Depression, this might have worked. Large numbers of the Scots have emigrated. Since the First World War, Scotland has lost approximately 1 300 000 emigrants to the five most favoured destinations of the 'White Commonwealth' and the USA. The figure is based on data supplied to the author by the Embassies and High Commissions of the countries, and is necessarily to be treated with caution. About 8 per cent of the Oxford Mobility Study of England and Wales had been born in Scotland. The question of emigration brings us full circle to this chapter's initial concern, namely, the notion of Scotland as a unit of analysis. For purely pragmatic reasons, the chances of mobility that are discussed in this study are those for people working in Scotland. The Scot born and bred north of the Border who leaves his native shores to work abroad, or in England, is excluded, even though he was once potentially part of the original supply side of the Scottish labour market at one time and is now part of the supply in another place. Of course, this problem is not unique; any national study has the same difficulty, although it is almost universally ignored (see, for example, Halsey *et al.*, 1980, and in particular the index). It only assumes prominence here because of the scale of Scottish emigration between the wars. We have the unusual situation among mobility studies of a society which has had a declining male workforce. Despite a higher birthrate between 1921 and 1971, the Scottish population grew by only 350 000 or 7.4 per cent compared with 28.6 per cent south of the Border; it fell from the equivalent of 12.9 per cent of the population of England and Wales to 10.7 per cent. The male labour force declined 170 000 over the same fifty years. We need to consider if this creates any special conditions of mobility. Even if the migrants are excluded, what effect did their moving have on those who stayed behind?

The first thing to establish is that, despite emigration, there has been a surplus of male workers over jobs, as evidenced by the high unemployment rate. Thus there is not a congruent decline of men and jobs so that the opportunity structure remains constant. Second, at a common-sense level, industries contract by shutting down plants and making men redundant. In milder forms, posts are frozen: chances to change posts are restricted and without growth of establishments or technological innovation, promotional avenues are blocked. The supply of men remains constant (or increases): the supply of occupations contracts. The workforce is thus confronted by a worsening of its position in the labour market – and thus a worsening of its class position. While strongly unionised occupations may resist longer, and white collar employees with contracts hold on in greater security, the events between the two wars were such a scale as to outweigh the power of workers' organisation, while the Trade Unions' political party did little to intervene. Despite the strength of the Labour movement in Scotland, the close identification of Clydeside's MP's with the ILP meant that Scotland was effectively a political wilderness even in the early days of Labour government.

In the general Depression between the wars, there were then two classes of depressed worker: the unemployed and those whose mobility chances were restricted. Which provided most of the emigrants is an open question, but inevitably some of the leavers were highly trained, impatient of constraint, and with ambition: the would-be occupationally mobile. This is not to argue that migrants are the 'best' of any society and that the less able, less educated, less imaginative and less achievement-oriented are left behind. Such an impression – to be found, for example, in Erikson (1972, pp. 22–4), Blau and Duncan (1967, chapters 6 and 7) or Uhlenberg (1973, pp. 296–311) – owes much to the conspicuous success of English-speaking migrants to the USA (as against the less successful European peasant migrant – see Richmond (1969, pp. 267–96) and Thomas (1973, chapter IX)). It also reflects the fact that internal migration over long distances is primarily a middle-class phenomenon, because of the organisational contexts of many middle-class jobs (Watson 1964, pp. 149, 153–4; Payne, 1973). It is typically such 'organisation men' who cannot directly inherit their positions and therefore are recruited from a wider range of backgrounds. Not least, most sociologists fall into this latter category and maybe predisposed to see all migrants as 'stars'!

At first sight, emigration may appear to reduce upward mobility rates further, since the successes would disappear from Scotland. In fact, drawing on economic ideas, this is not necessarily so. If, in a situation of unemployment, a man leaves a job to emigrate, this creates a vacancy for someone who is unemployed to fill. This emigrant ultimately removes one unemployed man from the region. His post may be filled by a promotion, or by a new hiring: in both cases it may admit someone less qualified or equally qualified but younger than his predecessor when *he* started. So the net effect is to allow easier access to the vacated post, much as in the manner of the American South where whites at given occupational levels have lower educational qualifications than whites in the North. But this is to assume that the post *is* filled. Between the two wars this was not always true. Thus, while stayers could be expected to have higher achievement for, say, lower qualifications, this would not be as marked in the inter-war period as in the American South where a power structure exists to reinforce their position. A second point is that every man who leaves removes his spending power from the country, so reducing demand.

The Historical and Social Context of Mobility 33

Thus 'there will be a multiplier effect on employment; and my guess is that, in a typical British region, one extra man will lose his job for every six or seven who go elsewhere' (Brown, 1969, p. 236). This again will restrict the White-Southerner Effect, so that if there is an effect, it can be looked for in the latter twenty years, rather than earlier. The loss of migrants, then, sets up a number of processes, both increasing and decreasing mobility with the result that their empirical detection is almost impossible, even if this represents a further distinctive feature of Scottish society.

SCOTLAND: A SEPARATE UNIT OF ANALYSIS

The strong emphasis on grounding the mobility analysis in Scottish social conditions is the outcome of an empirical and historical perspective on social events. Such an approach relies more on the concrete than the abstract, and the absolute complexity of social life seems, to the author, to demand descriptions and explanations that may sometimes be lacking in generality but are at least grounded in everyday experience. It may also owe something to a resistance to an over-metropolitanised and simplified view of British society.

The argument that Scottish society has a characteristic institutional and cultural existence and history, made in the first part of this chapter, seems well established. The argument for an analysis of economic phenomena on a separate basis is less clear: it can only be justified in terms of Scotland's connections with international capitalism, and the historical effects of its integration into that world-system, in particular with the English economy. This argument lies midway between the view that Scotland has been dependent on, or subordinate to, English interests since the Act of Union (Dickson 1980, p. 90) and the contrary view that Scotland's development is best understood as an example of an industrial society, only marginally connected to England (Kendrick et al., 1983, p. 21). The position adopted is closer to Lenman's judgement that Scotland has 'developed a very specialised regional branch of the British economy' (1977, p. 204), an economic position overlaid with cultural specifics so that Scotland can be treated separately (but still within a wider framework of international markets and capital flows).

Thus the second half of this chapter has tried to explore features which make the Scottish economy unlike the English. This has served three purposes, First, it has shown that one cannot simply generalise from one country to the other – as Goldthorpe (1980a) implies. Second, even if Scotland can be neatly classified as an 'industrial society', there are variations within that type that require consideration. Finally, since Scotland is regarded as both typical and unique, a separate analysis of her occupational structure and mobility is justified.

[Handwritten note: What about advant. for devel. of theory in using an extreme case?]

3 The Occupational Structure

A discussion of industrial employment, although commonly used to depict occupations (see Payne, 1986), provides only a partial picture of how groupings at various skill levels have expanded or contracted, The Census, albeit with confusing changes of categorisation, can be adapted to produce a decennial time-series which deals directly with occupations. This not only provides a grounding for the empirical analysis of occupational mobility, but also enables us to consider in more detail how the theory of industrial society accounts for occupational transition.

Among the various contributions that make up this school, one of the most useful summaries is W. E. Moore's *Social Change* (1974), from which it is possible to draw eight specific propositions about occupational transition. One of these – that there will be increased mobility both within careers and between generations – is left for discussion in a later chapter. Three of the others can be regarded as general propositions:

1. All economic operations – such as the subsistence agricultural sector – are incorporated in the nation market economy.
2. There is a transition of activity from primary to secondary, and secondary to tertiary, industrial sectors.
3. New occupations are created, and differentiation between occupations increases.

The remaining four propositions deal more specifically with occupations.

4. The proportion of workers in agriculture will decline.
5. An upgrading of minimum and average skill levels will take place, resulting in a structure with relatively few unskilled workers and 'the vast majority' of workers in various middle categories.
6. There will, none the less, be a shortage of skilled workers.
7. This will be accompanied by an increase in demand for professionals of all categories and in particular doctors, engineers and experts in organisation.

These propositions apply to countries both during industrialisation and in contemporary industrial economies (Moore, 1974, pp. 104–5).

They can be put to empirical test by considering how the Scottish occupational structure has changed this century. The main source of information available on this change is the decennial Population Census. Its data for the years 1921 to 1971 (1941 excepted) cover the working lives of the men in the Scottish Mobility Study sample (the oldest respondent was born in 1909 and began work in the early 1920s) and also coincide with the economic and social changes that have been discussed in the last few pages. It should be remembered, however, that direct comparison between census data and the sample data reported later cannot be made for technical reasons of classification, time points and ages of the population concerned.

A number of sources are already available for an examination of this period. Routh (1965) deals with the years up to 1951, while Bain (1972) has extended the analysis to include the 1966 sample census. Both deal with Great Britain as a whole. More recently, Goldthorpe (1980a), Routh (1980) and Brown (1978) have produced tabulations for England and Wales. None of these quite meets present needs, so that it is necessary to return to the Census Reports and carry out a re-analysis. This is a very time-consuming operation and care needs to be taken to ensure continuity in categorisation, as classifications have changed several times, most notably in 1951 and 1961.

The units chosen for the analysis are based on the Registrar-General's Socio-Economic Groups (SEGs) as used in the 1971 Census (HMSO, 1971a). Full details of the SEG classifications are to be found in the *Classification of Occupations, 1970* (HMSO, 1971b), but the labels used in this section should be self-explanatory. This scheme identifies seventeen groups on the basis of their occupations and the status attached to them. Like all occupational classifications, they have their minor peculiarities (Bechhofer, 1969; Hope and Goldthorpe, 1974, pp. 22–7); in this account 'armed forces' (which does not differentiate officers from other ranks) and the residual category seventeen of 'unclassified' persons are discarded and the very small numbers in the 'large' proprietors and managers category (SEG 1) have been merged with the 'small' proprietors and managers category (SEG 2). This leaves fourteen categories. Although the SEGs contain an 'own-account workers' category, the classification does not otherwise differentiate between those who own and those who merely manage enterprises. Its blindness to property obviously restricts any consideration of ownership, or the managerialism thesis in the present context. Previous census Occupational Tables were reprocessed to obtain comparable groupings. To achieve this requires the reclassification of over 900 occupational categories, each with four or more grades of seniority, at each census point. Obviously, the level of comparison with which one works is limited: if it is too precise, the accuracy of the reconstruction becomes crucially important, whereas if it is too general, the purpose of improving on crude di and tri-chotomies is lost. A note on some technical aspects of the reclassification is given in the Appendix.

As Kendrick *et al.* have observed in a preamble to using some of the data presented here (and published as an earlier paper: see Payne, 1977a), there are two types of problem with redeploying census data. The first is methodological: without returning to the raw data, the earlier census information as published in tabulated form can never be *exactly* translated into the 1971 categories, however careful and detailed one may be with the *technical* procedures. 'All one has to go on in performing the translation are common-sense assumptions of continuity between meanings, the concrete referents of the component occupational titles of the two classifications' (Kendrick *et al.*, 1983, p. 17). The second problem is an epistemological one. Even if one could solve the technical difficulties, the time-series still requires acceptance that the same conceptual category can be applied to phenomena fifty years apart. Industrial change changes the content and standing of occupations, so that only a detailed historical examination of every occupation over fifty years could even begin to tackle this problem of historical comparison. The reader must therefore proceed with all due caution, recognising that as in all such time-series, the new data can provide only a basic outline of a very complicated process.

For convenience, the exact SEG titles used below are slightly different from the census but this is intended as a convenient shorthand: the SEG number remains the same. The advantages of these categories should be fairly obvious. Since the debate about 'skills levels' in modern society has been conducted in an imprecise fashion, there is no guidance as to what, say, an 'upgrading of skill levels' means in empirical terms. At least the SEGs provide a specific framework in which to identify 'skilled manual workers' as having – or not having – the level of skill to which others are upgraded. Even though the original formulations did not intend to refer to the conventions of the British Census, this course of action should at least serve to clarify the range of meanings which could have been intended. At the same time, the construction of the categories is reasonably visible. In the past, the reader has been given little guidance whether one man's 'administrative employees in the non-agricultural sector' is the same as another man's 'white collar' and 'professional workers'. Most commentators on occupational transition have been willing to take such equivalences as non-problematic (see Garnsey, 1975, p. 308) despite a more general sensitivity to such nuances in mainstream sociology.

The analysis which follows concentrates on male, female and combined distributions for Scotland, as being most relevant to a study of mobility in that country: a parallel discussion of England and Wales can be found in Payne (1977a). At the same time, these can be used as a case study of occupational transition in industrial society, as Table 3.6 below specifically demonstrates.

OCCUPATIONAL TRANSITION: HIGHLY SKILLED NON-FARM OCCUPATIONS

The first occupations to be considered are those in which *expertise* derives from long periods of education, both formal and informal. Since these are not all 'salaried' or 'administrative' or 'professional' they are referred to as the 'highly skilled, non-farm occupations' – a title which also avoids confusion with the lower skill levels of intermediate or manual occupations. The numbers for these at the five census points covering the sixty years since the end of the First World War are given in Table 3.1.

Considering first the overall totals, the most notable feature of the highly skilled non-farm workers is their increase, more than doubling in size from 1921 to 1971, while the economically active sector increased by less than one-third. The second feature is that the four categories behaved differently: while salaried professionals and employers and managers have very similar growth profiles, the self employed professionals did not follow that pattern after the 1931 decline, and the semi-professionals have an equally distinctive pattern, one of more rapid expansion than the other groups. This is shown in Figure 3.1: it will be remembered that there was no 1941 census.

These patterns do not fit the conventional model of occupational transition that was encountered in the Introduction. In the first place, economic modernisation appears to have received a severe setback between 1921 and 1931, with only SEG 5 (the lowest skilled of the five SEGs) showing any growth. This is not in accord with two of the

Table 3.1 Highly skilled non-farm workers (SEG 1–5) in Scotland, by sex

SEGs	Occupations	Category	1921	1931	1951	1961	1971
1–5	All highly skilled, non-farm	Total	214 660	206 542	262 526	332 720	429 820
		Males	152 724	143 379	177 186	224 740	282 660
		Females	61 936	63 163	85 340	107 980	147 160
1 & 2	Employers and managers	Total	117 035	114 065	129 043	147 470	175 930
		Males	106 684	99 988	109 914	121 510	141 640
		Females	10 351	14 077	19 129	23 960	34 290
3	Self-employed professionals	Total	12 416	8 795	9 178	15 340	14 410
		Males	8 482	4 930	7 763	14 690	13 540
		Females	3 934	3 865	1 415	650	960
4	Salaried professionals	Total	25 953	21 689	33 470	38 710	60 650
		Males	21 666	19 494	28 598	34 660	54 380
		Females	4 287	2 195	4 872	4 050	6 270
5	Semi-professionals	Total	59 256	61 993	90 835	131 200	178 830
		Males	15 892	18 967	30 911	53 880	73 190
		Females	43 364	43 026	59 924	77 320	105 640
1–15	All economically active	Total	2 114 850	2 173 256	2 221 443	2 281 970	2 266 410
		Males	1 480 834	1 517 266	1 540 784	1 550 190	1 432 930
		Females	634 016	655 990	680 659	731 680	833 480

SOURCE: See text.

40 *Employment and Opportunity*

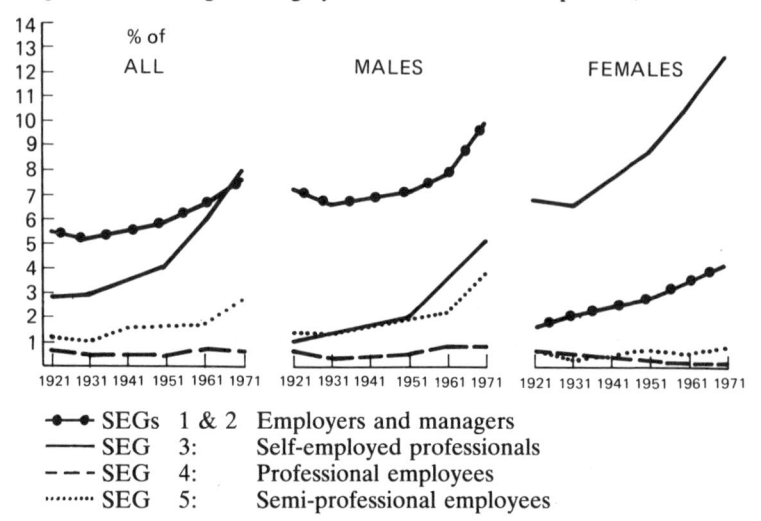

Figure 3.1 Changes in highly skilled non-farm occupations, 1921–71

```
% of        ALL                MALES              FEMALES
```

1921 1931 1941 1951 1961 1971   1921 1931 1941 1951 1961 1971   1921 1931 1941 1951 1961 1971

●—● SEGs 1 & 2   Employers and managers
—— SEG 3:   Self-employed professionals
– – – SEG 4:   Professional employees
······ SEG 5:   Semi-professional employees

propositions that were drawn from Moore above, namely, that there is an up-grading of average skill levels (unless something dramatic has happened in the next skill bands to weight up that average), and second, that there should be an increased demand for 'professionals of all categories, and in particular doctors, engineers and experts in organisation' (Moore, 1974, 104–6). The theory of industrial society has nothing to say directly on 'demodernisation'; its logic of industrialism is unidirectional.

Second, the increases in this sector during other parts of the period are quite different, particularly in the latter twenty years. The theory of industrial society gives no explanation of why rates of change should vary so much in consecutive decades in the same society. If the two propositions are meant to be descriptive statements of what actually takes place, then they are inadequate in that they do not describe rates of change. If, on the other hand, the propositions are meant to be a theory of industrialisation (and it is not clear which is the case for most of the writers mentioned above), then the theory does not provide an immediate explanation of why rates of change are so varied, as inspection of the graphs demonstrates.

A further problem involves the different performance of the four sub-sectors which jointly comprise the highly skilled non-farm workforce. These sub-sectors are not arbitrary categories but manifest an attempt to identify functionally different occupational units. One of the key propositions calls for an increase in demand for professionals, particularly doctors and experts in organisational skills such as lawyers. In Scotland, these are two self-employed professions. If there has also been a greater need for other professions (such as engineers, by the same proposition), we would also expect at least some (the new, most specialised consultants) to join the ranks of the self-employed. SEG 3 should therefore show both an absolute and relative growth. But as Table 3.1 shows, while absolute growth has been (erratically) from 12 500 to 14 400 its relative position has only fluctuated around half a per cent – and fell in the last decade.

Conversely, the semi-professions have outperformed their highly skilled partners, overtaking the managers as the largest single highly skilled group. SEG 5 has experienced almost perfect straight-line growth since 1951, and the semi-professions are now two and a half times bigger a proportion of the labour force than fifty years ago. The propositions of occupational transition do not describe/predict/explain this exceptional growth of one particular occupational category among the professions (in the American sense): indeed, in proposing that the 'vast majority' of workers will be in the middle range of skills (the remaining part of the other proposition that is relevant here), there is no allowance for the shift of nearly 10 per cent of the labour force out of the middle range of skills and into the highly skilled sector.

It would be perhaps a little unfair to criticise the theory of industrial society for not also identifying which of the highly skilled elements would expand by means of female labour. Both Table 3.1 and Figure 3.1 show that men and women have had separate experiences of occupational transition. Women in full-time employment as defined by the census have made little impact in any of the professional and managerial sector (SEGs 1–4) except the semi-professions. While their numbers in management have tripled, this is only an increase of around 20 000 during the time that male managers expanded by nearly 60 000. Because the males outnumber the females by more than 2 to 1 overall, the male trends are more or less the same as the general trends already discussed, except that their growth is little higher in all SEGs except SEG 5. Even here, the expansion is from 16 000 to 73 000.

THE LOW SKILLED

To some extent, grouping SEGs 7, 9, 10 and 11 together is a little arbitrary. It could be argued that skilled manual workers, having served formal training of periods in most cases lasting up to five years in apprenticeship, should be discussed with the 'intermediate' skill sector. Again, service workers are a more heterogeneous group and are not mainly concerned with industrial production, as are the other three. However, all four together comprise the non-farm manual sector and most sociologists accept that manual workers share greater components of life chances than skilled manual workers share with white collar or supervisory employees. It might have been more consistent to include agricultural workers in this section so that all manual workers would be considered together, but there is more heuristic advantage to be gained in concentrating on their industrial sector and so discussing them with farmers. The numbers of workers engaged in the four SEGs is given in Table 3.2.

The most striking feature of these data is the decimation of the skilled manual workers. Scotland has lost nearly 150 000 and this represents a drop from an index of 100 in 1921, to about 78 in 1971, while the economically active population has increased from 100 to over 107. To put this another way, had the skilled manual workers simply performed as the economically active population as a whole did, there would have been 729 300 of them in 1971, not 531 600. Clearly the expansion of the economy was not in this sector, nor was it unequivocally in the other manual sectors either, as Figure 3.2 shows.

These four SEGs are particularly relevant to the argument that minimum and average skill levels rise, leaving relatively few unskilled workers (proposition (5) above), that there is a shortage of skilled workers (proposition (6)) and that new jobs are created, while differentiation between jobs increases (proposition (3)). If the skilled manual worker is treated as low level on the skills continuum, then the 'non-farm low-skill sector' has contracted, in line with the usual transition proposition. However, the sector increased from 1921 to 1931, declined slowly up to 1951, and generally fell more sharply after that. But even this statement disguises the upturn of the unskilled manual category in the 1960s, the thirty-year rise in semi-skilled manual occupation from 1931 to 1961, and the upturn of the service worker sector since 1961. Moreover, one might reasonably expect the contraction of those sectors with minimum skills to bite first and most sharply into those with least skills – service worker and unskilled manual worker sectors – but it does not. Skilled manual workers were first and most affected, while service workers and unskilled manual workers are the two categories which have been most buoyant in the last ten years. In this respect minimum and average skill levels do not

Table 3.2 Non-farm manual workers (SEGs 7, 9, 10 and 11) in Scotland by sex

SEGs	Occupations	Category	1921	1931	1951	1961	1971
7, 9, 10, 11	All manual non-farm workers	Total Males Females	1 305 060 947 196 377 864	1 378 110 984 795 393 315	1 314 810 977 042 337 768	1 263 910 943 970 319 940	1 184 620 833 160 350 860
7	Service workers	Total Males Females	149 232 17 643 131 589	179 219 28 810 150 409	118 443 18 360 100 083	102 180 15 480 86 700	124 300 15 880 108 420
9	Skilled manual workers	Total Males Females	680 306 564 570 115 736	633 385 533 850 99 535	601 890 518 387 83 503	610 990 541 210 69 780	531 560 480 080 51 480
10	Semi-skilled manual	Total Males Females	297 508 187 786 109 722	284 138 186 131 98 007	308 673 215 772 92 901	342 490 232 640 109 850	303 190 189 930 113 260
11	Unskilled manual workers	Total Males Females	198 014 177 197 20 817	281 368 236 004 45 364	285 804 224 523 61 281	208 250 154 640 53 610	224 790 147 270 77 700
1–15	All economically active	Total Males Females	2 114 850 1 480 834 634 016	2 173 256 1 517 266 655 990	2 221 443 1 540 784 680 659	2 281 870 1 550 190 731 680	2 266 410 1 432 930 833 480

SOURCE: See text above.

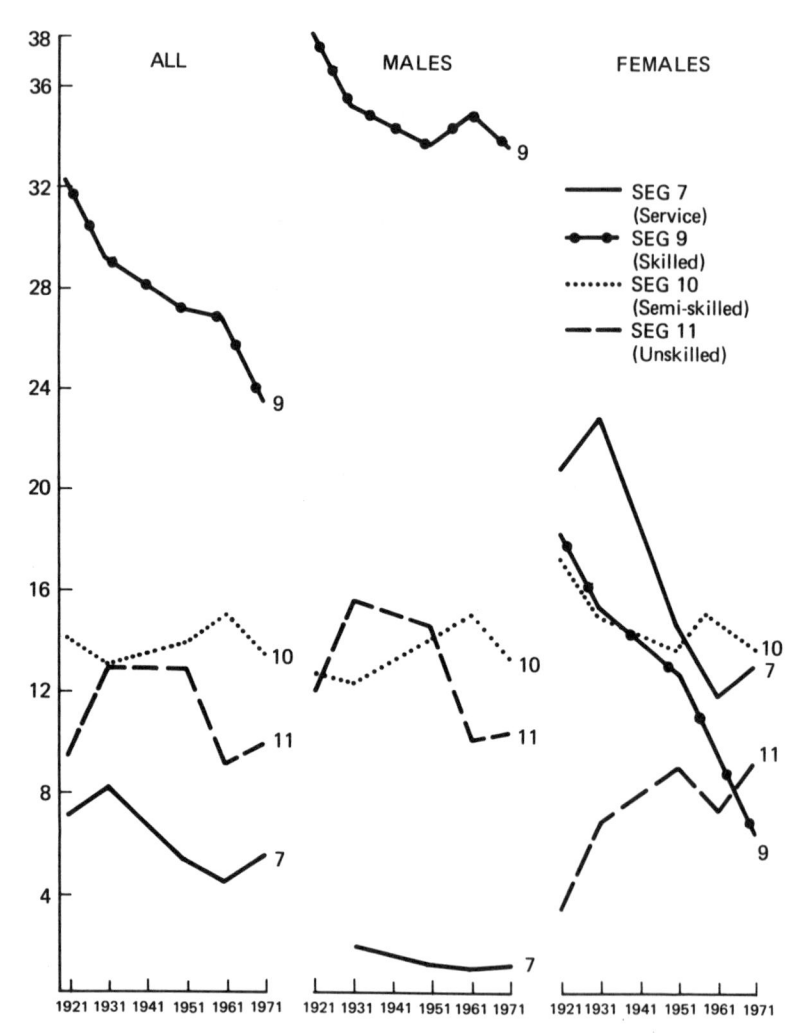

Figure 3.2 Changes in low-skilled non-farm occupations, 1921–71: percentage of labour force

SEG 7 (Service)
SEG 9 (Skilled)
SEG 10 (Semi-skilled)
SEG 11 (Unskilled)

rise in the appropriate transition pattern among the non-farm manual workers in Scotland.

Alternatively, skilled manual workers can be regarded as having 'intermediate skill level' on the occupation continuum. In this case, the long-term proportional contraction of the low-skills sector is only about 1.8 per cent which makes Scotland an embarrassing inconsistency to the theory of industrial society. However, we are still left with the 'recovery' of these sectors post-1961, while the contraction now bites first into the semi-skilled manual category (not the most skilled of the three low-skilled sectors): the unskilled manual category is proportionately still higher than in 1921; and the decline in this latter category is confined to the 1950s, whereas service workers decline most sharply before this, between 1931 and 1951. if the hidden hand of economic change is active for one category in this period, why is the obviously similar unskilled manual worker left relatively untouched until the next ten years – during which time the service workers begin to stabilise? The theory does not tell us.

These data also impinge on other propositions of occupational differentiation. If an occupation becomes differentiated, it presumably becomes more recognised, more specialised, requires a more specific system of recruitment (and training), and cannot just be taken on by any casual worker. If new occupations are created, they too presumably exist in an organisational framework, and by definition must fulfil a specialised work function that is now demarcated from other occupations. Among the most highly differentiated and restricted occupations are skilled manual occupations, entered only by prolonged apprenticeship, and safeguarded by rigorous Trade Union rules (supported by management practices in many cases). But there is not only no evidence of an increase in occupational differentiation, that is, in skilled manual occupations, but the evidence shows the reverse. Alternatively, semi-skilled manual occupations – which, it might be argued are the more likely occupations for new technologies to expand, as new skills are capital-intensive even if specialist – show a long-term and now accelerating decline. Unskilled manual and service occupations, with the lowest levels of skill requirement and therefore the greatest interchangeability of labour, typified by the labourer, the cleaner, and the casual all-purpopse hand, show an upturn in their numbers. Among the lower skill levels, which comprise about half of the labour force, there is no evidence at this level of analysis to support the proposition that occupational differentiation is occurring, let alone increasing.

While these data do not directly indicate 'shortages', or 'demand' for particular types of labour, it is difficult to see how a long-term decline in, say, the skilled manual category is compatible with a 'shortage of skilled workers' – unless, of course, skill in this case refers to professional skill only, something which is not specified. By Moore's first proposition, that all economic operations are integrated into the national market economy, any shortage of skills should be corrected by market mechanisms. Thus, while a long-term decline of a broad occupational category could be occurring, workers to fill specific occupations may be in short supply (and scarce in some regions but not others) in the short run. But one cannot imply the dominance of market mechanisms, on the one hand, and then explain away a fifty-year, long-term decline, on the other, as characterising numerous localised short-run shortages. Indeed, none of the writers in question even advances the adjustment thesis to account for this shortage, so that one is left to assume that they see a shortage as the precondition for the increase in skilled occupations which they believe takes place, since these are the only two items included in the propositions. In this sense, the proposition of skills-shortage is incompatible with the proposition of market incorporation and without further evidence of whether we are dealing with a supply or demand effect, the former seems untenable.

This discussion of the less-skilled occupations has so far concentrated on the perspectives derived from the theory of industrial society. It is equally possible to consider the same data as they impinge on Braverman's Marxist thesis of deskilling, in which the skilled manual worker in particular looms large.

In the first place, the decline in numbers of skilled workers (SEG 9) is as generally predicted by Braverman (1974). However, the rest of the picture is less clear, for rather than this decline being matched by an increase in semi- and unskilled work, to replace skilled workers in new production processes, the latter categories change little between 1921 and 1971. Taken together (in line with Braverman's rejection of the notion of a semi-skilled category) they increase absolutely, from 495 522 to 534 750, but decrease relative to the total labour force, from 23.5 per cent to 23.3 per cent. If we restrict ourselves to the male labour force, there is not even an absolute growth in numbers. And in the intervening years, the levels of less skilled manual workers fluctuate with the lowest category (weighted by labourers, cleaners, etc.) varying inversely to the slightly more semi-skilled category. A more plausible explanation for these figures would be that entire industries lost their prominant position in the economy: for example, a high proportion of female skilled labour was employed in the declining textile trades.

At best, Braverman's thesis can be sustained in a very weak form. The degradation of labour would appear to be contained *within* categories, with skilled status being attributed to reduce work tasks, and therefore invisible to this kind of analysis (although see Chapter 7 below). Braverman would have had to make rigorous use of this argument if he were to explain away the 215 000 increase in high skilled occupations that we saw in the previous section.

Before leaving the less skilled, it is worth noting once again the gender segregation of occupations. Not only are women much more reliant on service work (SEG 7) but the decline in skilled employment has been sharper for women, so heightening the segregation: in 1971, one-third of Scottish males were still skilled workers, whereas among females the figure had fallen from over a fifth to one-sixteenth. The number of women in unskilled work has generally been on the increase, the reverse of the trend in the other three manual categories among women. In other words, *within* the manual class, occupational degradation seems to be the main characteristic of the female labour force since 1921.

THE INTERMEDIATE SKILLED

In the previous section, it was suggested that the skilled manual worker might be considered part of the intermediate occupational sector: if this is so, then the proportion that this sector comprises has contracted in fifty years from 49 per cent to 47 per cent. This is clearly not in support of the proposition that the 'vast majority' of workers move into the intermediate categories. Only if SEG 5 is drafted out of the highly skilled set, and down into this version of the intermediate sector, could such a proposition be upheld, but this would make sociological nonsense by combining, for instance, teachers with degrees with clerks who have no post-secondary education and manual workers who finished full-time education at the minimum school leaving age: the intermediate sector would be too heterogeneous to have any meaning, except as the residual category left once 'true' professionals and unskilled manual workers have been accounted for – which is not a helpful concept. If SEG 9 is not included, the intermediate sector so defined has grown by 6.7 per cent, but this growth hardly represents the 'vast majority' of workers. The skilled manual workers have not been included in either Table 3.3 or Figure 3.3 but readers can, of course, make their own adjustment if they wish.

The junior non-manual occupations show a steep, indeed spectacular growth from 1921 to 1971 of 190 000. But in the last decade, junior non-manual occupations have seen a decline in the rates of expansion:

Table 3.3 Intermediate non-farm workers (SEGs 6, 8 and 12) in Scotland by sex

SEGs	Occupations	Categories	1921	1931	1951	1961	1971
6, 8, 12	All intermediate	Total	386 396	437 227	495 488	568 170	573 610
		Males	214 855	252 512	251 800	274 510	247 960
		Females	171 541	184 715	243 688	293 660	325 650
6	Junior non-manual	Total	282 822	320 812	403 610	473 040	472 230
		Males	145 241	161 656	175 207	191 300	161 090
		Females	137 581	159 156	228 403	281 740	311 140
8	Foreman and supervisors	Total	27 726	30 584	40 092	54 800	56 590
		Males	26 284	28 736	36 834	51 550	51 140
		Females	1 442	1 848	3 258	3 250	5 450
12	Own account workers	Total	75 848	85 831	51 786	40 330	44 790
		Males	43 330	62 120	39 759	31 660	35 730
		Females	32 518	23 711	12 027	8 670	9 060
1–15	All economically active	Total	2 114 850	2 173 256	2 221 443	2 281 870	2 266 410
		Males	1 480 834	1 517 266	1 540 784	1 550 190	1 432 930
		Females	634 016	655 990	680 659	731 680	833 480

SOURCE: See text above.

currently these occupations are about 21 per cent of the workforce. This again suggests that increases in skill levels and the supposed increasing dominance of the middle categories is not a uniform process, even if one wishes to argue that it does partially apply to the largest single intermediate category.

Figure 3.3 Changes in intermediate-skilled non-farm occupations 1921–71: percentage of labour force

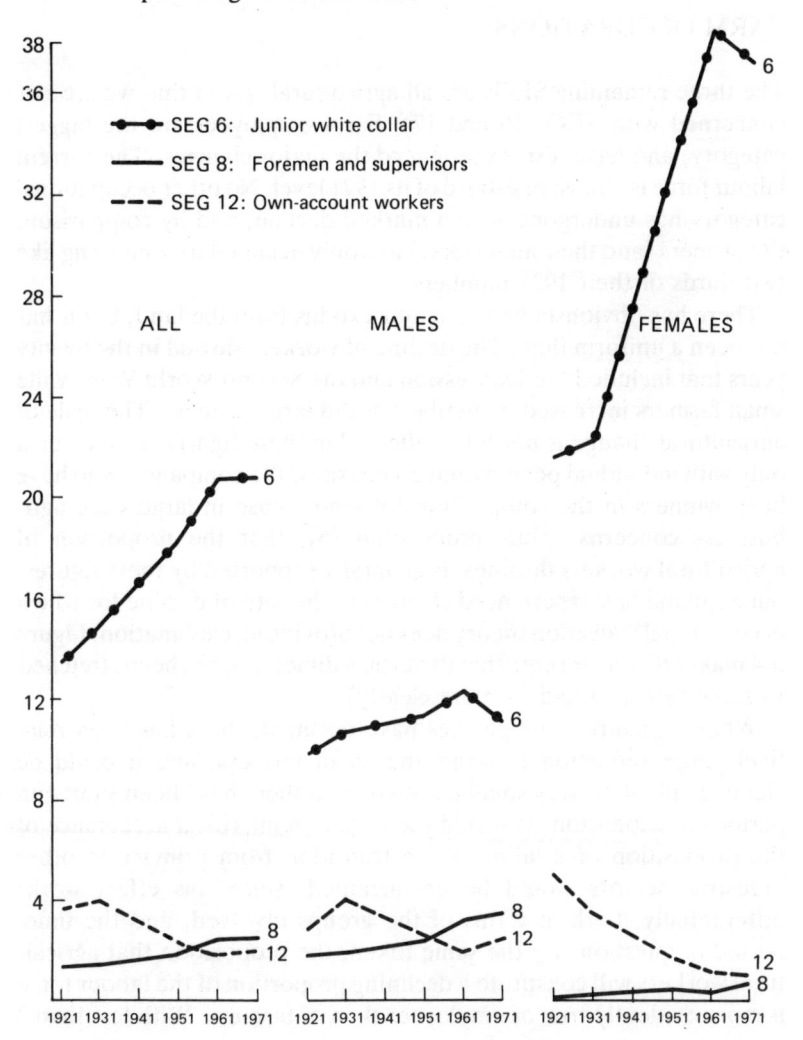

- SEG 6: Junior white collar
- SEG 8: Foremen and supervisors
- SEG 12: Own-account workers

Not only does SEG 6 show the greatest change, but it also manifests the most striking gender differences. At the start of the series men outnumber women, whereas by 1971 the women out number the men almost two to one. In the later decades, junior white collar work comprises in excess of one-third of all female employment, while SEGs 8 and 12 are of little significance. This stands out clearly in Figure 3.3.

FARM OCCUPATIONS

The three remaining SEGs are all agricultural (given that we are not concerned with SEGs 16 and 17). Farm employees are the biggest category, and have also experienced the major changes. The current labour force is almost one-third of its 1921 level. No other occupational category has undergone such a marked decline, and by comparison, the farmers (and their managers) have only declined to something like two-thirds of their 1921 numbers.

There has obviously been a major exodus from the land, but is has not been a uniform flow. The decline of workers slowed in the twenty years that included the Depression and the Second World War, while small farmers increased in number, as did large farmers. The scale of agricultural change is not fully reflected in these figures, as they deal only with individual persons and do not show the companies who have been winners in the competition for land to use in large-scale agribusiness concerns. Thus proposition (5), that the proportion of agricultural workers declines, is generally supported by these figures, but Scotland has experienced changes in the rate of decline for which occupational transition theory does not provide an explanation. Figure 3.4 makes this clear (note that its vertical dimension has been stretched to show SEGs 13 and 14 more clearly).

While agricultural employees have declined, there has been relatively little reduction in large and small farmers, and it could be claimed, albeit on very small numbers, that there have been short-run periods of expansion. It would seem that an uncritical acceptance of the proposition of a labour force transition from primary to other industrial sectors would be unwarranted, since this effect works differentially, both in terms of the groups involved, and the time-period in question. By the same token, the proposition that agricultural workers will constitute a declining proportion of the labour force is more evidently true of employees than of farmers. With less than 3

Table 3.4 Farm occupations (SEGs 13, 14 and 15) in Scotland by sex

SEGs	Occupations	Category	1921	1931	1951	1961	1971
13,14 and 15	All farm occupations	Total	190 683	154 371	148 785	117 070	78 700
		Males	168 058	139 580	134 922	106 970	69 150
		Females	22 625	14 791	13 863	10 100	9 550
13	'Large' farmers	Total	31 353	36 180	37 834	31 420	17 160
		Males	28 678	34 059	36 279	29 100	15 560
		Females	2 675	2 121	1 555	2 300	1 600
14	'Small' farmers	Total	25 722	13 397	16 679	17 660	16 810
		Males	23 384	11 495	15 464	16 470	14 710
		Females	2 338	1 902	1 215	1 190	2 100
15	Farm employees	Total	133 608	104 794	94 272	67 990	44 730
		Males	115 996	94 026	83 179	61 400	38 880
		Females	17 612	10 768	11 093	6 590	5 850
1–15	All economically active	Total	2 114 850	2 173 256	2 221 443	2 281 870	2 266 410
		Males	1 480 834	1 517 266	1 540 784	1 550 190	1 432 930
		Females	634 016	655 990	680 659	731 680	833 480

SOURCE: See text above.

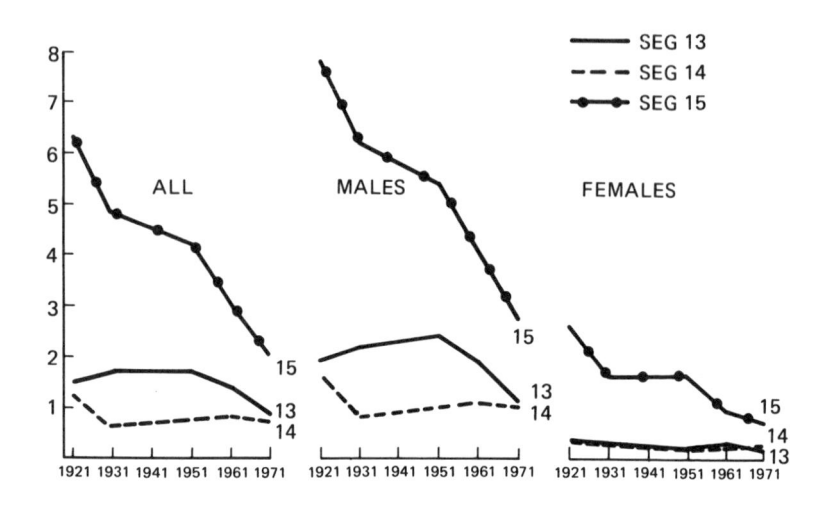

Figure 3.4 Changes in farm occupations in Scotland, 1921–71: percentage of labour force

per cent of men employed in farming, it is hard to imagine much future reduction in this sector.

Before leaving the set of propositions derived from Moore's work, it is worth commenting that even basic proportions can be less than explicit. The fundamental proposition of a transition of activity from primary to the secondary (and tertiary) industrial sectors may be a valid statement about 'activity' conceived of as 'number of employees' in agriculture. However, the value of the output of agriculture has been increasing at constant prices; the 1960s for example, saw an increase in output of around 10 per cent, with a drop in manpower of near 25 per cent. Both absolutely and in output per man this is an increase in economic activity (Johnson, 1971, pp. 103–4). Again, while capital investment in agriculture is only one-tenth of what it was 100 years ago, it has not changed greatly this century, consistently accounting for around 3 per cent of the nation's total fixed capital formation (Johnson, 1971, p. 199; Deane and Cole, 1962, p. 306). Thus while gross manpower levels have fallen in the primary sector (fishing being very much the junior partner in this sector), changes in the balance of general economic activity between this and the secondary and tertiary sectors must be due to greater growth in these latter, rather than absolute decline in the primary sector.

SOME CONCLUDING ISSUES

In Chapter 2 an argument for a separate consideration of society in Scotland was advanced, and the foregoing analysis has concentrated on that line of analysis. It remains an interesting question to consider whether the occupational changes are unique to Scotland or are also true for England and Wales. At a gross level, the latter is the case, with, for example, the time-profiles generally congruent and broad similarities for the major changes – the moderate expansion of the highly skilled and more rapid growth of SEGs 5 and 6 and the decline of SEGs 9 and 15 (see Payne, 1977a). This suggests that the same forces operate on the two economies.

This is certainly the view taken by Kendrick *et al.* in their extended analysis of the same time-series earlier produced by Payne (1977a), although their interest lies more in the manufacturing labour market for male and female workers, rather than all sectors (but mainly for male employees) as in this study. Their account stresses the decline of skilled manual employment and the use of non-manual employment. In particular, they conclude that 'there was an unambiguous deskilling of the industrial workforce in the 1920s', even allowing for the effect of the Depression on the 1931 Census. However, they may have overestimated the buoyancy of the Scottish economy in 1921 (see the previous chapter). They also note how SEG 7 changes in this period from being mainly domestic servants to other kinds of personal service worker (Kendrick *et al.*, 1982b, pp. 86–132). In addition to the SEG series, Kendrick *et al.* (1982b, pp. 95–7) present a shift/share analysis of changes between 1961 and 1971. This attempts to partition occupational change between changes due to the use of labour within industry, and the shift of employment between sectors. Perhaps the most striking result is the great complexity of movements, the main features of which are produced in Table 3.5.

The interaction of industrial change in occupations is clear in the middle two columns: gains of new occupations of *whatever* level are either in newer industries or widely spread, but not in mining, shipbuilding, or metals, and in fact only 2700 new jobs in semi- and unskilled manual work were recorded. Conversely, job losses were in the old staples, but also in transport, showing how the industrial heritage of the nineteenth century continues to be reflected in the occupational structure. At the same time, the non-manual SEGs (we omit some of the intermediate SEGs because of their small numbers for male workers) show a strong occupational effect, i.e. a response to

Table 3.5 Shift/share analysis of occupational change: Scottish males, 1961–71*

SEG	Gains	Losses	Shift/Share
Non-manual; 1–5	Professional & Scientific Services, Various manufacturing	None	⅔ occupational
Skilled manual; 9	Newer industries, e.g. engineering	Old staples, distribution & transport	More industrial than occupational
Semi-skilled manual; 10	Various, but not old staples except textiles	Old staples (esp. mining), transport	⅔ industrial
Unskilled manual; 11	Various, but not old staples except textiles	Transport, old staples, public admin.	⅘ occupational

*Adapted from Kendrick et al. (1983, pp. 107–29). The reader who wishes to consider more recent changes, to 1981 (i.e. the period of less interest to us here because we shall be dealing with completed mobility) should see Kendrick (1986).

technological innovation which applies across the board and not just the specialist new service industries. These results, which will be important for an understanding of the changes in mobility rates discussed in later chapters can be summarised as follows: 'the non-manual groups, it is safe to say that the occupational component of change predominated. . . . for male manual workers, industrial change tended to be the main factor' (Kendrick et al., 1983, p. 132). Kendrick et al., also point to long term similarities between Scotland and the situation south of the border, a broad similarity which must be acknowledged.

On the other hand, there is not a complete coincidence of patterns, with differences of levels, rates of change, and even small-scale, short-run counter trends. These can be summarised by examining the degree to which the several occupational categories are over- or under-represented in Scotland, as against England and Wales, using a simple comparison of actual numbers and the expected frequencies if there were no differences between the two countries. Table 3.6 makes this clear: it gives the number of jobs in each SEG, and the percentage of these which are in Scotland for the census year in question. This can be thought of as first an expression of social justice, in that if Scotland is, say, 10 per cent of the mainland UK's labour force, it should have 10 per cent of the desirable or skilled occupations and 10 per cent of the undesirable or unskilled ones: Table 3.6 suggests the scale of national imbalance. Second, the figures can be taken as an indication of convergence or divergence of industrial structures over fifty years – although the interim fluctuations must be borne in mind.

The occupations in Table 3.6 have been arranged in a very rough hierarchy of 'desirability': those towards the top tend on average to be more skilled, to receive better income, have greater security, have superior working conditions, receive better holidays, fringe benefits, and flexibility of working hours, and to be popularly recognised as more desirable (i.e. following the argument of the Hope–Goldthorpe scale). Some readers may wish to adjust the hierarchy to suit their own perceptions, as the arrangements given here is recognised as a very approximate solution and not one which is inherent in the OPCS definitions of the SEGs: the exact order of heirarchy is not crucial to the argument.

What Table 3.6 shows is that Scotland's position *vis-à-vis* England has changed in the last fifty years, on the whole for the worse. Among the top 50 per cent of 'more desirable occupations', Scotland started with a better share of large farmers, self-employed and employed professionals: only in the large farmers, a relatively closed group, has Scotland maintained an advantage, and this in a small and currently declining sector. Scotland was deficient in managers and in semi-professionals: the latter are now in balance with England, but the former have fallen even further behind. The other employed highly skilled category, the salaried professionals, started with a 'surplus' in Scotland but since 1961 has also moved into 'deficit'. Scotland, therefore, does not now have any advantage over England in the highly skilled non-farm sector, and despite a relatively good performance in the semi-professions, the situation in this sector has deteriorated since 1921.

In the intermediate occupations, relative advantage among foremen, and junior non-manual workers has given way to disadvantage. Scottish own-account workers have dropped further behind, while small farmers have ended a period of considerable fluctuation with a much reduced position. In each of the four intermediate categories which form the second part of the more desirable 50 per cent of

Table 3.6 Deviations between observed and expected frequencies in Scottish SEGs*

SEGs	Occupations	1921	1931	1951	1961	1971
13	Large farmers	+3.8	+7.4	+12.6	+7.3	+3.1
3	Self-employed professionals	+2.1	−2.1	+1.1	+0.7	+0.1
4	Employed professionals	+2.5	+2.5	+0.1	−2.1	−1.2
1 & 2	Employers and managers	−2.0	−1.2	−1.5	−1.4	−1.6
5	Semi-professionals	−0.8	+0.5	+0.7	−0.1	0.0
8	Foremen	+0.2	+1.5	+3.0	+0.1	−0.2
6	Junior non-manual	+0.9	+0.2	−0.2	+0.2	−0.5
12	Own-account workers	−3.3	−2.2	−4.2	−3.9	−4.3
14	Small farmers	+6.8	+0.4	−1.4	+0.5	+1.7
9	Skilled manual	+0.1	+0.2	+0.1	+1.0	+0.6
10	Semi-skilled manual	−1.1	−0.4	−0.1	−0.1	+0.1
11	Unskilled manual	+0.9	+0.4	+1.1	+1.3	+2.5
7	Service workers	−1.6	−1.0	−0.3	−0.4	+0.1
15	Farm labourers	+4.0	+3.7	+4.0	+5.6	+5.5
	Scotland /UK (%)	11.3	10.5	10.1	9.4	9.4

*Each cell gives the difference between the percentage of the SEG for Scotland, England and Wales that is located in Scotland (the observed), and the percentage of the total labour force of England, Wales and Scotland to be found in the latter country, as shown in the bottom row (the 'expected' frequency). For example, Scottish large farmers in 1921 numbered 31 353, or 15.1% of the 208 113 large farmers in the three countries: the difference between 15.1% observed and 11.3% expected is 3.8%.

occupations, Scotland has lost ground to England.

In the 'lower skilled half', the biggest change has been the growth of Scotland's excess of the lowest skilled occupations, the unskilled manual and the agricultural, together with an increase in the semi-skilled. Of course, in this context, these occupations are 'undesirable', so that an 'excess' is unwelcome. Scotland has positive scores on all five manual occupations for 1971, and although the excess of skilled workers throughout the period is the least unwelcome feature, in that these are the most skilled of the lower half, even this is another declining sector.

Clearly, Scotland has become more working class in occupational terms and its population is now less skilled, *vis-à-vis* England, than at any time since the First World War. In ten out of fourteen SEGs, the skill distribution in 1971 is in England's favour (two of the remaining cases are farm occupations, and three of the four involve ownership of capital: in twelve of the fourteen SEGs, Scotland's position has actually worsened since 1921. This suggests that an inter-country economic relationship which benefits the South at the expenses of the North has been the outcome of the unified economic policy. The cumulative effect of the small differences in each SEG has been shown to be considerable.

The data given in Table 3.6 can also be regarded as impinging on the convergence thesis. One of the peculiarities of this thesis is that while independent nation states are expected to converge, very little is said about how regions within a state are expected to behave. If a more extreme form of technological determinism is advanced, 'regional convergence is the outcome'; a weaker form of the argument would be that functional specialisation of regions (divergence) could occur as part of an overall national convergence. Scotland does not unambiguously fit either model. Ten out of the fourteen SEGs are now closer to the 'norm', which appears to mean that the occupational structures of the two countries are now more alike than fifty years ago. But conversely, there are four SEGs which have diverged (mainly in the lower part of the hierarchy), and the growing similarity between both sides of the Border should not be allowed to obscure the marked shift of the balance in types of occupations.

Again, if occupational convergence is said to have occurred up to 1971, why has the institutional differentiation observed in Chapter 2 above remained intact? Although functional regional divergence seems a more plausible proposition on the present evidence, this has not arisen as a result of public or private official economic policy, which has been to encourage a 'balanced' growth. Furthermore, the institutional differentiation, while not uniformly being a hindrance to economic efficiency, has been a source of some difficulties in the areas of law, religion (especially the Sabbath), dual centres of administration, and possibly in education. Without a more precise statement of what are the essential institutions and units of convergence, no progress can be made on these lines.

A better model of explanation, in the style of the historical account used in the previous chapter, stresses the interplay of technology and decisions about the use of capital and the relative autonomy – or should one say the inertia – of social institutions. At least, such an account goes some way to explaining Scotland's subordinate status and the reasons for her declining occupational position. The synthesis of the several perspectives and the empirical evidence show that an industrial society can expand its high-skilled labour force while at the same time being relatively proletarianised (in occupational terms) in the wider context. Neither a Braverman-type degradation, nor (to a lesser extent) a Moore-type expansion of the middle range seems to be a major feature of such a change, as far as Scotland's concerned. One of the most striking and unexplored avenues for further analysis in this context is the way in which later industrialisation has coincided (to put it no stronger) with the mobilisation of women into the paid labour force. In Scotland, the total increase was nearly 200 000 over fifty years, or 31.5 per cent on a base of 634 000, during a time when the male labour force actually fell by 47 000.

The results of these changes, if conceived as changes in social class rather than just in occupations, are considerable. Between 1921 and 1971, the patterns of change are 130 000 increase in the upper middle class, 11 000 increase in the intermediate classes, and over 190 000 decrease in the manual working class, all in a period of relatively little change in total size of male labour force. Even allowing for migration and unemployment, these figures indicate a framework in which upward social mobility is fostered. Where else were the extra 141 000 middle-class employees to be recruited, except by a combination of reduced downward mobility and increased recruitment from below? The composition of the new middle class is not a uniform one of traditional middle-class backgrounds and must contain at least a substantial minority of people with origins in working-class families.

This historical and occupational context brings us face to face with the question of social mobility. We now need to know how much mobility there has been in the various decades since the First World War, together with the total amount of mobility. This provides the central focus for the next chapter, before we go on to look at the way in which the particular patterns of economic development have influenced the roots and flows of mobility in current Scottish society.

4 Occupational Fluidity and Class Structure

Social mobility is commonly measured as movement between two social identities. The origin identity is normally defined by the occupation of a person's father when that person was at minimum school leaving age. The destination identity is defined by the person's own occupation at a later stage in life. This intergenerational mobility will be our main focus of interest, either as movement to the person's first job or to his job at the time of interview.

The empirical analysis will use two main occupational classifications. One is the familiar manual/non-manual dichotomy, and the second splits the manual class into three occupational categories, with the non-manual class having four categories. The labels to the tables in this chapter give a general idea of which jobs go into which categories; the schema is a fairly conventional one, while the job allocations and class boundaries are determined by scores on the Hope–Goldthorpe scale. Details are given in the Appendix.

The choice of origin and destination points, and of class schemes, is not just a technical matter of concern for the empirical researcher; it colours the reader's perception of what is going on. For example, if we talk about upward mobility across the manual/non-manual line to present job, we have a figure of 23 per cent, i.e. 23 out of every 100 in the sample made that move. But if we take upward mobility across all seven categories, then the rate becomes 43 per cent, a much more impressive flow. Alternatively, if we are dealing with manual/non-manual flows at first job, the figure drops to 13 per cent, impressive for quite the opposite reason.

Most sociologists work with a basic assumption that mobility rates are fairly low. This is based on the highly influential study by David Glass, published in 1954 as *Social Mobility in Britain*, which reported little mobility. It has survived because most sociologists have been predisposed to believe that there was little mobility. And it has been partially reinforced by Goldthorpe's account of mobility in England and Wales, despite the greater flows of movement which he found.

It is necessary to examine these three claims in more detail. First, Glass was an outstanding individual, working at LSE which was the dominant sociology department in those days of small-scale social science in Britain. His colleagues went on to set up new departments, taking the message of his conclusions with them. His findings were used by later writers on social class, like Bottomore, Parkin and Westergaard. It was more than twenty years before the next major study was made of Britain.

However, there are problems with Glass's results, problems that an occupational and historical approach immediately identify. Given what we know about occupational transition, both in general and historically in Britain, an intergenerational mobility table must show more non-manual sons than non-manual fathers, because the former are working in a society with more non-manual jobs. All mobility tables show this (the pattern is also caused by class differentials in fertility). All, that is, except Glass's main table, which is symmetrical. His attempts to explain this do not stand up to examination and may well have contributed to the devaluation of the occupational and historical style of analysis, which has its origins in early work by Sorokin (1927). A much fuller version of this critique of Glass can be found in Payne (1986).

The second claim made above was the tendency of most sociologists who wanted to believe that there is little mobility. This stems from British sociology's central interest in social class. This interest has chiefly manifested itself in a critical concern with structured social inequalities, within which low rates of mobility have been taken as confirming the rigidity, continuity and closedness of the British class system. In so far as there has been discussion of mobility, it has been in the context of class, not occupation. The main theoretical models of the class system in the corpus of contemporary sociology in fact depend on scant empirical support when they deploy mobility in their arguments. As a reviewer has said of one attempt to assemble data on mobility, it confirms 'what every sociologist knows' about the lack of mobility in Britain (Scase, 1976, p. 515). This is not to argue that there has been a wilful disregard of the truth, but rather that the limited available evidence, pointing towards a closed society, fitted the theoretical orientations of most subsequent writers on class.

This brings us back to the third of our assertions above, that Goldthorpe's work has in fact only served to reinforce this partial view of mobility rates. Again, Goldthorpe does not suppress his findings, but because he is more concerned with some problems, such as class inequalities, rather than others, he *writes* more about certain features of his data, and uses those *indices* which throw most light on those features. Thus although he reports a 43 per cent gross upward mobility rate, the reader can be excused for taking away an impression of a very closed society.

This is because Goldthorpe's interest is 'the implication for class formation and action' which mobility has, and he wishes to show the necessity of 'collective action on the part of those in inferior positions' (1980a, pp. 28, 29). He chooses to look largely at 'relative' mobility chances; comparing the chances of a given number of non-manual sons getting non-manual jobs, with the chances of the same number of manual sons getting non-manual jobs. At times he discusses these net of structural effects, i.e. that part of mobility which is left over, after allowing for changes in occupational structure, rather than concentrating on the real mobility thus generated. He therefore offers his reader the interesting paradox of increases in absolute mobility, but no improvement in relative mobility rates.

Goldthorpe is also mainly concerned with his 'service class' of managers and professionals, as well as wishing to avoid an excessively hierarchical view of his occupational categories. This leads him to make relatively little comment on mobility in the middle ranges, a mobility which in the Scottish data is quite considerable because of genuine career structure links. His concentration means that in general his analysis will 'speak of upward mobility only in the case of movement into classes I and II' (1980a, p. 42). Once again his data are presented in tabular form and there is no deliberate distortion whatsoever. None the less, our perception is to some extent guided towards the model of a closed class system, because Goldthorpe is interested in only part of the total mobility.

The analysis in this book is oriented in a different way (and is, of course, open to a similar complaint that its commentary is selective in its coverage). Because it is concerned first and foremost with occupations and not class, there is no ideological hang-up about talking about high levels of occupational fluidity. Indeed, for this author, the striking feature is the wide range of origins from which the present incumbents of the non-manual categories have come. This is largely the result of the occupational transition process, and therefore it receives more attention in the form of absolute and inflow rates of mobility than the lack of movement which can be demonstrated by relative and outflow rates of mobility. That does not in itself constitute an argument that Britain has an open society in class terms; it is instead an argument for a wider view of what mobility is really about.

INTERGENERATIONAL MOBILITY AMONG SCOTTISH MEN

The data discussed in the following sections follow the convention of dealing with male mobility between the respondent's job at the time of interview, and his father's job when the respondent was 14 years old. In cases of unemployment, or where the father had been called up into the wartime armed services, the last civilian job was taken instead. Respondents were asked 'What is your job now?' as one of a series of occupation questions, all of which required a job title, a job description, ('What exactly do you do as a . . . ?') an industry, and an employment status. The question concerning the father, or Head of Household where there was no father living with family, was 'And what was your "father's" job at that time? I mean, what exactly did "he" do?'. No distinction has been made between those giving a 'last civilian job' or having non-father heads of households in preparing the tables which follow.

The first feature to observe is the difference between the marginal distribution of the fathers (the row totals given on the right of the tables) and those for the sons (the column totals forming the bottom line). As already argued in the previous section, these do not reflect occupational transition alone, but they do indicate considerable structural shift between the two 'generations'. All three of the manual categories (V, VI and VII) have higher numbers for fathers: 1336 as against 939; 923 as against 899; and 787 as against 660. Conversely, the non-manual categories are all larger in the sons' generation. In total, the shift is an expansion of the non-manual sector of 548 − or alternatively a contraction of 548 in the manual sector: about 12 per cent of the total sample. The largest expansion (264) lies in category I, the professional/managerial group; the largest contraction (397) is in category V, the skilled manual class. This is presented diagrammatically, in Figure 4.1.

If we total the cells below, on, and above the main diagonal from top left to bottom right, Table 4.1 shows that 42.3 per cent of the sample were upwardly mobile by at least one category, 27.4 per cent were immobile, and 30.3 per cent were downwardly mobile. It might be more informative to split the 'immobiles' into those who retained some kind of advantage by remaining immobile in the non-manual class, and those who retained some kind of disadvantage by remaining in the manual class. This yields the figures of 9.8 per cent and 17.5 per cent respectively. Even so, on the basis of these gross mobility rates, about

Figure 4.1 Distribution of origins and destination to scale

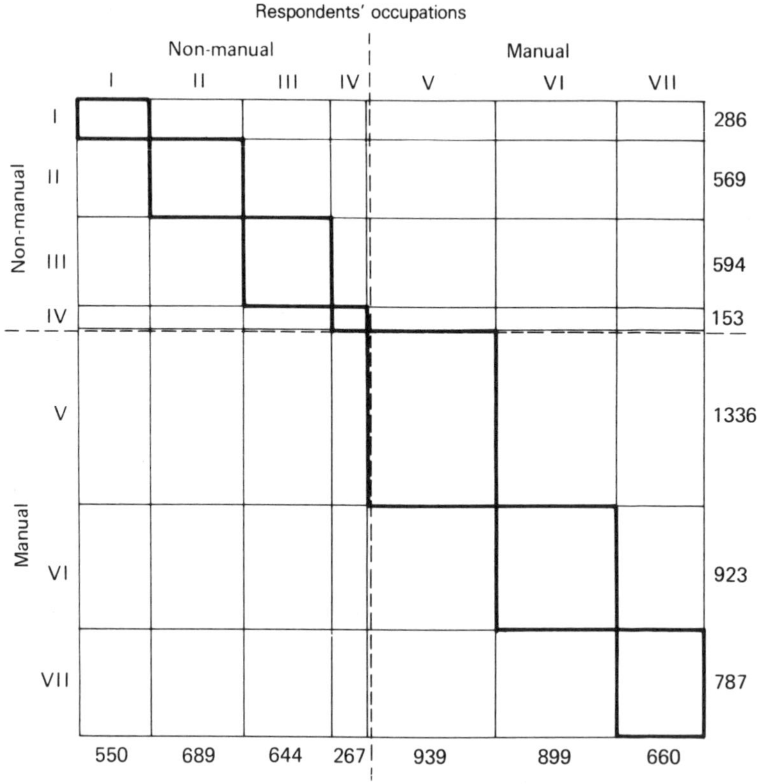

		Non-manual				Manual		
		I	II	III	IV	V	VI	VII
Non-manual	I							286
	II							569
	III							594
	IV							153
Manual	V							1336
	VI							923
	VII							787
		550	689	644	267	939	899	660

(Respondents' occupations across the top)

three in every four men experience some kind of disjunction between their family background and their own occupational identity (forgetting for the moment any additional respondents whose earlier career took them away from their origins before they returned to the same category at the time of interview). This we regard as a relatively fluid condition.

Of course, had we used a smaller number of categories, such as 'manual' and 'non-manual', the appearance of the results would be different. In this case, 23 per cent of the sample were upwardly mobile, 65.7 per cent were immobile and 11.3 per cent were downwardly mobile. We might hesitate to call this 'fluid', but this still shows one in three men being mobile. Conversely, if we were to operate exclusively with the twenty categories which were used for parts of the analysis, the upward mobility figure would be 51 per cent and the downward 34

Table 4.1 Intergenerational male mobility: numbers and percentage inflow

		Respondent's occupation at time of interview							
		I	II	III	IV	V	VI	VII	Totals
I.	Professionals; Managers; Senior administrators	128 23.3	71 10.3	18 2.8	29 10.9	14 1.4	14 1.6	12 1.6	286
II.	Semi-Professionals; White collar supervisors	108 19.6	193 28.0	62 9.6	45 16.9	54 5.8	72 8.0	35 5.3	569
III.	Formen; Self-employed artisans	76 13.8	95 13.8	121 18.8	26 9.7	91 9.7	110 12.2	75 11.4	594
IV.	Routine white collar	41 7.5	35 5.1	16 2.5	15 5.6	21 2.2	14 1.6	11 1.7	153
V.	Skilled manual	91 16.5	128 18.6	172 26.7	63 23.6	400 42.6	265 29.5	217 32.9	1336
VI.	Semi-skilled manual	51 9.3	92 13.4	131 20.3	47 17.6	193 20.6	257 28.6	152 23.0	923
VII.	Unskilled manual	55 10.0	75 10.9	124 19.3	42 15.7	166 17.7	167 18.6	158 23.9	787
	TOTALS	550 (100)	689 (100)	644 (100)	267 (100)	939 (100)	899 (100)	660 (100)	4648

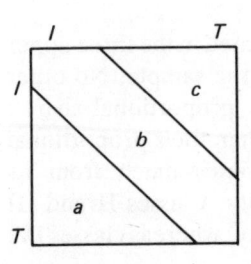

Father's occupation when respondent aged 14

a = upwardly mobile = 42.3 per cent
b = immobile = 27.4 per cent
c = downwardly mobile = 30.3 per cent

per cent. Thus the selection of a seven-category model of the occupational order directly influences both the detail of the findings and also the way the reader interprets the level of mobility.

Parts of this mobility can be attributed in a direct way to the changes in the occupational distributions between the two generations. While it is not possible to make a direct equivalence between the SEGs discussed in the previous chapter and the sample data, for reasons of age and date of survey, as much as definitions, it is possible to establish that the bulk of SEGs 1 to 4 lie in class I; SEGs 5, 13 and 14 in class II; SEGs 8 and 12 in class III; SEG 6 in class IV; SEG 9 in class V; SEGs 7, 10 and 15 in class VI; and SEG 11 in class VII. On the basis of what one knows about changes in the size of the SEGs, one would therefore look for upward mobility fuelled by expansion particularly in classes I, II and IV (although less so here than if women were being considered), but little upward mobility in class V which should reflect the decline in skilled manual work, or in the fluctuating classes VI and VII. To allow for the different sizes of these classes, the share of overall upward mobility to be found in each class is compared with its size in the sample. In this way, the components of mobility can be allocated to the relevant class. This is shown in Table 4.2, which also includes immobility and downward mobility.

Table 4.2 Proportions of mobility associated with classes

	Expanding occupations				Contracting occupations			
	I	II	III	IV	V	VI	VII	Totals
% of all Upmobility	21.4	21.6	22.5	7.7	18.2	8.5	n.a.	100 (1968)
% of all Immobility	10.1	15.7	9.5	1.2	31.5	20.2	12.4	100 (1272)
% of all Downmobility	n.a.	5.0	5.7	7.1	12.8	33.7	35.7	100 (1408)
% of sample	11.8	14.8	13.9	5.7	20.2	19.3	14.2	100 (4648)

Two-thirds of the upward mobility is concentrated in the three upper classes which consist of just over one-third of the sample. No other class has substantially more mobility than its 'proportional share'; contracting classes have less upward mobility than their proportional share. None of these classes except V deviates much from its proportional share when it comes to immobility. Classes II and III have a relatively low share of downward mobility, whereas classes IV,

VI and particularly VII are sites for disproportionately high levels of downward mobility; some kind of 'ceiling' and 'floor' effect may be present in these numbers. Even so, in considering the mobility characteristics of the various occupational groups, Table 4.2 helps to identify that the profiles are quite distinct and generally compatible with an explanation that draws on occupational transition.[1]

However, one would not expect these data to show exact correspondence between occupational size and mobility because the 'occupational' approach is not one that deals only in changes in size. It also includes ideas about other facets of occupational change, such as changing standards of recruitment, or shortages of labour supply, or unemployment. The changing occupational distributions are the framework within which these 'rules' – and others less directly to do with labour, like access to schooling – operate. Occupational transition is neither a simple, nor a monocausal, explanation of mobility.

Tables 4.1 and 4.2 both present a picture of considerable readjustment of employment level over two generations, with a consequent mixing of people with different backgrounds, and a need for them to learn new mores. Although this is not to say Scotland is an 'open' or egalitarian society, it does show that direct inheritance of occupation is relatively rare, even at this level of general categories. Exceptions do occur: for example, farming and small businesses are heavily recruited from among the ranks of farmers and 'small businessmen', presumably because they involve property inheritance. But the general rule is to the contrary, so that there must therefore be important mechanisms for allocating sons to their occupational destinations over and above parental intervention to maintain status stability.

To some extent, in that it has become 'normal' *not* to follow in one's father's footsteps, occupational inheritance ceases to be problematic. Nevertheless, if sons are relatively free agents who can decide their own occupational destinies, the data still show that constraints operate on job choice, so that the net effect of these choices is to allocate more non-manual jobs to non-manual sons than to manual sons.

Table 4.1 also shows from where the present members of each class have come (the percentages in brackets). Thus clearly class I is not a closed category. Three out of every four of its members have come from other origins, one in three from manual backgrounds, and each of the manual categories contributes about 10 per cent or more. It is true that its largest source of recruitment is from itself, followed by the adjacent class II. But this is a totally different picture than one gets from Glass's work. There one finds that apparently only one in ten of the upper middle class have manual working-class origins, and half are self-recruited (Glass, 1954, p. 183). This is one of the more significant findings because it shows that 'long range' mobility, from low in the hierarchy of backgrounds to a much higher ranked occupation, is not only possible but does indeed happen. This is a point to be returned to in the later discussion of existing assumptions about the British class structure.

In contrast, while class II (consisting mainly of semi-professionals and technical workers with high levels of skills, plus managers of small enterprises) also recruits from a wide range of origins, it shows the highest degree of self-recruitment of any non-manual class. This is due in part to the component categories (not shown in Table 4.1) which include farmers and small businessmen, the two occupational groups with exceptionally high self-recruitment – presumably due to the key role of property inheritance.

Among present-day farmers, 56 out of 84 (67 per cent) were born the sons of farming fathers, while 41 out of 146 (32 per cent) small proprietors came from a small business background. Among the semi-professionals and technical workers who make up the rest of the class, the self-recruitment figure is only 5.2 per cent. A similar discontinuity occurs in the marginal distributions: the two property-based occupational groups contain 480 niches for fathers and 230 for sons, whereas the semi-professionals increase from 189 to 459. This tends to confirm the two conclusions already drawn: first, expanding occupations not only provide routes for upward mobility, but recruit from a wide range of origins, while conversely contracting occupations – and here those with a petty capital basis in particular – are more likely to be self-recruiting. It is as if on a contracting market, either a disproportionate number of sons of that class 'apply' for the jobs, or they are in some way specially favoured.

Class III consists of foremen and self-employed artisans, i.e. those work-roles which represent 'realistic' career ambitions for at least some of those who start work as (chiefly skilled) manual workers. 'To be your own boss' will in practice mean being a one-man band for most such workers, while a shop-floor supervisory position is about as high in the ranks of management as most workers could expect to rise in their own lifetimes. Not surprising, therefore, class III in some ways resembles the skilled manual class (V) more than classes II or IV (semi-professionals and routine white collar). Two-thirds of its number are from manual origins, its self-recruitment is low – presumably because the advantages that parental career achievements confer are not readily convertible into career advancement for the sons – and few class I sons arrive in this kind of work. This seems to be a good example of genuine occupational mobility, in which the mobility table reflects exactly what would be expected both from common-sense observation and from a more developed argument about the occupational basis of social mobility. The finding of a high proportion of mobility focused on this class can be explained, not by class expansion, but by structural connection of career significance to the manual worker, and of no little significance for the way capitalist production is able to mobilise parts of the labour force to bring its technical expertise into play on behalf of a less expert (in this context) management. In the same way, the system offers a space for the one-man operation in the interstices between large-scale production, which can occasionally allow an individual to graduate from being a manual worker to being a proprietor of some significance. It seems likely that such a development may be more important to capitalism as a pacifying and legitimising myth for the working class than as a new source of entrepreneurial dynamism.

Class IV, routine white collar work, is here the smallest (because many such workers are female) and has a recruitment pattern more in line with the non-manual sector than the manual. It recruits less than its 'share' from manual backgrounds, i.e. on the expectations of no association, and more from the non-manual. However, it has an unusually low rate of self-recruitment. This is only 5.6 per cent (the next lowest is class III with 18.8 per cent) and its recruitment from all classes is very close to the appropriate proportions.

In contrast to the routine white collar category, skilled manual workers are both the largest class and the most self-recruited. This is a contracting class; 1336 sons came from skilled manual families, but there were only 939 niches for them. As we shall shortly see more clearly from Table 4.3 below, the 'natural' connection with class III accounts for 172 of them, while 42.6 per cent of the present skilled workers are self-recruited. This may reflect an ability to pass on limited occupational advantage (*vis-à-vis* the rest of the manual labour force) to the next generation, by means of manipulating the apprenticeship scheme. It is not conventional to conceive of this kind of self-recruitment as self-interested closure – in the way that elite recruitment is normally treated. None the less, the basic principle would seem to be operating at a secondary level lower down the scale. No evidence is presently available, however, to substantiate this.

What is evident is that class V is substantially the largest in both generations and, other things being equal, would be expected to have prominent interactions with all other classes as a source of their recruits. Interestingly the converse does not hold true. Table 4.1 shows that less than 2 per cent of the skilled category come from class I (a pattern shared with the other two manual classes). In all, about four out of every five skilled workers come from a manual background; again, a pattern common to all manual classes.

The semi-skilled, and the unskilled, manual classes resemble each other, and indeed the decisions to call one job semi-skilled rather than unskilled was sometimes hard to justify. The main difference in inflow is that each recruits more heavily from among its own sons than from the other. Both are also contracting sectors, although the contraction of the semi-skilled category is somewhat less marked. Neither recruit as much as 2 per cent from class I, and only around one in five of their numbers come from non-manual backgrounds.

The central point about Table 4.1 is that it shows a high level of movement, a much higher level than one would expect from most sociological writing in Britain. Within the *system* of occupational stratification there is considerable *individual* mobility. If we regard mobility as one index of the rigidity of that system, then it is necessary to modify our conception of class in Britain (or strictly speaking, Scotland). Even at the most modest level of the manual/non-manual transition, more than one in every three male adults personally experienced occupational mobility. That is to say, he has been a member of two different classes. If we conceive of the stratified order as consisting of smaller units such as the seven categories that we have used above, then nearly three in every four adult males has moved across group boundaries. It does not seem plausible to regard this as a rigid system, except in so far as one concentrates strictly on the perpetuation of a system.

However, the dichotomy between the properties of a system, and the characteristics of the elements contained within that system is not so neat as is sometimes assumed. Of course, it matters that social inequality exists, and continues to exist over successive generations. But it is at one level also a property of that system of inequality that individuals and families experience different parts of that system. Inequality is easier to bear when either one's own life, or one's children's (or parents') lives have involved other social circumstances. The reality of *familial* experience of occupational mobility goes some way to explain away the problematic of why social inequality continues to exist. And that familial experience is a property of the system, as much a characteristic of the actors caught up within it. On this evidence, the general rigidity of the British class system is not as great as has been suggested: a later question for this research is to locate where rigidity is still established.

The second general point to be made on the basis of Table 4.1 concerns class formation and the generation of class consciousness. Occupational mobility tends to result in people experiencing different life-styles: one in their families of origin and one – or more – in their own adult careers. Let us make the not unreasonable assumption that early experience does have an effect on later life, in the sense of contributing to ideas and values, providing a frame of reference for evaluating 'progress' in one's own life, influencing social relationships (e.g. with parents and others from neighbourhoods of origin, and so on). In other words, childhood socialisation 'sticks', despite the overlay of more recent events such as re-socialisation into new occupations or grades as part of promotion within an organisation (Watson, 1964; Nichols, 1969; Offe, 1976). It may be that an intergenerational shift between two adjacent categories of the seven-category scheme is unimportant in this context, but a move from one end of the scale to the other clearly is. What Table 4.1 (and to a lesser extent, Table 4.3 below) shows us is that the backgrounds in question are for the present middle class very variable, and therefore any notions of social homeogeneity and shared values which draw on what is brought to the current class situation from family of origin, might be suspect. It is not possible to entertain ideas of a non-manual class developing as a class 'for itself' when its collective experience is restricted to much less than a single lifetime. With heavy recruitment from the manual sector, the non-manual class may wish to stress its difference from and superiority over manual workers – but that is a far more dynamic and at the same time constrained situation, than one in which successive generations of a class are overwhelmingly self-recruited.

However, this situation is less true for the working class. Although there is some downward mobility, the main pattern is that manual workers are the sons of the previous generation of manual workers. There is considerable interchange between the levels of manual work (skilled/semi-skilled/unskilled) between generations (and as we shall see, within careers) and this may provide some kind of heterogeneity of life experience in the way that we have seen for the middle class. It certainly is not provided by the inflow of sons from above, and manual workers have more basis for a common identity and consciousness than do non-manual workers.

The continuity of working-class membership is also well illustrated by the patterns of outflow from manual class origins. The discussion so far has concentrated on absolute and inflow measures of mobility, which reflects a concern with one strand of the problem, namely, what are the implications of mobility for the present structure of the classes. The emphasis on inflow shows up most clearly that heterogeneity of origins is far more prevalent than was expected, and that there is greater fluidity in the system. But while this is important – and perhaps one of the main contributions of the present study is to demonstrate these basic facts – it would not do to ignore that other strand of British mobility writing, the differential access to desirable jobs. To put it more strongly, a sense of moral outrage informs much of the writing on mobility and stratification, and while the inflows may show considerable movement, they show much less about those who are not so successful in the mobility competition. For this, we need to turn to the outflow table shown below as Table 4.3.

Table 4.3 Intergenerational outflow mobility

		Respondents' occupation at time of interview							
		I	II	III	IV	V	VI	VII	Totals
Father's occupation when respondent was aged 14	I	44.8	24.8	6.3	10.1	4.9	4.9	4.2	100 (286)
	II	19.0	33.9	10.9	7.9	9.5	12.7	6.2	100 (569)
	III	12.8	16.0	20.4	4.4	15.3	18.5	12.6	100 (594)
	IV	26.8	22.9	10.5	9.8	13.7	9.2	7.2	100 (153)
	V	6.8	9.6	12.9	4.7	29.9	19.8	16.2	100 (1336)
	VI	5.5	10.0	14.2	5.1	20.9	27.8	16.5	100 (923)
	VII	7.0	9.5	15.8	5.3	21.1	21.2	20.1	100 (787)
	Totals	11.8	14.8	13.9	5.7	20.2	19.3	14.2	4648

Outflow analysis can be misleading because the flow percentages are more obviously constrained by the size of the destination categories. Thus, for example, the small values in the class IV column say more about the fact that there are only 5.7 per cent of all occupations in that category, rather than any process of connection between white collar work and other origins. It is not proposed to explore this table in the same detail as Table 4.1 but certain features do stand out.

Despite the earlier emphasis placed on movements between occupations, the children of both the higher classes – and particularly class 1 – have a much better chance of good jobs than other children. Only about 14 per cent of the sons of managers and professionals and 28.4 per cent of the sons of semi-professionals ended up in manual work. In contrast, roughly 65 per cent of manual workers' sons became manual workers, i.e. in absolute terms they were four times more likely, and man for man twice as likely, to be manual workers than the sons of professionals. Nearly half of those born into class I held their position and another quarter ended up in the adjacent class II. Less than one in every fourteen sons of manual workers made it to the upper middle class.

The immobility of many of the sons of manual workers can be seen as being that part of the outcome which would be expected even if there was no parental advantage involved. Thus if, say, skilled work is about 20 per cent of employment, then about 20 per cent of the sons of each class would be in skilled manual work – including the sons of skilled manual workers. In fact, the latter's proportion is about 30 per cent, an 'overload' factor of 3:2. But the flow from both semi- and unskilled manual origins into skilled work is 'about right', while those from the non-manual classes are low. Given the earlier observations about self-recruitment in contracting classes like skilled manual work, it is interesting to speculate whether these patterns represent some kind of excessive self-recruitment, or the outcome of a blockage preventing a distinct proportion of able skilled manual workers' sons from entering the non-manual class.

This kind of analysis, which obviously draws on Glass's idea of perfect mobility and the index of association, tends to reduce much of the apparent disadvantage of lower-class sons in the competition for better jobs. Nevertheless, that disadvantage is real and enduring in the 1970s. It is still true that even in its 'reduced form' there is a class differential. And whatever the shape of the class structure, one must not lose sight of the fact that a chance of one in fourteen of getting a good job is singularly poor odds, when the rewards attaching to good jobs are so much better.

The evidence of absolute and inflow mobility rates, even when balanced against the outflow measures, suggest a basic pattern quite different from those normally attributed to Glass, namely, that movements over long distances are rare, and that the level of movement is relatively limited. The rejection of these statements is important, because in addition to the general points about rigidity and class formation, there are a number of specific models of stratification based on these assumptions about occupational mobility. The three main models are those of a mobility barrier, or threshold, between manual and non-manual occupations; that the intermediate range of occupations act as a 'buffer zone' between the middle class proper and the working class, which takes two generations to cross, and that the upper reaches of the occupational hierarchy are increasingly closed to entry from below, until the highest echelon is almost completely self-recruiting. Each of these models is considered in turn in the next section.

MODELS OF MOBILITY AND THE CLASS STRUCTURE

The simplest of these models proposes the existence of a mobility 'threshold' at the manual/non-manual boundary. Westergaard and Resler – who ironically have done much to bring social mobility to centre stage by the attention they give it in *Class in a Capitalist Society* – claim that there is a 'persistence of some mobility threshold along the line dividing manual from non-manual labour, even if it is lower than before . . . That line in fact has something of the character of a barrier against mobility' (1975, pp. 302, 301).

In the first place, as has already been shown, about one-third of the sample moved across that line in one direction or the other. This does not seem like a serious mobility hurdle. Second, within each of the four non-manual classes, there is considerable recruitment from the other side of the threshold: 35 per cent, 42.9 per cent, 66.3 per cent and 56.9 per cent respectively. The reverse is less clear-cut: the three manual classes recruit 19.2 per cent, 23.4 per cent and 20.2 per cent from the non-manual sector, about one in every five.

Third, if the manual/non-manual line is to be regarded as a key hurdle, it should presumably be a more formidable obstacle than exists elsewhere in the occupational structure, i.e. the mobility flow across it should be lower than between any other two points in the mobility table. So, for example, it should be harder to move from manual to non-manual, than from 'semi- and unskilled' into 'skilled and non-

Occupational Fluidity and Class Structure 75

manual' occupations. But whereas the former has a mobility flow of 34.3 per cent, the latter is only 38.7 per cent and again the flow between the sector comprising classes I, II and III and that comprising IV, V, VI and VII is 34.2 per cent. In other words, moving the threshold up or down one category does not seriously change the mobility flow.

The logical extension of this critique is to redichotomise the seven-category classification at each of its six possible points. In such an exercise, the closer one moves to the top or the bottom of the classification, the smaller becomes the number of cases which could in theory be mobile: for instance, the maximum mobility value for class I is achieved if all sons born in class I (286) enter other classes, while all the present class I occupations (550) are exclusively filled by sons from those other classes. The maximum value in each cell is, of course, dependent on the marginals. It follows from this consideration that at the supposed threshold between manual and non-manual sectors, those who are mobile make up a smaller proportion of all those theoretically at risk of being mobile partly because the number of people theoretically at risk is higher in the middle of the table.

We can extend this analysis by using the outflow rates in Table 4.3. Each of the three manual classes exports more than one third of its sons into non-manual occupations. While this is less than would be expected on a no-association assumption (when one would look for nearer half of such sons to be in non-manual work), it is still a considerable flow. The counter-flow is slightly smaller for classes II and IV, bigger for class III, and only about one in seven from classes II. If the supposed threshold were drawn one class lower, the outflows from semi- and skilled manual backgrounds would be substantially increased, so that nearly 60 per cent of their sons crossed the barrier. If the threshold were drawn one class higher, the flows would be slightly reduced, by about 5 per cent on each class; this would then be balanced by the added outflow from class IV which would also export about 60 per cent of its sons to classes I, II and III. These rates of movement only seem limited against the absolute standard of perfect mobility. The idea of the threshold does not receive sufficient support from these data to be accepted. Perhaps a semi-permeable membrane might be a better analogy.

The second model which has been advanced as representing the main features of mobility is Parkin's 'buffer zone'. In this model

> The children of manual workers who cross the class line tend to assume fairly modest white-collar positions – as clerks, salesmen,

shop assistants, schoolteachers, and the like. Recruitment to the established middle class professions requiring long periods of training and education is far less common . . . We could sum up these remarks by suggesting that there is what might be called a social and cultural 'buffer zone' between the middle class and working class proper. Most mobility, being of a fairly narrow special span, involves the movement between the class extremes. (Parkin, 1971, pp. 51, 56)

The effect of this buffer zone is to insulate the 'middle class proper' from the culturally disruptive incursions of large numbers of ex-working-class incomers, so securing the middle class's privilege and also maintaining class values and identity. In the seven-category classification, the buffer zone can be equated with classes III and IV, and the dominant pattern of movement should, therefore, be between these two and classes I and II, or classes V, VI and VII. However, if we examine inflows (Table 4.1) to classes I and II, there is a larger flow direct from classes V, VI and VII than from classes II and IV, in fact, almost exactly double (39.7 per cent of the total, compared with 19.9 per cent). However, the flow into the two intermediate classes from below is heavier than the flow from classes V, VI and VII into the upper two categories: 579 cases compared with 492. A strict test of the buffer zone model would have to be that not only was this latter condition fulfilled, but the intermediate-to-upper flow would also have to be greater than the manual-to-upper flow, which it is not.

Parkin does not say much about the function of the buffer zone in *downward* mobility. Here the picture is the reverse of the upward pattern, with a smaller direct flow from classes I and II to the manual classes than that from the intermediate classes, but with a larger direct flow than that into the buffer zone. Again, only one of the two required conditions is met.

Even if one takes the outflow figures, the model cannot be clearly substantiated. The percentage flows direct into classes I and II from the manual classes are 3 per cent greater than those into the buffer zone classes. The downward flows from class I direct to manual occupations are slightly smaller than to the intermediate zone (14.0 per cent as compared with 16.4 per cent) but those from class II are much larger (28.4 per cent and 18.8 per cent).

The heart of the problem for the buffer zone model is its more general assumption that all mobility is predominantly over a short range. If Parkin were correct, each class should have intakes which consist mainly of recruits from the immediately adjacent categories. But if the immobile are discounted, then all but one of the categories draw only one-third of their remaining intake from the categories immediately shown above and below them: the notable exception is the semi-skilled group with double this level of 'local' recruitment, which may in part be due to technical problems of deciding the limits of semi-skilled occupations. Intergenerational mobility does not predominantly consist of a series of one-place, short-range steps, from one category to the next: recruitment draws instead from a wide spectrum of origins – although as was noted above, manual occupations have higher levels of mutual intake.

This means that the heterogeneity of origins is not just the heterogeneity caused by drawing on the two adjacent classes which have relatively similar origins, but is more complex and extensive, particularly in the non-manual sector. The diversity of composition thus not only applies over the whole range of categories, but is in each case extensive, although again, the important caveat about the manual groups needs to be made. These are 40 per cent of the total workforce who inter-recruit extensively, but who have added to their own numbers just over 10 per cent of the total workforce drawn from different origins. In this half of the society, then, only one in five has been mobile over a 'long distance' which includes crossing the manual/non-manual line. Conversely, the non-manual half consists of 25 per cent of the total workforce which is inter-recruited, with an equal amount added from manual origins: one in two is a long-distance mobile in this half, so that the heterogeneity of the non-manual sector is far greater than in the manual. Thus while Parkin may be correct in saying that not many semi-skilled or unskilled workers are recruited from the sons of professionals, managers and so on (but still nearly one in ten in this case), 36 per cent of the present category I, and 43 per cent of category II come from the other side of the buffer zone.

The thesis of a buffer zone, in which cultural resocialisation of the mobile is either unnecessary or can take a whole generation, and which protects the upper middle class from social dilution, is not supported by experience of present-day Scots. It may be that the mobility over two generations and the intermediate classes does serve the functions which Parkin proposes, but it is not the dominant pattern of mobility. Such a process might be better pictured as a kind of fairly effective safety net, or perhaps a non-return valve, against downward mobility rather than a filter against upward mobility. This would be to change the significance which Parkin attaches to the buffer zone analogy very substantially, and to stress protection for offspring rather than closure against incomers.

The third model of mobility, to be found in the writings of Miliband and Bottomore, for example, suggests that a kind of 'graduated closure' operates as one moves closer to the top of the stratified order until at the last, the narrow elite is almost totally self-recruiting. Any additional members are recruited only from those groups most like the elite, which in turn are nearly as closed-off to others below, as the elite is from its neighbouring groups. This model needs to be considered in some more detail than the previous two, for several reasons. In the first place, it has its particular relevance to theories of industrial society and the expansion of the new middle class. Second, reports of higher general rates of mobility need to be carefully qualified when it comes to identifying elite recruitment. And third, Goldthorpe's promotion of the idea of a service class has drawn attention to this upper part of the class structure.

RECRUITMENT TO THE NEW MIDDLE CLASS

An important first step must be to clarify the relationship between the study of 'elites' and the study of mobility. In fact few mobility studies can say much about elites, because elites are by definition small and unlikely to show up in discernible numbers in a national sample. There is, therefore, a natural temptation for sociologists to redraw the boundary of the elite 'lower down' the class hierarchy, in order to have sufficient cases to analyse: this has led to some confusion over definitions. In the present case, this temptation has been resisted, not least because of the considerations discussed in Chapter 2, namely, that Scotland is unlikely to contain many of the British elite, which is either metropolitan or internationally based (see Giddens, 1974, p. 15). Careful scrutiny of our nearly 5000 questionnaires located two, and possibly three, individuals who could be safely said to belong to Giddens' elite, and perhaps up to twenty who might in an independent Scotland be recast in a more powerful mould. Power is both vertically and geographically concentrated in Britain, and Scotland is as much a depressed area in power terms as in other fields.

But this is already to beg several questions about the nature of the powerful. In the first place it is assumed that there are relatively few people who are 'really powerful', and that they should not be confused with the middle or upper middle classes (see Pahl and Winkler, 1974;

Lee, 1981). Because we wish to include writers who operate with elite and ruling-class models – and some writers who use the two together – we do not distinguish sharply between them, or insist on one at the expense of the other. The difference between the two *is* important, but the precedent of Giddens and Bottomore shows that at times there can be advantages in operating at a less precise level (Giddens, 1974, pp. x-xi).

The first step is to review several empirical accounts of elites, and the boundary with the upper middle class, in order to show where confusion has arisen over the size and function of elites, and therefore coloured debates about recruitment. Consider, for example, the literature on inequalities in wealth, income and inheritance. The contributors to Urry and Wakeford (1973, pp. 18–60) refer variously to over 1 per cent, 2 per cent, 5 per cent, 7 per cent, 10 per cent and 12 per cent of the population as being the high earners. It is true that such measures help to demonstrate the steepness of the income gradient 'at the top', but is the reader to conclude that the elite or ruling class consists of one person in a hundred – or one person in ten?

Westergaard and Resler (1975, pp. 156–9) suggests that the 1.5 per cent of all adults aged 25 and more, with holdings in excess of £5000 in 1970 (and more so the 0.6 per cent holding £20 000 or more) are the only people who can actually exercise any influence on business policy – and *that* within an arena in which the largest blocks of share holdings are held by companies and not by individuals. Do the interests of these powerful individual share-owners coincide with the larger group (about 7 per cent) with smaller holdings? If we assume that this is typically so, we effectively have an 'active' and a 'passive' division within the stockholding class: the former have a degree of power, while the latter can be thought of as a reserve group which provides some kind of ideological support and legitimation.

A similar confusion can be found in the work on recruitment and access to positions of power. In his chapter on 'Economic Elites and Dominant Class' Miliband rejects the notion of a separate managerial class, partly on the grounds that their social origins are the same as those of the large-scale capitalist owners. His managerial element includes 'all layers of management' and the origins cover both upper and 'upper middle class' families (Miliband, 1969, pp. 36–8).

This seems to be a confusion of *senior* management with management in general. As other writers, such as Nichols (1969, p. 61–2) and Westergaard (1975, pp. 161–5) have pointed out, it is one thing to argue that a group of senior managers have day-to-day charge of capital, if this refers to that small category of directors who make up the boards of large companies. But that is not the same thing as saying that such men are a separate class, nor is it to say that *all* levels of management are included in this (still less is it to include all 'technical, planning and other specialised staffs' as having managerial power, as advocated by pluralists such as Galbraith (1967, p. 69), Lenski (1966, pp. 364–5), Burnham (1945) or Crosland (1956)). Equally, the debate in recent Marxism on the professional/managerial class raises similar problems (e.g. Poulantzas, 1973; Hunt, 1977).

Miliband (1969, p. 39) writes of advanced capitalist societies that 'elite recruitment in these societies has a distinctly hereditary character. Access from the working class into the middle and upper class is generally low'. It has already been observed above that this version of mobility is attributable to Glass, but to a degree it is Miller's representation of those data that has been influential. Miller links the Glass findings to other studies of elites, suggesting that a general feature of all societies is that there is little movement from the manual strata into elites of various sizes.

The first objection to his conclusion is that the percentages are misleading. Taking the original data for Britain, the '0.6 per cent' flow from manual backgrounds into Miller's 'Elite I' consists of twelve men now in Glass's category I, out of all 2200 men born to manual backgrounds (categories 3b–5) who were 'at risk' of being able to move from 'manual' to 'category I'. But since Elite I has only 103 members, the maximum flow could only be $103/2200 = 4.7$ per cent. Again, Miller's 'Elite II' is shown as taking 2.2 per cent of the manual class (49/2200): by the same logic, its maximum flow is 262/2200 or 11.9 per cent. These percentages depend on the size of the class of origin, in this case the manual class, in relation to the size of the elite: the larger the manual class for the same size of elite, the smaller will seem the flow. In presenting the data as percentages without immediate comment on the range of possible values, it seems that Miller may have contributed to a misreading of elite recruitment.

By extension, what if Miller had expressed recruitment as a percentage of inflow rather than outflow? The two figures for the elites would have been 12/103 and 49/262: 11.7 per cent and 18.7 per cent of the current elites were recruited from the working class. The theoretical upper limit of this measure would be 100 per cent. It may well be that 11.7 per cent and 18.7 per cent would still not be regarded as large flows: after all, how 'big' is 'big'? But a common-sense view of perception would suggest that 11.7 per cent is likely to seem a lot more

than 0.6 per cent; and 18.7 per cent to seem more than 2.2 per cent.
Third, there is the question of Miller's use of the term 'elite' to refer to groups of very different sizes. Thus eleven studies are taken as operating with an elite of under 4.6 per cent, eight with elites between 6 per cent and 8.5 per cent, three with over 10 per cent and three over 15 per cent. The inclusion of such different categories, all under the term 'elite', is not only an inconsistent usage of the term, but is a potential source of considerable confusion. It is one thing to discuss *mobility into the top-decile of occupations*: it is another to talk about *recruitment or access to elite positions*. The high reputation of Miller's work may well have produced the unintended consequence that subsequent writers on elites have failed to differentiate between occupation-based general categories such as the 'upper middle class', and their own more rigorously defined conception of elites.

Goldthorpe has addressed this problem by means of Renner's concept of the 'service class' – or more exactly, by means of Dahrendorf's version of Renner's work. Although Goldthorpe clearly recognises the elite boundary problem (1980a, p. 45) he is surprisingly brief in his theoretical statement of the service class model. On page 40, the reader is told that Goldthorpe's class I (of seven classes) can be

> taken as very largely corresponding to the higher and intermediate levels of what Dahrendorf, following Karl Renner, has termed the 'service class' (*Dienstklasse*) of modern capitalist society – the class of those exercising power and expertise on behalf of corporate bodies – plus such elements of the classic bourgeoisie/independent businessmen and 'free' professionals as are not yet assimilated into this new formation.

Goldthorpe's class II, he goes on to say, are the subaltern or *cadet* levels of the service class, while class III is not part of it (pp. 40–1). Upward mobility will be defined as only those movements into classes I and II, and while there is some initial discussion of each of these classes separately, this is soon superceded by a style of analysis which treats them together as one service class. This is justified on the pragmatic grounds of needing to simplify the analysis (p. 51). The collapsed three 'class' model dominates the remainder of the book. Although the reader will pick up several comments on the mobility and employment characteristics of the service class, there is almost no further explication of the basic category being used, although Goldthorpe has since added to this (see Goldthorpe, 1982).

Although Goldthorpe is careful to distinguish between the elite and the service class, his solution raises as many problems as it solves. First, we now have a major boundary drawn *below* class II, so that the service class is a large one, including a number of relatively less influential managerial and technical occupations, all of which are said to exercise 'power and expertise on behalf of corporate bodies'. This must run the risk of confusing the extensive control and very considerable expertise of the class I managers and professionals with the lesser powers and skills of the class II. Second, although Goldthorpe thereafter talks about the service class, his classes I and II include 'elements of the classic bourgeoisie' which are not in Dahrendorf's original formulation (Dahrendorf, 1964, pp. 244–52). Third, the entire emphasis of mobility analysis is shifted because of his particular redefinition of what he will accept as mobility, i.e. moves into and out of classes I and II.

A more conventional approach is adopted here, which concentrates more narrowly on the upper echelons of the managerial and professional class, i.e. class I, the 'upper middle class' (UMC). This term, together with the distinctive label 'lieutenant class' to identify the specific operationalisation used in analysing the Scottish data, specifies that part of the middle class which typically does not own or exercise strategic control over large blocks of capital, and does not occupy key command positions in the state apparatus: when we say 'managers', we do not mean the *most senior* management in the major companies in the economy. Nor, at the other end, are routine clerical workers, foremen, 'one-man businesses', or even semi-professionals (teachers, social workers, etc.), managers of small firms, or farmers included: all routine and intermediate skill levels (and reward levels) are excluded. This leaves professionals (both self-employed and employees); managers and administrators of large organisations (both commercial and governmental); and senior supervisory staff – in all, about 12 per cent of the male workforce.

By defining the upper middle class in this way, there is no danger of mistaking it for the elite theorist's idea of 'really powerful' groups in society and it can be analysed, if not in isolation from the upper class, at least independently. It will rapidly become apparent that the generally acceptable sociological wisdom about where, and how much, mobility takes place in Britain is seriously open to question. This applies particularly to the position adopted by Bottomore and Miliband, who regard the occupational hierarchy as increasingly closed in its upper reaches. The former has written that movement into the class which includes company directors, landowners, professionals, higher civil servants and others of similar social position (i.e. at least some of our category 'I'), is 'very limited in any society and notably so in Britain' (Bottomore, 1965, p. 38), while Miliband – who, it should be said, is more concerned with elite recruitment and political power – argues that the 'upper and middle class in these (capitalist) societies is still largely self-recruiting and therefore to a marked degree socially cohesive' (Miliband, 1969, p. 44).

If we re-examine the data in Tables 4.1 and 4.3, we see that less than one-quarter of the present UMC has been recruited from its own ranks and more than one-third come from manual working-class origins. While there is a degree of concentration at the top (classes I and II are the biggest contributors), the composition suggests considerable openness, and mobility for one in three is of a 'long-range' character across most of the occupational structure. As far as origins are concerned, the UMC cannot be said to be either closed or homogeneous.

In terms of outflow, less than half the sons of the UMC retained their occupational advantage. Most of the less successful sons did manage to preserve a non-manual position, but again, this is not the picture of overwhelming self-recruitment and inheritance of advantage that earlier writers had assumed. It is all the more striking, in that the data cover a period of rapid expansion of UMC occupations so that the conditions for the maintenance of occupational privilege should have been relatively favourable.

This occupational privilege is considerable and consists of several elements. By definition, the UMC is popularly seen as having the most desirable occupations, with greater security, autonomy, satisfactions and rewards. Incomes from employment are higher, there is more chance of ownership of shares and property and personal possession of housing, consumer durables and privileged education are more common. The UMC may not occupy positions of power in the sense of an elite or ruling class, but they are undoubtedly important material beneficiaries of the current forms of state and industrial organisation.

However, not all families in the lieutenant class are equally successful in maintaining their position. The 'track records' of the four constituent occupational categories of the UMC in placing their sons are somewhat varied. Forty-six per cent of the sons of professional employees have made it into the UMC, as did 44 per cent of managers' and proprietors' sons: however, the sons of the self-employed professionals did much better, with 61 per cent, and the sons of other senior staff did rather worse, with only 35 per cent. On this outflow evidence, the self-employed are the most secure in their privilege, while the bureaucratic technical experts are less so, particularly those senior staff who are only marginally of managerial or professional status.

One thing that is striking about these various rates of self-placement is that they bear almost no relation to strict self-recruitment. Professionals have placed 29 per cent of their sons in the professions, and 17 per cent in other UMC occupations. Both self-employed professionals and managers and proprietors have about 18 per cent of their sons in their own sector, but whereas the former have a further 43 per cent in the UMC, the latter have only 26 per cent; so that while the sons of managers and proprietors maintain their privilege to the same extent as professionals, they do so more by transfer to other sectors, most notably to that of professionals, than by narrow self-recruitment.

Thus inheritance is not 'direct' even for those categories – the self-employed, and managers and proprietors – where the question of property inheritance might be involved. The occupational advantage of the father is converted into a general currency of advantage which does not rely narrowly on personal influence or ownership for occupational entry. The family's privilege is maintained by the son's entry into an occupation of comparable status (or more accurately, general desirability). This is perhaps most surprising for the self-employed professionals, dominated by the old professions, where less than one in five sons followed their fathers, choosing instead to follow mainly salarised professions.

We know from sources such as Kelly (1976), and Cruickshank and McManus (1976) that the mechanisms of recruitment still strongly favour father/son succession among some of these self-employed occupations, and the operation of 'practices' provides a property resource (of apparatus, clients, etc) for the marketing of professional skills, which the sons can either take over, or use as capital for entry into another professional business. But most of the sons of self-employed professionals have not taken this option, and among the UMC respondents as a whole, we appear to be talking about only 6 per cent who could possibly have made direct use of property inheritance for job entry. There may, of course, be some delay in taking over from the father, which would depress this last percentage.

A second aspect of these flows between sectors relates to the managerial revolution thesis that a new class has emerged. At this 'below senior management level', there is no evidence to suggest that managers per se presently constitute a new closed group with inherited privilege. Less than one in five managers' sons have become second generation managers; nearly half the sons of managers are downwardly mobile; the rest have converted their privilege into wider professional (and mainly bureaucratic) employment. Even if the writers on industrial and post-industrial society were correct about the significance of technical expertise and the division of ownership and control, these UMC managers have yet to show any signs of consolidating their new economic power into dynastic security of the kind presumably enjoyed by the owners, and without this achievement (on lines pointed out by Mills, 1963) their participation in a 'revolution' is incomplete.

Furthermore, these same patterns of inter-sector recruitment do not support what Westergaard and Resler (1975, p. 170) have characterised as 'the thesis of benevolent managerialism' namely that the new managers bring with them a social ethic of responsibility to temper the owners' need for profit maximisation. This reorientation of policy criteria depends on

> an increasing recruitment even to top level management from among professionals and technical specialists. For they *par excellence* can be expected to be job, product-, and growth-orientated rather than dedicated to profit maximisation (Westergaard and Resler, 1975, 155)

But as we have seen above, despite the growth in the managerial sector (one new recruit needed for every three managerial origins), there is little sign of significant flow from professional and technical specialist *backgrounds* (i.e. those who would be expected to have an ingrained family culture of professionalism) into management. The flow has been less than 9 per cent of the absolute potential, and such ex-professional incomers are only 6 per cent of all managers. Conversely, a quarter of managers' sons have joined the professionals and they make up nearly twice as big a proportion of current professionals as the ex-professionals do of current managers. If anything, the professionals are being infiltrated by the managers, not the reverse, so that wherever the social ethic in manageralism is supposed to come from, it is not from intergenerational intersector recruitment.

A further difference between the two groups is the outflow of sons who are downwardly mobile. More than half of both the professional groups' downwardly mobile sons found jobs in class II (semi-professionals, small proprietors and managers), compared with less than 40 per cent of the sons of managers and senior staff. A quarter of the senior staff's downwardly mobile sons and a third of managers' downwardly mobile sons are in manual work, a fate that befell only one tenth of self-employed professionals', and only slightly more of salaried professionals' sons. The latter two categories also exported a smaller proportion to the 'supervisory and self-employed artisan' class III, which may be the result of a lack of a connection between the worlds of professionals and industry. Putting it somewhat oversimply, the less successful sons of the professionals go in for semi-professional and white collar jobs; while the less successful sons of senior staff and, even more markedly, of managers, are just as likely to end up in lower grade industrial occupations.

In contrast to this picture of openness in downward mobility, there are signs of growing maintenance of privilege in recent years. Whereas at the start of the period (those born before the end of the First World War), only 42.9 per cent maintained their station in the UMC, by the end 70.6 per cent of those born during the Second World War were achieving this. And of those who did not, most were in class II (semi-professionals) and none had become manual workers (classes V–VII). In the oldest cohort, the sons had a 60/40 risk of downward mobility; the middle cohorts (1919–38) improved to 45/55, and the youngest cohort (albeit on the basis of small numbers) had made it to 30/70. So that while not dominating the UMC in the sense of making it their exclusive preserve, the upper middle class appears to have become increasingly successful in maintaining its intergenerational privilege.

However, in terms of inflows, self-recruits have never been more than 36.4 per cent of the total and they were generally less, at around 20 to 25 per cent. There is no sign of a consistent trend for the incomers' share of UMC occupations to increase or decrease, although the total size of the UMC has tended to expand. The first conclusion from this is that, since the First World War, the lieutenant class has *always* been predominantly drawn from 'other ranks': we are not dealing with a new phenomenon, but merely one that has previously been underestimated. Secondly, as the size of the class has expanded, the expansion has worked to enable more of the lieutenant class to remain in the class of their birth.

The picture of privilege maintenance that these various figures present is not one which can support a simple model of the closure of the UMC. First, these UMC sons who 'make it' into the UMC are not following in their fathers' footsteps: whatever cultural or other capital they have is a general currency. Secondly, while there is inheritance of advantage, in that a greater proportion of UMC sons 'made it' than the children from any other background, the majority of UMC sons have been downwardly mobile, albeit by a small majority. Thirdly, there is some signs of privilege maintenance becoming more common, but this is at the same time associated with inward recruitment from the lower classes. Thus the extent to which it can be said that a specific inherited culture is shared by all UMC sons is severely limited, since this culture is being exported into other occupational groups and also attenuated by heavy in-recruitment from other classes. The new recruits to the UMC outnumber the 'immobile', or 'self-recruiters' by three to one. This is the reverse of the pattern which Miliband (1969, p. 44) has described in reference to elite recruitment, which is one where 'the upper and middle class in these (capitalist) societies is still largely self-recruiting and therefore to a marked degree socially cohesive'. Nor does the current evidence accord with Bottomore's (1965, p. 38) view that access to a rather broadly defined upper class is 'very limited in any society and notably so in Britain'. Even allowing that a different definition of the 'upper class' is being employed in this second case, it is clear that recruitment patterns are very different from what both Miliband and Bottomore have assumed.

Is this difference crucial? In the first place there is the plain matter of empirical evidence and specific statements: recruitment does not operate in the lieutenant class in the way which, say for example, Miliband has said that it did. Secondly, there is the question of how such specific assumptions underpin general models of a ruling class or elite. In the work of Bottomore, Millibant and others like them, there is a sense of graduated insulation about the rulers. Recruitment is either from their own ranks, or from the group closest to them, which is almost as closed as the elite itself. The tumult of the multitude has to pass through many baffles before it can disturb the peace of the inner corridors of power. Against this, the new data on mobility rates seem to suggest that the lieutenant class is already open to the other classes: it is filled with men from humbler backgrounds. So the Masses are at the Gates, and their clamour fills the Palace. With these alternative impressions guiding them, sociologists would expect to find differences in the ways in which the power-holders protected their continuity and exercised their power – if indeed they could continue to do so.

However, the Masses (and not even *all* of them) are only at the Gates: they are not yet inside. There is a striking dissimilarity in accounts of closed access and self-recruitment among those supposed to be the holders of large blocks of capital and the occupants of key command positions, on the one hand, and the new indications of openness in the lieutenant class, on the other. There is clearly a considerable difference between the lieutenant class, recruited 25 per cent or at the very most 45 per cent, from the upper parts of the middle classes, and the elites recruiting at 85 per cent, 80 per cent, 66 per cent, 75 per cent or 72 per cent from the higher echelons (see Stanworth and Giddens, 1974).

How can this be explained? It may be a methodological artefact: the mobility data refer to origins since 1909, and destinations in 1975: respondents are aged 20 to 64 years, and so are at all stages of their careers. The elite data, on the other hand, were collected mainly in the late sixties or 1970, and presumably deal with mature men at or near the peaks of their careers. So the differences in recruitment could be due to the time of the research, or to some career factor. The first explanation we reject as implausible; we know of no supporting evidence that recent years have seen the sort of dramatic democratisation required to bring the two patterns into agreement. The second explanation would require that many young middle-class sons start work at lower levels, and then later in their careers recover their upper middle class status in such numbers as to balance out (presumably not displace) the incomers.

As Goldthorpe has shown for England and Wales, there is a degree of this later counter-mobility (Goldthorpe, 1980a). However, unless one assumes actual displacement, the return flow could not be large enough to produce sufficient adjustment to bring the two patterns into line and as Chapter 7 shows does not happen. So while the mobility survey may underestimate self-recruitment because of the career effect, the difference between elite and lieutenant class recruitment patterns would still be between 15 per cent, 20 per cent or 25 per cent when the most generous (or implausible) allowances are made. It seems reasonable to infer that the elites, narrowly defined, are much less accessible than the lieutenant class, that their backgrounds and recruitment systems are very different, and that the elites are not 'like' other occupational groupings because of this.

Now it is important to remember that what one has here is a discontinuity between evidence about family backgrounds in some positional elites, on the one hand, and a set of occupations, on the other. This is not in itself direct evidence for the existence of an elite, or that the positions discussed by the contributors to Stanworth and Giddens have in some way been shown to be powerful because self-recruitment is high. At best, these recruitment data are compatible with such as interpretation, but mobility studies are about jobs, careers and backgrounds, and it is dangerous to overextend their findings.

The importance of the discrepancy in the recruitment patterns is twofold. It would seem that this kind of formulation of the problem, i.e. contrasting the 'really powerful' with the 'not quite so powerful' – might be a fruitful line to follow, provided an adequate conception of power could be made. In other words, as Giddens has implied (Giddens, 1974, p. xii), the study of careers and avenues of connection may sustain positional analysis. Secondly, if the 'top people' and the lieutenant class are rather different, their inter-relationship – dependent, supportive, legitimative, recruitment pool, etc. – therefore now seems more problematic.

SOME CONCLUDING REMARKS

This account of mobility has not revealed a neat or simple pattern. On the one hand, there are elements of fluidity, while on the other hand, we find sharp class differentials in access. These are not purely artefactual, despite the earlier observations about the way certain techniques tend to emphasise one view or another: not for the first time, the real world has proved to be complex.

The three models of the class structure that have been re-examined in the light of the Scottish data have all been found to be inadequate. There is almost no evidence of a threshold effect, only a little more for a buffer-zone, and the thesis of progressive closure seems to survive only as an observation about elites narrowly defined. Underlying all three of these models is the basic misconception, drawn from Glass, that almost all mobility is short range. Once it has been demonstrated that short-range mobility is not the dominant feature, these theoretical constructions require rebuilding. A similar view of short-range mobility (which dates from Sorokin) also appears in the writings of others like Parkin and Giddens, but in a more diffuse form, and some implications of this will be drawn in the final chapter.

Although one or two images – safety-net, semi-permeable membrane – have been suggested, the complexity of the actual processes does not easily lend itself to handy metaphor. The basic pattern is a product of several tendencies:

(a) Nearer the 'top', there is high self-recruitment and low export of sons to the lower levels.

(b) Nearer the bottom, there is fairly high self-recruitment and fairly high export of sons to the upper levels.
(c) At all levels, a majority of sons enter other classes, and in all classes, the incomers heavily outnumber those whose fathers were in the same class.

In discussing these results (indeed in conceptualising them in this way) the chapter has followed the main tradition of mobility research, namely, the identification of class boundaries, inequality of access to non-manual classes, and the components of class formation, that is to say the investigation of upward mobility and the lack of it, particularly in reference to the higher groups.

The latter part of the chapter has attempted to develop aspects of the sociology of the new managerial and professional class. Their backgrounds are fairly diverse, and their capacity to pass on occupational advantage, although relatively high, is still limited. It follows that their ability to generate a cohesive identity or class position seems very restricted as far as mobility is a factor, so that there is a disjunction between functional necessity under a technological system, and capacity to act as social class. Of course, the processes of selection and resocialisation work to counteract this, but such processes clearly must be accorded much more emphasis than hitherto because the mobility rates are now seen to be so high.

The present chapter has attempted to answer what can be seen as the most fundamental question about mobility, namely, how much movement is there between origins and current status? In examining some of the implications of that answer, the dimension of occupational change has not always been paramount, because the initial question is framed in static, if historical, terms. Occupational transition has been included either by reference to the father's distribution or by implication rather than explicitly: mobility rates are the results of a background process previously described. Now that the basic pattern is clear, we can deal with the second of the main mobility questions, is society becoming more or less open? This is a dynamic question, and one that lends itself to a more explicit answer in terms of the dynamics of economic change, as we shall see in the next chapter.

5 Trends in Occupational Mobility

Changes in mobility can be thought of as caused by one of three processes. Mobility will respond to:

(a) a change in the 'rules of recruitment',
(b) a change in the occupational process which expands/contracts the proportion of non-manual jobs, and
(c) an expansion/contraction of the industry which is under discussion.

This can be presented dramatically, as in Figure 5.1.

The first part of Figure 5.1 (top left) shows an industry with two levels of job, manual and non-manual. The latter is subdivided into two by virtue of its recruitment: one part is filled by workers from non-manual origins and the other is filled from manual origins (although this can be generalised to any number and structure of classes). The number of those coming from manual backgrounds can be expressed as a percentage of all those in the industry, for an industry-specific mobility rate, or more commonly aggregated with their equivalents in all other industries to give a total mobility rate. On the left of the industry 'block' is a representation of the 'recruitment process'. This is a catch-all title to cover everything from the hiring and firing policies of the industry's personnel departments, through the aspirations and values of the total labour force, to the exigencies of the educational system.

In the second part of Figure 5.1 (top right) the *total size* of the same hypothetical industry has increased, as represented by a broadening of its width. the industry-specific mobility rate remains the same, but the industry's contribution to total mobility in the society is greater, because more people are going through the expanded industry's 'mobility route'.

In the third part of Figure 5.1 (lower left) we have returned the industry to its original scale, but modified the recruitment process. Now more of the available non-manual jobs go to the upwardly mobile. Both the industry-specific and the total mobility rates increase. The change in the recruitment process could be something completely external to the industry and thus 'forced' on the employer,

Figure 5.1 Diagrammatic representation of factors in changing mobility rates

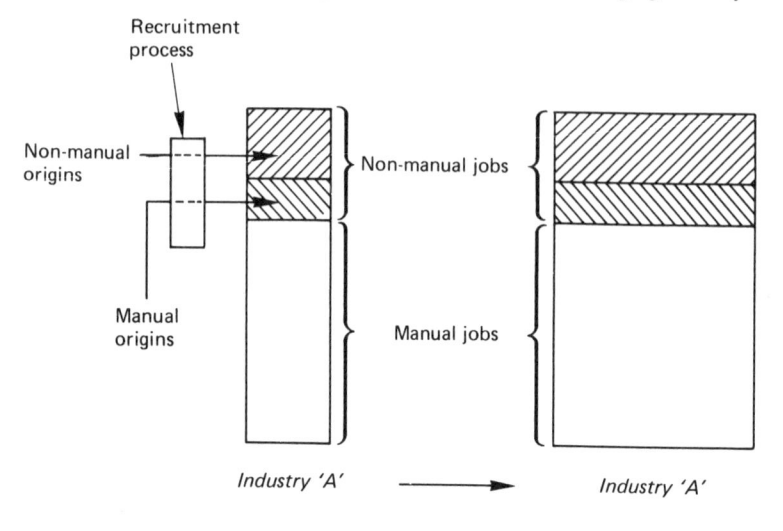

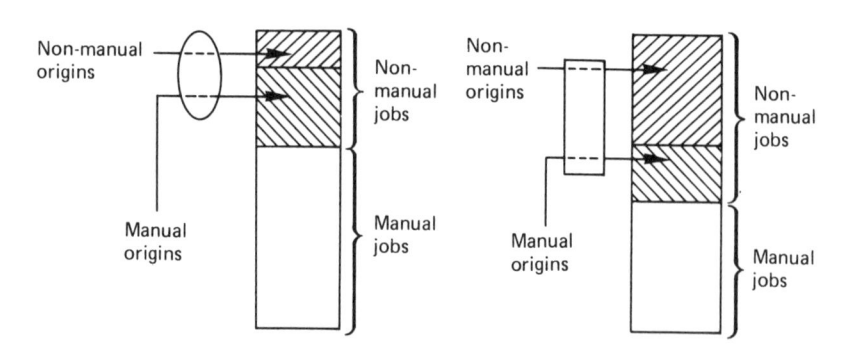

or it could be a conscious change in personnel policy which had the (possibly unintended) consequences of opening up access to the children of manual workers.

Finally (lower right) we have an industry of the same size, with the original recruitment process, but with an expanded non-manual sector. If these jobs are filled in the same proportions of recruits from manual and non-manual origins as before, there are, none the less, more opportunities for upward mobility in the expanded sector, so that again both the industry-specific and total mobility rates rise. Although each of these processes is analytically separate, in practice they are all operating, to various extents, at the same time. Nor have we exhausted all logical possibilities in identifying these three sources of change. For example, a drastic change in the distribution of origins (by means of a demographic shift or a change in occupational structure) would alter the supply of labour with particular backgrounds, and who could be said to be 'at risk' of being upwardly mobile. However, while fathers' occupations, when the respondents were 14 years old, tend to become relatively more non-manual from 1930 on, there are no sharp shifts in the distributions which coincide with the key period that interest us.

SOME METHODOLOGICAL CONSIDERATIONS

In practice, implementing this model is far from easy. To start with, the whole enterprise of connecting sample data to external time series or historical accounts is rendered impossible, certainly at a high level of precision, by problems of comparability. It is therefore necessary to restrict ourselves to cautious, indirect and general points of reference in alternative sources like those used in Chapters 2 and 3. Second, any discussion of 'demand' for labour which depends on evidence from a later sample must be incomplete, because jobs will have gone to other men not included in the analysis (who have in the interim died, emigrated or who had worked already and so do not count as men 'first entering the labour force' (see below)). For this reason and the practical limits of maintaining large cells values, it is necessary to simplify the analysis and to use broad groupings, such as 'non-manual workers', or 'manufacturing industry', etc. The cohort numbers dealt with in this chapter range from 450 to 500, with any one cohort containing one-eighth of the sample.

This use of less specific categories also helps to avoid the objection of Crompton (1980) that certain jobs (e.g. clerks) had very different tasks and status in the past, so that any trend analysis is misconceived because a given job cannot be regarded as having a constant value in the occupational hierarchy over forty years. For the time being, Goldthorpe's (1980b) reply will suffice: cases of dramatic deskilling are few and only a relatively small proportion of the labour force is involved.

A more substantial problem resides in the career data that can be used in analysing trends. The different lengths of respondents' careers means that older men have completed their careers while younger men still have some way to go. Any account of historical changes or trends which might promote greater mobility can be hidden by this career development factor. Again, the Scottish study in following the Nuffield example has only a limited set of information on each respondent: lacking full career histories, we can compare only a small number of 'job points'; in practice first job and job ten years after starting work. Nor is the 'first job' necessarily what a common-sense view would expect. Jobs taken between leaving school and starting apprenticeships ('butcher's delivery boy', etc.) are discounted as temporary, while apprentices are classified as skilled manual workers from the start, rather than when they became skilled men in their own right, at the age of 21. This is because the Hope–Goldthrope scale follows the OPCS conventions of classifying trainees with the occupations for which they are being trained. By using the first job and the job ten years later, we control for differential career length but necessarily truncate the careers of older respondents. The mobility that is explained is, therefore, only apart of the mobility discussed in the previous chapter, which together with its often cruder categories means that direct comparison cannot be made. Mobility between first and last jobs is tackled in Chapter 7 below.

To balance against these limitations, the methods of analysis used here offer a considerable improvement on more traditional accounts. First, conventional trend-analysis of mobility typically uses fixed cohorts, starting with the year of birth of the oldest respondent and reckoning ten-year blocks forward to the present, from that date. Thus Glass's cohorts run 1890–9, 1900–9, 1910–19 and 1920–9, while Goldthorpe's are 1908–17, 1918–27, 1928–37 and 1938–47. One difficulty with this is that these dates are determined by the year of the survey, rather than by an interest in a period of historical event. Therefore, the cohorts may straddle countervailing trends and disguise chronological patterns (the cohorts have to be ten years long to retain large numbers for analysis). One way around this is to use 'rolling cohorts', i.e. moving averages based on successive, partially overlapping, groups of years. Instead of a table showing four cohorts, the data are presented as lines on a graph, as in Figure 5.2 below.

Second, rather than using dates of birth to define cohort membership, year of entry to the labour market has been used. This enables us to talk more directly about the state of the occupational context at any one time because the data then refer to all men starting work, whether ages 14 or 24. Although men born in the same year share certain experiences (e.g. early school education) they do not all start work at the same time and under the same economic conditions.

Figure 5.2 Five-year moving averages for non-manual employment and mobility, ten-years after entry to labour market

```
    % Non-manual first employment
—·—·
    % Non-manual first employment
———   and recruited from manual family
        (i.e. upward mobility)
    % Non-manual first employment
————  and recruited from non-manual family
```

When looking at the graphs it is important to remember that the five-year cohort is plotted at its mid-point: thus 1930–4 is plotted as 1932. The change between two adjacent points reflects the net effect of dropping out the oldest year and introducing a new one (1930–4 becomes 1931–5) so it is important to look on either side of the points to see the period in question.

OCCUPATIONS AND MOBILITY, 1930-70

Although our explanatory Figure 5.1 was presented as a series of statements about an industry, the basic approach can be applied at an aggregate level and indeed the first step is to grasp the overall picture, before considering its components. Figure 5.2 shows the pattern of changes in occupational distribution and in mobility for the first jobs of men entering the labour market from 1930 through to the late 1960s. Allowing for an odd kink here and there, the upper line shows a decade of expansion of non-manual occupations, from an origin around 18 per cent. This was followed by a decade of contraction, but the fall was not to the former levels. Finally men starting work from about 1950 on did so during a considerable expansion of non-manual work, rising to a point in excess of 40 per cent.

If we examine the lower line, showing the percentage of upward mobility from manual backgrounds to non-manual employment, the first part of the pattern echoes the occupational distribution line, with a decade of increase followed by a decade of decrease. However, although mobility begins to increase in the fifties, it levels off at around 15 per cent by the mid or late fifties. This is double its earlier levels, but the apparent association of mobility and opportunity disappears.

Instead, the expansion of non-manual occupations is filled by men from non-manual backgrounds. This is shown by the middle, dotted, line which hovers between 10 and 15 per cent until the late fifties but then takes off at a similar rate to the expansion of non-manual employment line. In short, as far as mobility across the manual/non-manual line at the first job is concerned, the upward mobility rate has ceased to improve. Indeed, in the last decade of the period covered by the SMS, it has worsened *vis-à-vis* that rate at which the sons of the non-manual class gain access to non-manual work themselves.

The general characteristic of the pattern ten years after starting work resembles those in Figure 5.2, but with two main differences. First, the last part of the data in Figure 5.2 cannot be plotted in Figure 5.3 because respondents entering the labour market between 1964 and 1974 had not, at the time of interview, yet had a job 'ten years from starting work'. Therefore, the sharp change in recruitment, from around the early sixties, does not show up in Figure 5.3, although there is a hint of it in the last few points plotted. Secondly, the percentage values in the latter figure are, as expected, higher than those in Figure 5.2 as a result of the career effect. What is striking is that the later patterns closely follow those of the first employment, showing how the

Figure 5.3 Five-year moving averages for non-manual employment and mobility, ten-years after entry to labour market

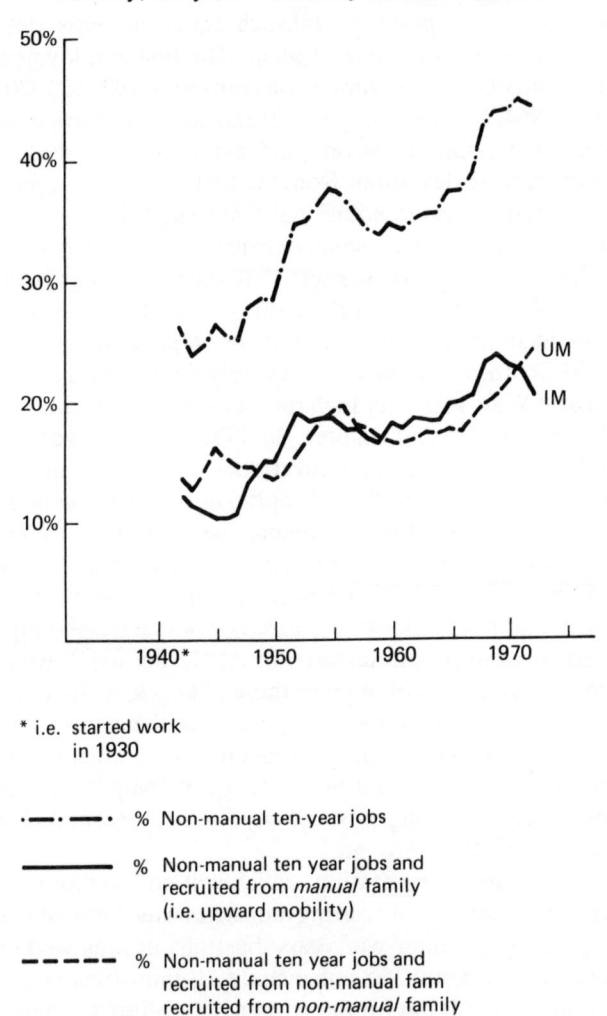

```
50%


40%


30%
                                                        UM
20%                                                     IM


10%

       1940*       1950       1960       1970
```

* i.e. started work
 in 1930

—·—·— % Non-manual ten-year jobs

———— % Non-manual ten year jobs and
 recruited from *manual* family
 (i.e. upward mobility)

— — — — % Non-manual ten year jobs and
 recruited from non-manual fam
 recruited from *non-manual* family

initial structure is carried forward into the career. There is no evidence that the advantage derived from family background weakens after ten years, to be replaced by the respondent's own qualities of achievement. For that to be true, the upward mobility line in Figure 5.3 should be markedly higher than the immobility line than it was in Figure 5.2. The same relationship between the two figures also suggests that the later 'achievers' do not outperform their equivalents whose careers came earlier historically (see also Chapter 7).

Because the two job points reveal such similar patterns, details will be reported below for only one of them. The first employment point has been chosen because the time-series runs from 1930 to 1970, rather than 1930 to 1964. Parallel analyses were consistently carried out using the ten-year job point, however, and evidence from these is used wherever there were deviations from the first employment pattern, or the analyses demonstrated additional features of interest.

Both time-series indicate a small expansion of non-manual employment during the 1930s. To suggest that there was a growth in the proportions of non-manual work in this period seems on the face of things to be incompatible with the facts of Depression. As Chapter 2 showed, the Scottish economy was severely depressed right up to the Second World War, with very high rates of unemployment. However, as was also observed in that chapter, the 1930s were years of increasing productivity, of technological innovation even in declining old staple industries, and of concentration of capital into larger organisations of production. Following this argument, the transition to increased proportions of non-manual employment can perhaps be partially explained in terms of the occupational requirement of the new technologies and new scales of organisation which despite high levels of unemployment were maintained through the decade. It would seem that young workers benefited from these changes, while their elders tended to remain unemployed, trapped in their now redundant careers. Second, it follows that changes in non-manual employment and upward mobility do not seem to be incompatible with high unemployment, with rising productivity, or with marked changes in the nature of capital.

One 'test' of this interpretation, which will not be reported in any detail here, is to take manufacturing industries which were declining or expanding during the inter-war years, basically as indicated by Leser and Silvey (1950). These do not include all industries (e.g. service industries are omitted) but for the remainder it offers a chance to look for any pattern of association between economic performance (growth or contraction of labour force) and either percentage of non-manual jobs or upward mobility. A full list of which industries are included can be found in Leser and Silvey (1950, pp. 171–3). Broadly speaking, declining industries include the old staples, plus some foods and printing while expanding industries include electrical engineering, chemicals, building materials, vehicles and 'consumer goods'.

First, we observe that as far as young men are concerned, there is no evidence that consistently fewer were recruited into the declining industries, even if the total labour force in those industries was falling. Second, while the proportion of non-manual jobs was lower for this group, it grew from around 5 per cent to 10 per cent during th 1930s, of which around one-third involved upward mobility. In the expanding industries, non-manual jobs made up about 20 per cent of all jobs for those first starting work, with a slight tendency for this to be higher in the later years. Up to half of these jobs went to the upwardly mobile. We therefore conclude that while expansion and relative economic success are associated with growth in non-manual occupations and mobility, the same process is going on, to a lesser extent, even in contracting and economically unsuccessful industries. This conclusion applies, however, only to those entering work for the first time (and the first ten years of their careers): the experience of older men may be much less optimistic.

But if the transition to higher levels of non-manual employment is sufficiently robust to stand up to the effects of the Depression, how is one to explain the collapse of this trend (and mobility rates) in the late forties and 1950s? We would like to suggest that this is the result of a quite separate process, namely a 'war effect'. During the war, the war economy differed from that of peacetime in several important ways. First, a very large part of the male labour force was not available for employment because they were in the Armed Forces. Calder records that one-sixth of men under 40, and more than half of men in their twenties, had been called up by July 1940. Second, 'non-essential' enterprises were run down or suspended, while industries directly relevant to the war effort were modified and expanded. Third, the need for co-ordination, rapid change and controls generated new state bureaucracies and company record-keeping departments.

The processes through which school-leavers were recruited to fill vacant jobs were thus completely different during this period. The school leaver taking a civilian job between 1939 and 1945 found himself able to consider jobs which, under normal circumstances, would not have been available to him. Men of fighting age were being replaced by women, by old men past retiring age, and by these youngsters. In a situation of economic upheaval and labour shortage, established practices were in abeyance and the inexperienced could find themselves taken on in offices or stores, or (given the prevalent attitudes of the time) used to direct the labours of women (Pelling, 1963; Cole and Postgate, 1961).

Thus the rise shown in Figure 5.2 in the numbers of non-manual occupations and in the upward mobility rate do not reflect so much an expansion of the non-manual sector, but in the increased employment of young men in those non-manual occupations that were available. What we are witnessing is a temporary change in the recruitment patterns. To put it another way, the graph shows at this point an improvement in the chances of the young worker getting a non-manual job as well as any structural shift caused by this newly created machinery of state regulation.

Conversely, after the war, the reverse was true. Not only were there the demobbed armed forces back in contention, but those who had done so well at home during the war were also well-ensconced in their careers (as Figure 5.3 shows). The opportunities for young men entering the labour market for the first time in the post-war period were blocked by older men who had stronger claims than they did. If this supposition is correct then the peak and trough that lies between 1938 and 1949 (i.e. cohorts 1936–40 to 1947–51) is a direct product of the Second World War, and in that sense a deviation from mainstream trends. Its effects in terms of career entry, and therefore subsequent life chances, persists until the end of the 1940s.

From around the early 1950s, non-manual growth is fairly consistent, as one might expect in two peaceful decades marked by more or less steady economic growth, further technological innovation, the flowering of the welfare state, and ever greater economic concentration. What is interesting about this period is the relative decline in upward mobility which appears from the 1955–9 cohort onwards. Since we have no wars or major depressions to provide an explanation, we must look elsewhere.

One possible cause of this new trend might be that the fathers' occupations become so influenced by occupational transition that the *supply* of manual sons who could by definition be upwardly mobile has been dramatically reduced. On closer inspection, however, this does not hold water. First, previous peaks and troughs on the mobility curve have not been associated with changes in the father's distribution. For example, during the peak in upward mobility in the early 1940s, and the trough that followed in the late 1940s, the percentage of manual fathers was virtually unchanged, from 68.4 per cent to 68.6 per cent. Second, although there is a decline in the proportion of manual fathers, it is not a sharp major one. In the five-year period immediately before mobility began to plateau, the percentage of manual fathers ran at was between 68 and 70 per cent. From 1955–9 to 1964–8, it dropped ten percentage points, from 69.4 per cent to 59.6 per cent, an annual average drop of marginally under 1 per cent, with no single fall of more than 2.1 per cent. There was no sudden plunge in the late 1950s, and at the end of the time-series there were still six out of ten fathers – or more precisely six out of ten sons – with manual backgrounds who were theoretically 'at risk' of upward mobility. A supply side explanation of the plateau effect is not substantiated.

Our second line of explanation is to disaggregate the main trend into some of its component parts. We have already observed that the non-manual class is a combination of four categories of white collar work. Given that the SEGs discussed in Chapter 3 did not move in a uniform manner, we might expect some variation between classes. Again, we have observed that industrial sectors have very different histories of growth and contraction. Figure 5.1 alerted us to the interplay of occupational, sectoral and recruitment policy factors, i.e. to the significance of size as well as to rate of mobility. Each of these is interesting in its own right, as well as its interaction with the others, which may explain the static mobility rate of the 1960s.

DISAGGREGATING NON-MANUAL MOBILITY: OCCUPATIONS

The four non-manual occupational categories are plotted in Figure 5.4 for comparison with the overall change in the proportion of non-manual occupations. As we might expect, the four 'classes' have different profiles. Classes I and II are the most similar, showing small but fairly steady growth: class I has very slightly more of the peak and trough effect during the 1940s, while class II shows rather faster growth in the 1960s. In contrast, class III is more volatile, with a marked peak and trough, followed in the main by an increase through both the 1950s and 1960s. It seems class III's decline during the 1940s is a major factor in the early part of the overall non-manual profile, while together with class II it is an important contributor to the upswing in the later part of the overall profile. Class IV shows an earlier (but very small) growth than the others, which soon fades: it is not until the late fifties that it recovers, but the last part of the profile is downwards.

Where the mobility percentage line begins to deviate from the overall non-manual line, the class lines are generally still upward. Then, in the cohorts plotted for the years 1958–62 (cohorts 1956–64),

102 *Employment and Opportunity*

Figure 5.4 Percentage sample in each of the four classes
(five-year moving averages for year of first employment)

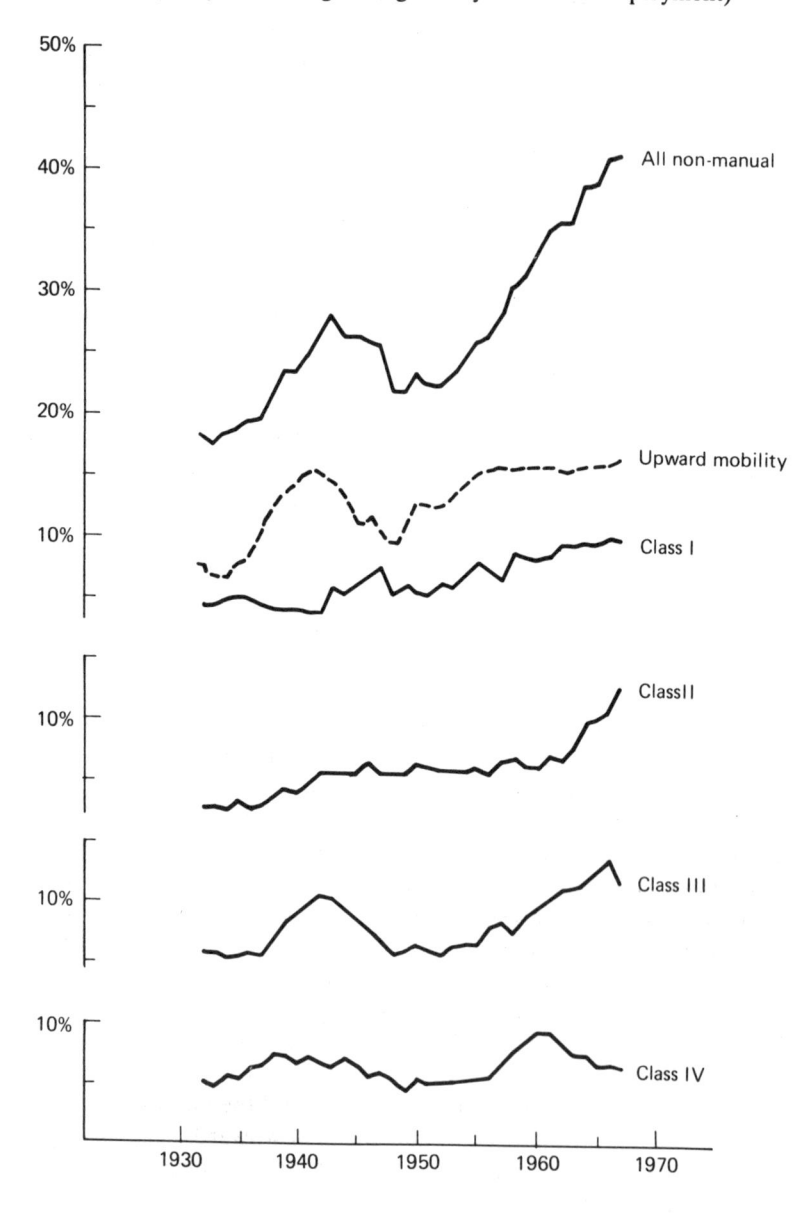

classes I and II show less growth than III or IV. Thereafter, class IV declines, while class II climbs (cohorts 1961–70).

What does this imply for our model of mobility? The later trends in mobility that we are seeking to explain coincide with rather different periods in occupational terms. In the late 1950s, the faster growth is in the size of the two classes III and IV (which according to the buffer zone thesis should contain the most mobility: instead mobility shows little growth). In the 1960s, the mobility trends does not change much (if anything it rises), despite a decrease in class IV and an increase in class II.

This can be clarified by looking at the mobility flows into each of the four classes, as in Figure 5.5. Unfortunately this breakdown results in small cell sizes (with less than ten cases at some points) so that the percentages are volatile. Figure 5.5 has been plotted at half the vertical scale of the earlier graphs, but the extent of the variation is striking: for example, class II goes from 18 per cent upward mobility to 62 per cent upward mobility in a period of only seven years.

A comparison of Figures 5.4 and 5.5 should help to explain the patterns of mobility. For example, class I combines a small increase in scale with a decrease in recruitment from manual origins: the net effect is that its contribution to upward mobility tends to be relatively stable and if anything very slightly less towards the end of the period than earlier. Class II's contribution seems to be mainly dominated by its fluctuations in recruitment rather than by its expansion, although this generalisation does not hold true for the last five years when the size increases while its recruitment decreases. This is shown in Figure 5.6.

The third of the classes has a more profound effect on overall mobility. Although it is not noticeably larger than the other classes (Figure 5.4) it contributes at least a third of all mobility (Figure 5.6) rising to about half in the early 1940s. Throughout the period, with only three exceptions, half or more of its members are recruited from manual backgrounds (Figure 5.5). The pattern does vary, showing a trough in the late forties (like the overall trend), followed by a very considerable peak in the early fifties, declining to a low around 1960 and then beginning to recover. However, in the 1950s this is not strongly reflected in its contribution to overall mobility (Figure 5.6) because these years were a time when class III was relatively small, and it is only in the sixties that there is a coincidence of expansion in its scale and in manual recruitment. It is worth noting, on the other hand, that class III shows the most marked peak and trough effect of the four classes during the first two decades, and that this roughly coincides

Figure 5.5 Percentage of each non-manual class recruited from manual origins
(five-year moving average, first job)

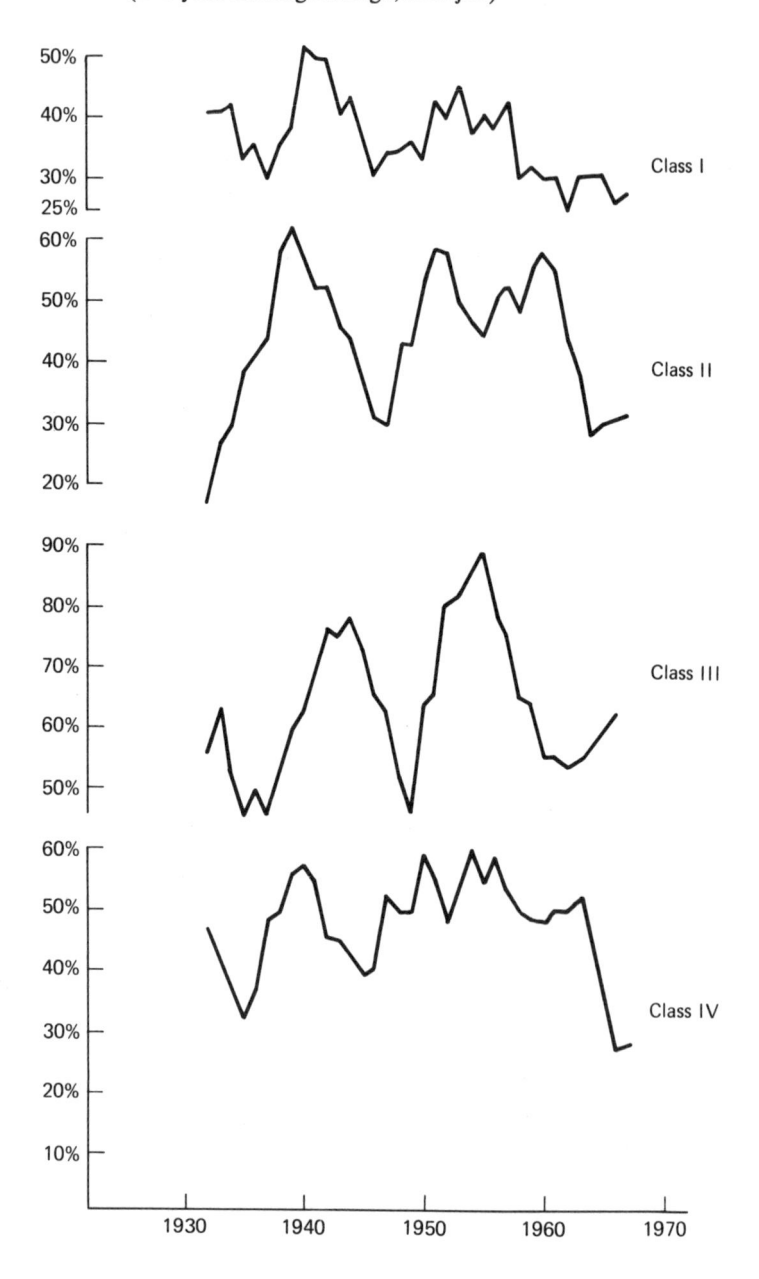

with a similar (if slightly later) peak and trough in its recruitment from manual origins. This goes a long way to localise the 'war effect'.

In the first two decades, as we observed earlier, class IV also has in much milder form this peak and trough effect, and while its recruitment pattern runs two or three years in advance, this helps to explain its comparatively large contribution to mobility in the first half of the period. Again, its numbers increase in the late fifties, when its recruitment from manual origins was running at about 50 per cent, but then the class contracts, its upward recruitment drops sharply and its contribution to overall mobility goes from 29 per cent to 5 per cent in seven years (the years, coincidentally, when the overall mobility stabilises and then begins to climb slowly).

Are there any general conclusions to be drawn from these data? First, at a general level all the classes make important but dissimilar contributions to upward mobility which vary considerably over time. Second, there is no evidence to suggest that when a class is expanding, manual workers' sons automatically stand a better chance of recruitment than those with non-manual origins. This *may* happen (classes III and IV in the thirties) but not necessarily (e.g. class II in the sixties). Conversely, when a non-manual class is declining in scale – which really only applies to classes III and IV for part of the period – this seems to disadvantage those from manual origins more than those from non-manual backgrounds, as the 1940s for both classes, and the 1960s for class IV, show.

As far as the change in relationship between overall occupational distribution and mobility post-1960 is concerned, it appears that this is initially repeated in classes II, III and IV, with no further increases in their mobility rates in the second half of the 1950s (plotted at years 1955). In the late sixties, classes II and III begin to recruit a few more upwardly mobile personnel but class IV is less available both in terms of scale and recruitment. Thus, as argued in the previous chapter about mobility to 'present occupation', it is the combination of a change in occupational distribution and the rules of recruitment which determines the mobility rate. The two factors may operate in the same or contrary directions: the logical set is given in Figure 5.7.

Expansion in size is a more common pattern than contraction, and to a lesser extent so is expansion of manual recruitment although here there is much more fluctuation in rates of changes.

Explanations of why the occupational distribution and rules of recruitment change are therefore needed. It is tempting to seek the latter in terms of the former: as the demand for labour in one class

Figure 5.6 Percentage of total upward mobility distributed among four classes
(moving averages by year of first employment)

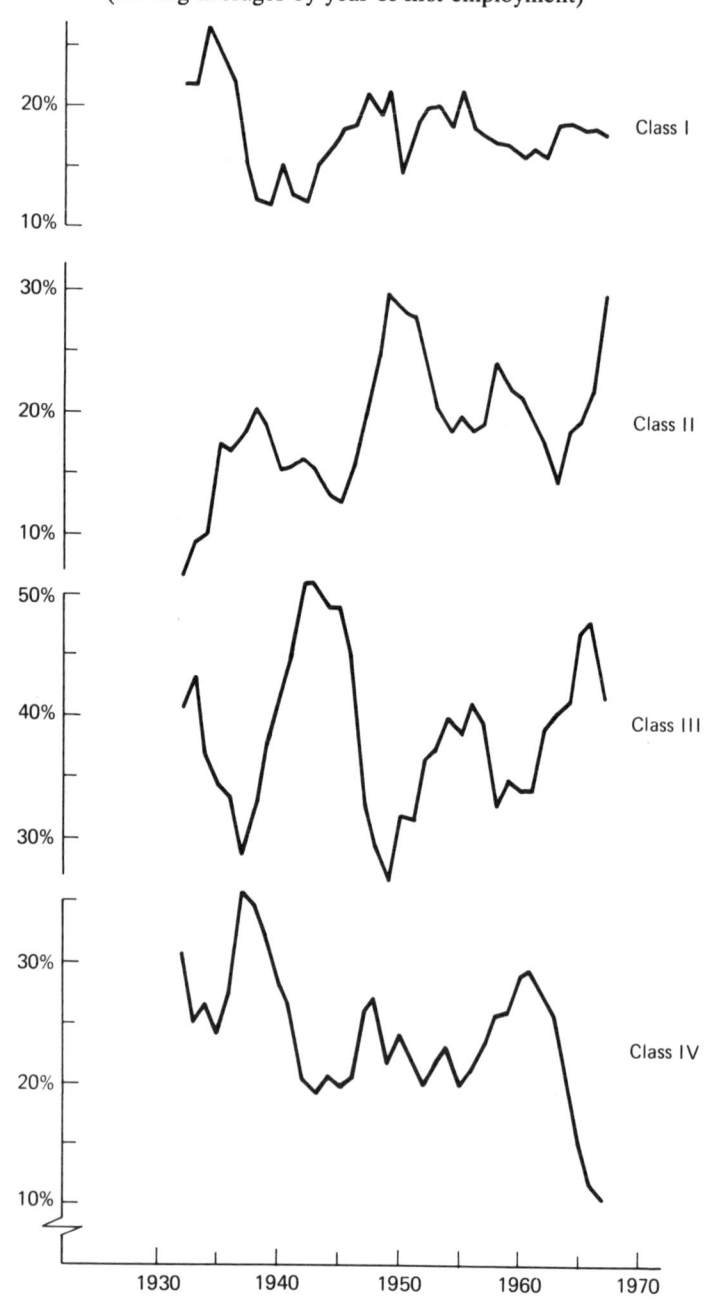

Figure 5.7 Mobility factors

	manual recruiting expanding	manual recruiting contracting
size of non-manual class — expanding	Mobility INCREASES (e.g. cl. III & IV in 1930s)	Mobility may INCREASE or DECREASE (e.g. cl. III c. 1940 versus cl. I in 1960s)
size of non-manual class — contracting	Mobility may INCREASE or DECREASE (e.g. cl. III c. 1950 versus cl. III in late 1940s)	Mobility DECREASES (e.g. cl. IV in late 1960s)

varies, it produces excess demand or supply for the other classes by releasing or drawing off job applicants from them. In the late 1960s, the contraction in size and recruitment in class IV would result in what previously would have been upwardly mobile recruits to class IV becoming competitors for classes II and III (in a market perhaps made easier because more of class I members are recruited from the non-manual sector, so reducing their need to seek class II and III jobs). We certainly need to remember that the four classes are part of one economic system, but it is premature to adopt a displacement model. That would imply that the whole of the non-manual sector is a single labour market: if that were unequivocally the case, one might expect more uniformity of profiles across the four classes. Even if such a displacement model were acceptable it would still be an explanation dependent on changes in the occupational distribution, that is to say, on the organisation of production of goods and services.

DISAGGREGATING NON-MANUAL MOBILITY: INDUSTRIES

We can now look at the shift in industrial employment from primary to secondary sectors, and from secondary to tertiary sectors. This can be done for the whole period, but it is the later part that is of the most interest. To simplify the task, primary industry can be virtually discounted as a contributor to national upward mobility trends. The numbers of mobile men in primary industry in some of the cohorts are, quite literally, ones or twos, and therefore no basis for any talk of trends. At its maximum (in the inter-war period), primary industry's share of the total labour force was only just over 20 per cent and for much of the period it was less than 10 per cent. Of these, barely one in ten were 'non-manual' jobs, and almost all of *these* were taken by the sons of non-manual workers. Of course, we know that this sector contains many small enterprises where the term 'non-manual' is an inappropriate synonym for 'ownership' and first jobs do not normally involve ownership. The farmer's son who works the farm often does so in the confident expectation of taking over from his father in due course. As agriculture, fishing, and mining are either rural, coastal or geographically focused occupations, their importance in some regions would be greater. Where that were true, the net effect would be to reduce mobility opportunities for the local labour force. On balance, however, we shall not discuss primary industry any further, despite its contribution to immobility and its 'release' of potential workers caused by its decline after the war (for details see Payne *et al.*, 1983b).

As Figure 5.8 shows, the three sectors[1] contribute very different amounts of mobility. Between 2 per cent and 5 per cent of the sample were upwardly mobile on entering manufacturing industry: this represents between about 15 per cent and 30 per cent of all mobility. In service industry, mobility fluctuates between being about 6 per cent and 13 per cent of the sample, that is, accounting for between 70 per cent and just over 80 per cent of all upward mobility. More obviously, the difference between the two sectors varies, with the wartime peak

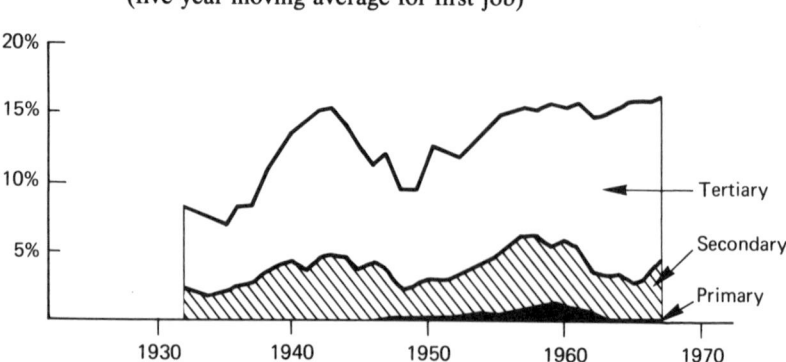

Figure 5.8 Proportions of upward mobility in industrial sectors (five-year moving average for first job)

being more noticeable in the service industries, and a widening gap after the late 1950s as the secondary sector contributes less mobility while tertiary sector mobility increases.

On the other hand, tertiary industry accounts for more non-manual jobs than other sectors; during the thirties this was about 14 per cent of all employment. This 14 per cent represents about one in every four tertiary sector jobs. Secondary sector non-manual jobs are only about 4 per cent of the total labour force, and this kind of work is only about one in every eight jobs in the sector. Although the overall size of the sectors is fairly stable despite the war, the pattern of non-manual jobs changes. In the service sector, non-manual work increases from a quarter to more than a third, while in manufacturing the increase is from one-eighth to one-fifth. In other words, although in both the two sectors there is an expansion of non-manual occupations, the greater absolute size of the tertiary sector means that its total expansion was greater.

The same logic applies to the mobility rates. Secondary industry has a higher rate of upward mobility, but its total contribution is lower because it contains fewer non-manual posts. Even though it offers its employees between a 66 per cent and 75 per cent chance of upward mobility (that is, between two-thirds and three-quarters of its non-manual jobs went to the upwardly mobile), compared with a 45 per cent to 60 per cent chance in service industry, the latter is four or five times bigger, and so has a bigger absolute effect on mobility overall. Thus, the 'war effect' (which is when the higher of the above chances of mobility occurred) may be more dependent on scale than on changes in the recruitment process.

However, in the early post-war period, while the overall balance between the broad sectors does not change much, the proportion of non-manual secondary industry jobs available to those starting work falls from around 20 per cent in the war to about 10 per cent by the early 1950s, before recovering towards the end of the decade. In the service industries, although there is a slight fall in the proportion of non-manual first jobs, it is only a few percentage points, and that only to the mid-fifties. The distribution of non-manual opportunity thus shifts in favour of tertiary industry particularly by around 1960.

If we now turn to the final part of our period, the 1960s, something different again is happening. As the decade proceeds, the size of the tertiary sector as a whole expands from about half to almost 60 per cent of all employment, while the secondary sector falls from just over a third to about 30 per cent. At the same time, the share of its employment which is non-manual increases from about 20 per cent to 27 per cent, whereas the non-manual proportion of tertiary sector jobs increases from just over a third to nearly a half. The net effect is to further shift the weight of available non-manual employment across to the tertiary sector (from around 75 per cent by the late 1950s to about 80 per cent ten years later).

We saw in Figure 5.8 that during the decade more of the total mobility had been generated in the tertiary sector. This can now be explained in terms of the balance between the sectors and the sector-specific mobility rates. We have already observed that it is manufacturing industry which has the higher mobility rates: manufacturing industry is in *relative* decline compared with the service industries, although its non-manual component is still showing net absolute increase. However, the proportion of these jobs going to the sons of manual workers declines steeply after the late 1950s, from around 66 per cent to about 40 per cent. In contrast, not only is service industry non-manual employment increasing but its upward mobility rates do not change so drastically, showing a drop of about 5 per cent at most, to a final level similar to that of the manufacturing sector, i.e. 40 per cent. The net effect on mobility is therefore a product of several processes, of which the overall growth in the tertiary sector is the main contributor. If we project the patterns of the 1950s on to the cohorts of the 1960s, it is clear that the more marked deviations between expectations and observations are those arising from this structural change. This is not to say that the mechanics of recruitment, i.e. the decline of all upward mobility, has no effect: rather, its impact is less than might be expected on the basis of more traditional mobility analysis.

There has been a tendency in some discussions of mobility to talk in terms of 'the middle class exploiting their initial advantage of birth and converting it into occupational advancement'. This rhetoric is inappropriate for a description of mobility of the 1960s. The middle class does not control service industry in that way; it would be the worst kind of conspiracy theory to suggest that the expansion of the tertiary sector was a result of anybody's attempts to improve mobility chances for their offspring! Similarly, the decline in secondary industry's share of employment has the hidden effect of reducing mobility and so indirectly it impacts on the class structure. But that decline is an outcome of general processes in the development of capitalism, not specifically class or even labour policies. In this perspective, strategies of professional closure or educational investment do not seem to be the crucial issues in explaining mobility, as against general changes to the labour market caused by processes internal to the major sectors.

DISAGGREGATING NON-MANUAL MOBILITY: THE OCCUPATION–INDUSTRY INTERFACE

The final stage of the examination of trends in mobility is to recombine the two perspectives of occupation and industry. To some extent, the industrial perspective includes the occupational because it has involved discussion of the proportions of non-manual occupations. However, a more detailed account of the components of the non-manual class should help to establish a better connection between the industrial trends and the contents of the more conventional mobility table.

Unfortunately, the problem of small cell size again arises, not least because we also are interested in exploring the sectors in more detail by separating out the old staples and newer services. Even with a tenyear moving average, the 900 or so available cases rapidly become subdivided. The sectors range in size over time from 15 per cent to 40 per cent, so that at some points an individual sector will employ only about 135 men. Each of the four classes makes up about 20 to 30 per cent of that total, or as few as twenty-five cases. With upward mobility as low as 10 per cent, we end up talking about two or three cases. While it is true that the more typical levels are around twenty-five men, and can be double that, a detailed presentation of graphs of percentages would not only be stretching the data very thinly, but would also be tedious for the reader. We shall therefore report some general patterns without providing an extensive treatment.

As we also use them later, this is a good point to identify the new industrial sectors. In manufacturing, the old staples – which featured so predominantly in the account of Scotland's economic history – are distinguished from the rest of the sector and joined with coal mining. Tertiary industry has also been dichotomised to give one group that is more clearly knowledge-based, and another with which is more closely related to production.[2] This also permits a direct link to the theories of industry society discussed above, by identifying those 'advanced' industries that are regarded as typifying modern society.

Taking each of the four sectors in turn, what general patterns are visible despite small cell size? First, the staple industries have used a distinctive mix of labour throughout the period, predominantly characterised by a smaller proportion of managerial and professional grades. This may be a result of the production process; for example, coal requires fewer highly developed technological tasks to be carried out because its relatively simple and stable technology involves little research and development work. Furthermore, much of its innovation arises from mining engineering, which is carried out by firms or research workers *outside* mining per se who service the needs of the coal production industry. It may also be a result of the organisation of the sector in large units, servicing a market that is not fixed (in that it is a declining market) but which changes slowly as far as product specification is concerned. To the extent that a nation or a region has a high proportion of its labour force engaged in staple industries, the employment opportunities are concentrated in relatively lower ranked occupations.

The second conclusion to be drawn is a modification of the first. The distinctive profiles of the staple sector are not constant. The later years have shown a tendency to use fewer male routine white collar workers (from 50 per cent of non-manual employees, to 20 per cent), but a marked increase in semi-professional and technical staff. The latter is most marked after the war, suggesting – if we accept the rational for conclusion one – that the need for more technologically advanced skills has increased since that time. This has been concentrated in class II rather than class I, suggesting not an increase in managers so much as an increase in high grade technicians (from 10 per cent to 40 per cent). It may be that it is still too early for the new post-war intakes to manifest themselves as managers: after all, comparatively few workers are taken on as managers in their first jobs.

If the employment profile of staple industries is distinctive, does this mean that their patterns of mobility are also different? Staple industry recruits more working class sons to its class I jobs than the all-sector average from the Second World War on, whereas its recruitment in class II and III are more typical, even if the latter has slightly lower rates at first and slightly higher rates in the post-war years. Class IV, apart from a dip during the late 1940s, also tends to be recruited more from the working class than the national average. In general terms, staple industry contributes more to upward mobility for its size than does the rest of Scotland's industries.

The other part of the manufacturing sector will, for convenience, be called 'light industry', to contrast it with coal, steel, textiles and ship building, although it includes chemicals, vehicle manufacturing and other large-scale production processes. Here the deviations from the overall pattern also concern classes I and II, in that the former initially runs at a lower level before changing to a higher level around 1950, whereas the latter shows the opposite of this with a smaller proportion in the later years. However, class II's decline happens later ($c.1955$) and it is not so marked a turn-around as that of class I. The other two classes are closer to the overall pattern, but class III runs at a lower level for most of the period. This is rather unexpected, as class III contains the foremen and manual supervisors that one associates with manufacturing. As in the case of the staples, class III is not strongly represented in secondary industry. Compared with the old staples, light industry, particularly post-war, has employed more men in those categories requiring higher levels of skills: a larger proportion of men in class II occupations before the war, and a larger proportion of men in class I post-war. These findings lend support to the argument that light industry, being based on newer technologies and selling to a more changeable market, employs a more highly skilled labour force (as far as the non-manual sector is concerned) than does the old staple sector.

On the other hand, in both light and old staple industries mobility to class I is relatively low until around the Second World War but relatively higher thereafter, particularly after the late 1940s. This propensity to recruit from the working class is to some extent hidden by the comparatively small proportion of these highly skilled occupations in secondary industry as a whole. In each of the classes, the main changes in the broad patterns seem to be concentrated in the post-war years.

Indeed, we can extend that generalisation to the 'basic service' industries of construction, transport and distribution, the third of our industrial groupings, but the changes are less marked. Class I grows more similar to the overall pattern in the 1950s and 1960s while classes II and III increasingly tend to diverge. Class IV is as close to the typical pattern as might be reasonably expected, given the small numbers used for the calculation of the percentages. The major distinctive feature for basic service industry, particularly ten years after starting work, is class III: this reflects the structure of construction (and distribution to a lesser extent), where firms operate in small teams with a supervisor – the site foreman – or where workers can operate as self-employed. While we have not dwelt on the actual levels, it may be worth noting that in this case the difference between the class III line for basic services and that for all industries is of the order of twenty to twenty-five percentage points towards the end of the time-series.

In the two most highly skilled categories, there is another case of one being higher (class I) and one lower (class II) than the average, although this is less evident in the post-war years. This high and low effect is the same as light industry (post-war) and staple industry (except that in this latter case it is class I that is low, and class II that is high). Class IV in the basic services also resembles the other two industrial sectors in being the class most like the overall pattern. However, overall basic services displays its own characteristic profile.

This observation is all the more interesting when the mobility rates are taken into consideration, because these *are* much closer to the overall pattern than either of the manufacturing groupings. Thus a dissimilar occupational mix is recruited in a fairly typical way. Classes III and IV are particularly 'typical', and even class I, which runs at a higher level of upward mobility for over 90 per cent of the time-points, does not show a marked level of difference.

Those service industries based on knowledge and organisation in the state and commerce contain a larger share of non-manual jobs than do the others, because a higher number of all non-manual jobs are found there and a bigger proportion of the sector's employment is non-manual than in the other three groupings. This produces two effects in the profiles. First, the 'new services' have a greater weighting on the overall pattern, because their non-manual jobs outnumber those of the others. At the start of the time-series, new services contained just under 40 per cent of all non-manual jobs; by the 1950s this had increased to 45 per cent, and by the later 1960s it had risen to over 50 per cent. We would therefore expect its profiles to be close to the overall pattern. Here the immediate post-war years are highlighted as a point of transition. Up to this point, classes I and II were slightly smaller shares of the new services, but then the difference disappears and slightly more of these classes are recruited than the overall pattern. In classes III and IV the reverse is the case: 'over-recruitment' becomes 'under-recruitment' at about the same time.

The balance of numbers between this sector and the other three helps to summarise the distinctive nature of new services: compared with all others, this most important grouping (in the sense that it does contain so many of the non-manual opportunities) does not emerge as a markedly high employer of the highly skilled (i.e. class I and II) until relatively late. This suggests that the general upgrading of skill levels also happens in the other industries, so masking the difference until relatively late, or that the key processes of post-industrialism are features of a comparatively recent past. In other words, the new services, which most closely approximate to Bell's quarternary and quinary sectors, blossom in the 1950s, while Moore *et al.*'s managerial and technical specialist economy operates from a much earlier point (and continues to do so).

However, despite containing so many non-manual jobs, the new services do not resemble overall patterns of mobility, only class III is a close fit with class II falling into line in the 1940s. Class I and IV are consistently lower in their recruitment from the working class than in the other industrial groupings. Indeed, even if classes II and III *are* taken as being close to the norm, they are on average just below it rather than above it. Less than one-third of the observations are higher than those for all industries. It is only in the last three or four points plotted that a new picture emerges with closer similarities between the new services and the total, and even then class I is still different. The similarity reflects the increasing impact of the sector rather than radical shifts in the other groupings.

DECIPHERING DISAGGREGATION

In view of the density of the data presented in the preceding pages, it may be useful to restate some of the main findings of the chapter here. First, it has been demonstrated that when the mobility of a national sample is disaggregated by industry sector – into groupings which have a sociological coherence and identity – the profiles of mobility which result are dissimilar. Not only does each industrial sector have a distinctive occupational mix, but the amounts of mobility into those occupations varies from industry to industry and from time to time.

Second, it has become evident that there are few simple relationships or principles which apply across industries or time. For example, when occupations or industries expand they do not manifest a consistent tendency to increased mobility, nor is the reverse true. Again, industries recruiting higher proportions of class I do not necessarily recruit lower proportions of class II – or vice versa. One key to understanding the mobility process as a whole must be to disaggregate and consider the 'local' conditions operating in each sector, rather than operating with aggregated data and using statistical techniques which average out these differences.

This is not to say that there are no broad tendencies or that using the data in aggregated form is never illuminating. It is possible to see three such broad tendencies present in each industrial sub-set. There are four *phases in the time-series*: slow growth of non-manual employment and mobility in the 1930s (despite the Depression); a war effect of accelerated and subsequently decelerated growth over the 1940s, presumably affecting younger men only; a 1950s period in which new patterns emerge; and a late period in the 1960s, generally less clear perhaps that the previous decade but marked more by relative changes in mobility than in relative occupational mix. All four of the sectors identified in the last section show these time effects. Next, *occupational profiles* also demonstrate common tendencies: class IV, for example, declines as a proportion of the non-manual sector in all industries while class I increases. Except for basic services, class II also increases (in basic services it is marginally down) whereas class III tends to decline (in basic services it is markedly up). As indicated in the body of the chapter, the construction industry seems to be very influential in the old service's deviant figures with its high proportion of self-employed artisans.

The third broad tendency is for *mobility*, after considerable fluctuations, to culminate in a lack of growth, even when the less precise and truncated ten-year moving average is used. This is not only apparent in mobility associated with classes III and IV, but also holds good for the other two classes with the exception of class I in staple industries (on a very small number of cases) and class II in light industry.

Such broad patterns pose a problem for how the process of occupational mobility is to be conceptualised. On the one hand, we can regard the process as a whole, demonstrating features which arise from universal causes even if there are occasional untidy exceptions to the rule. The universal causes in this case would be manifested in each industry: the sectors would merely be convenient sites in which to search for the common elements. On the other hand, we can treat the totality as only the aggregate of several different parts. Here the 'rate of mobility' is nothing more than the outcome of a particular combination of separate components.

This is not an idle intellectualisation of the analysis because a predisposition to one or other leads to the development of different kinds of hypotheses. For example, if one takes the 'third broad tendency' of mobility to decline in the 1960s, a holistic view might indicate that some general social change in the recruitment rules *external* to the industries had made society less open. Such an explanation might be a modified credentialist one, in which qualifications had become universally more important but were increasingly the preserve of the middle classes. However, if one adopts a

Trends in Occupational Mobility

disaggregational approach, one might be more inclined to seek an explanation in terms of the occupations which make up each industrial profile. Thus the expansion of non-manual employment in each sector could consist of a growth only of those occupations in which the sons of the middle classes have always done well, and a non-expansion of those other occupations which provide a better mobility route. On balance, the present author prefers to retain *both* these approaches but as the next chapter will show, even if the aggregate is only the result of its constituent parts, it can still be a useful level of analysis in its own right, not least for purely pragmatic reasons of sample size.

Before leaving this problem, it is interesting to examine the example just given of a disaggregationalist argument. If one wishes to attribute the decline in total mobility to a decline in some element of the total, then the data should show some tendency for the change to be concentrated in one sector rather than another. It is intuitively less plausible to propose that the expansion of the non-manual sector, consisting of only those jobs which advantage the sons of the middle classes, should operate in each of the four classes and in each of the four industries. The evidence is not conclusive: as we have observed, there is a tendency across all occupations and sectors for a decline in mobility, but there is also the rise of the 'new services' to consider. As we know (because of the disaggregationalist style of the chapter) this sector has always been a large one in terms of its non-manual composition, and one which has grown to comprise more than half of all the non-manual jobs reported in the sample, and almost half of all mobility. This would not be immediately apparent from its *total* employment: at the start of the time-series, its share of total employment, i.e. manual and non-manual, was less than 16 per cent and even at its peak barely reached 30 per cent. Its numerical dominance is the non-manual sector represents both a focusing of the universal or total change on to one key part, and also the advantage of seeing how the several parts react differently to economic and technological constraints.

In this connection, it is interesting to observe how the occupational changes, said to be characteristic of modern society, are neither evenly spread across all industries nor concentrated in the most advanced sector. The increases in the proportions of highly skilled male jobs are uneven and paradoxical. One sees staple industry increase its class II jobs but not those in class I, while light industry at first follows the same practice and then reverses it. Meanwhile, basic services are shedding class II and new services are adding both classes. Clearly, the relationship between requirement for high skill levels and the modern economy must be reconceptualised to take account of the industrial mix. It may be true that there is a tendency for skills up-grading, and another for a shift towards tertiary industry, and the two tendencies may even be mutually reinforcing and so the most important features. But there are other interactions also at work at the same time, and if one wishes to account for the changes in any one society, it is necessary to 'unpack' the industrial and occupational elements and discover what weights should be attached to each of them. Not least in such an exercise it will be apparent that upward mobility does not automatically increase with modernisation as, say, Moore has suggested.

This having been said, the present chapter has not primarily been concerned with an exact statement of such relative weights. In its central section, service industry was identified as the major influence, and in the last section it was implicit that the new services were the key part of the tertiary sector in this process. Because we have been interested in the trends (which proved to be somewhat complex) and in investigating how each sector is distinctive, the account has been less concerned with precise statements of the various contributions to total mobility. In other words, while the observations represented in Figure 5.1 have been used as a general frame of reference, there has been a deliberate policy of not staying too close to that original formulation in order to keep open several avenues of exploration.

It would be confusing to present comparisons for the whole of the time-series, so instead two selected points have been taken to contrast the early and the late phases of the trends: 1930–9 and 1960–9. Table 5.1 gives the share of mobility attributable to each of the four industrial sectors.

The largest shifts in contribution have been between basic and new

Table 5.1 Sectoral share of upward mobility, 1930–9 and 1960–9

		Old staples	Light ind.	Basic ser.	New ser.	
1930–9	Mobility	13.8	15.0	43.8	27.5	n=80
	Size	24.0	18.5	41.9	15.6	n=725
1960–9	Mobility	8.4	16.0	27.7	47.7	n=119
	Size	14.8	20.5	38.4	27.5	n=701

services, with a reversal of their positions. Light industry is virtually unchanged, both in terms of mobility and number of jobs. But whereas basic services were initially contributing a share of mobility consonant with their size, they are now not much smaller but with a large drop in mobility, while new services have nearly doubled both employment and mobility. Old staples have dropped sharply on both counts.

How have these results arisen? The dynamics within each sector are presented in Table 5.2 which can be regarded as giving a concrete example of Figure 5.1. Each sector is shown with its actual ('observed') numbers of non-manual or mobile men compared with a series of expected values derived from projecting the earlier pattern on to a base figure for the later period. The 'observed' numbers have in fact been standardised to the 1930s level by weighting up each observation by 725/701 (i.e. 1.034) and rounding to the nearest whole number. Where expected values differ from actual observations, we know that the relationship present in the earlier period no longer holds. If one expected value is close, but a second is not, this shows which of the Figure 5.1 factors has changed most.

Table 5.2 Intra-sectoral changes, 1930–9 and 1960–9

		Old staples	Light industry	Basic services	New services
No. Non-manual	Obs	33	35	73	157
	Exp*	11	23	54	106
No. of Upmobiles	Obs	10	20	34	59
	Exp**	20	21	42	58

*$\frac{\text{Non-manual 1930s} \times \text{total 1960s}}{\text{total 1930s}}$

**$\frac{\text{Upmobiles 1930s} \times \text{total non-manual 1960s}}{\text{total non-manuals 1930s}}$

Perhaps the most straightforward pattern is to be found in the light industry column. Here there are more non-manual jobs for the size of the sector in the 1960s than would be expected on the basis of the 1930s (35 compared with 23). But once we know the actual number of non-manuals, we can accurately predict the number of upwardly mobile men (20 observed against a prediction of 21). We can say, in terms of Figure 5.1, that light industry has expanded its base (Table 5.1, 18.5

per cent to 20.5 per cent), has more of its jobs now non-manual (Table 5.2, 23 to 35) but has retained basically the same pattern of recruitment to those modified jobs. Precisely the same logic applies to the new services: the internal recruitment rate is unchanged, but the scale of process has been increased so that more individuals experience mobility and the overall mobility rate is increased. Thus a substantial part of each of the two intakes can be thought of as part of a changing mobility experience governed more by scale changes than by association changes.

The picture for the other two sectors – the two industrial groupings which by contrast are in relative and absolute decline – is that the observed levels of non-manual employment are also higher than expected on the basis of the 1930s rates, but the mobility rates are lower. This suggests that there is an increase in the non-manual sectors but that the recruitment rules change, making it less likely that upward mobility will take place. The analysis in the previous section suggested that in old staples much of the non-manual growth was in class II and in the basic services it was class III. In each class, the mobility associated with these changes tended to be at or below the overall trends, i.e. the added non-manual jobs were precisely in those classes where less mobility was taking place.

This leads to the other observation that can be made concerning Tables 5.1 and 5.2. In light industry the proportion of non-manual jobs going to the sons of manual workers is about 57 per cent at both points, and its share of all mobility and non-manual jobs does not change much. But in the new services, with a mobility rate of about 37 per cent, the share of all non-manual jobs rises from 15.6 per cent to 27.5 per cent. In contrast, the old staples and basic services start with higher internal mobility rates, 61 per cent and 57.4 per cent (barely higher in this latter case it must be said), and lose their initially higher share of non-manual jobs while their mobility rates drop. Thus in the earlier part they are a bigger source of non-manual jobs *and* recruit more from the working class, job for job, and by the later period are a smaller force and one which no longer recruits more from the working class than do the new services and light industry. This see-saw effect combines with the new services' numerical domination to depress mobility rates in the latter stages.

The reader should be cautious in taking these statements as an adequate summary of a very complex series of changes running over some forty years. In the intervening gap several other trends have manifested themselves, but there are limits to the quantity of information that can be assimilated. At this stage one other general point will suffice. The new patterns that emerge in the post-war period are broadly in line with the thesis of post-industrial society, but it is only in the 1960s that the basic industrial and occupational changes reach anything approaching a quantum leap. It would seem that it is not until this point that the twin processes of industrial and occupational transition combine to change the basic character of society. Part of that new character is a levelling off of upward mobility, at least as measured here, rather than the increase earlier writers have anticipated. Moving back from a sectoral and occupational analysis to class, it is clear that instead of class continuing to diminish, its significance for the new society shows signs of increasing. That this should happen around 1960 – at a time of expansion and economic growth – suggests that we are not dependent on inflation, recession and unemployment to explain the lack of opportunity for the children of manual workers. The scene for structural disadvantage had been set well before the troubles of the last decade.

6 Education and Mobility[1]

Most writing on the relationship between education and mobility has accorded primacy to the former in a double sense. On the one hand, education comes chronologically before occupation and is seen as a precondition for mobility. On the other hand, if qualifications are seen as the ticket that allows entry to desirable jobs, and education is placed at the heart of the process of individual achievement (said to be increasingly replacing a system based on ascription), then education becomes the most important variable in the explanation of mobility patterns. Variations on this theme are considerable. Examples can be found in the recent (and earlier) work of Halsey (1980), which regards the operation of the school system to be central; in that of Blau and Duncan (1967) which treats qualifications as one variable in a set which enables the sociologist to model the mobility process by means of path analysis; and in Parkin or Giddens' view of credentialism as a closure mechanism employed by the professional/managerial class. These (and many other accounts) all share what is an intuitively attractive starting point, namely that education is increasingly necessary to achieve mobility or to maintain social advantage. In the debate about British mobility this is referred to, as one writer has put it, as 'the familiar hypothesis that "tightening links" between education and economy reduce the degree of occupational inheritance' (Ridge, 1974, p. 27). The thesis of the 'tightening bond' can be traced to a T. H. Marshall lecture which was first given in 1949 and published in 1950 (see Marshall, 1965).

As an argument, it can be stated in a range of various 'strong' or 'weak' forms. The stronger version takes access to desirable occupations as being normally only possible for those with qualifications, or in other words, education determines mobility outcomes (although family background may in turn determine access to education). Weaker versions see education as merely a further dimension of class inequality, or regard the process as less well advanced. As Raffe (1981) has recently observed, much of the debate has singularly failed to specify terms or to state exactly what the bond consists of in empirical terms.

These approaches to education accord it a primacy which the present author regards as misplaced. This is not to say that class inequalities in education are not a proper topic for investigation, nor that the relationship between education and mobility is of no interest. On the contrary, they are of great importance, but the view of mobility which has been propounded here is one which starts from the occupational end of the chain of connection. As we saw in the previous chapter, the industrial composition of a society must be regarded as a central factor in any explanation of mobility. Certainly the stronger versions of credentialism, which see mobility as a product of the educational process, are not compatible with this: instead the prior question is what are the recruitment requirements of a changing structure of jobs? It may be that these involve different levels of qualification, but the supply of qualified manpower – at any given level – will be less important than the demand created by the economy for jobs to be done. Indeed, it follows that we might expect a *mis-match* of qualifications and occupations, just as well as a neat credentialist fit.

We can develop this point by two kinds of analysis. The first will deal with the incumbents of class I – or upper middle class – positions, and follow fairly conventional lines by examining the educational experience of men who move into, or out of, or remain in, that class. Class I is selected for this analysis, rather than the whole sample, for a combination of pragmatic and theoretical reasons. Pragmatically, it affords an abbreviated indication of the basic argument without covering the whole of the sample at length, in a way which would distort the shape of the present study. It also avoids overlap with the research activities which are the preserve of colleagues in this area. Theoretically, concentrating on class I is a logical outcome of both this study's approach and that of the tightening bond thesis itself. The upper middle class occupies the most desirable jobs which require the greatest degrees of expertise in their execution. As argued in Chapter 4, if any stratum can be said to typify modern society, it is this group: its positions depends on its advanced technical knowledge. It would be expected, therefore, that credentialism should be most manifest among the members of class I.

The second line of analysis develops out of the occupational perspective already presented. In the previous chapter it was suggested that mobility needs to be disaggregated into its industrial types. At the very least then, one needs to investigate whether the tightening bond thesis applies equally to all industrial sectors. This relegates education to a secondary place in the causal hierarchy but opens up the credentialist thesis to new empirical exploration. If we encounter inter-industry differences, then this will be due to some feature of industrial organisation which modifies the extent to which the bond may be seen as tightening. Whereas the analysis of the upper middle class concentrates on the respondent's most recent employment, this second section will be concerned with early careers.

Quite deliberately there will be virtually no discussion of other sources of Scottish data on educational mobility. A few such sources do exist: the follow-ups to the 1947 Scottish Mental Survey (MacPherson, 1958; Maxwell, 1969; Hope, 1984) and the work emanating from the Centre for Educational Sociology (see Gray *et al.*, 1982, in particular) are cases in point. However, their main function in this account would be seen as a source of collaborative (or otherwise) information, and as such any comparison would be dependent on definitions, time-periods and samples. Sadly, the exercise of establishing comparability would be too great to justify its inclusion: to give one or two illustrations, the Scottish Mental Survey uses a different and changing definition of father's job, together with a class coding derived from the 1948 British Maternity Study, while most of the CES data are drawn from the 1970s, i.e. after the education of the SMS sample. The exercise is not impossible, but some of the difficulties can be ascertained by a careful reading of Kendrick *et al.*'s very interesting discussion of fee-paying secondary education and recent trends (1982).

The general pattern of class differentials in access to schooling is also not part of our main concern. Details are available elsewhere (Ulas, 1983); broadly speaking, the sample's experience resembles that of English samples. Perhaps the only significant difference is that more working-class sons enter selective schools in Scotland, but much of this advantage disappears in terms of qualifications achieved.

THE 'LSE APPROACH' TO EDUCATION AND MOBILITY

Before presenting the findings on education and mobility, it is necessary to amplify the introductory remarks about the way British sociologists have treated the problem. Among the fairly extensive contributions to this aspect of the sociology of education, the work of Glass, Floud and Halsey, and Little and Westergaard seems particularly relevant because they have all in their various ways addressed the problem of occupational change. Additionally, they have all been concerned with the extent to which educational reform can modify the class structure, a concern which dates from their common experience of the sociology department at LSE in the 1950s and early 1960s when many of the basic ground rules for the study of the sociology of education were laid down.

During this period, writers like Floud and Halsey (1958) were looking to educational reforms like the 1944 Education Act to change society by providing a better opportunity for the bright working-class child to succeed in school, and so take his rightful place among the ranks of the middle classes. After all, that major reorganisation of English secondary education in 1944, to cater for three levels of ability, had formally removed discrimination and opened up free post-primary education for all. The chances of obtaining qualifications were clearly less class-dependent than before the war and it was not unreasonable to speculate as Glass (1954, p. 24) did, that 'given the diminishing importance of economic and social backgrounds as a determinant of the type of secondary education a child receives, social mobility will increase, and probably increase greatly'.

It would not be unfair to describe this approach as 'Fabian' in its basic concerns with applying sociological analysis to social problems, with studying the results of social reforms and with advocating the equalisation of opportunities for the working class.

The importance which Glass attached to education as the enabling factor in social mobility is explained by a second strand in British sociology of that time. This was a concern with the occupational character of industrial society, and in particular the increasing requirement for high levels of skill and therefore for education. Advanced technologies, on which an industrial (or post-industrial) economy depends, require the application of high levels of complex knowledge. That knowledge can only be acquired and developed through long years of education and training, and mastered only by those with the intellectual capacity to handle it. Equally, the expansion and internal differentiation of large-scale organisations requires new kinds of specialist functionaries and managers.

To quote Little and Westergaard in 1964 (p. 302): 'As professionalisation, bureaucratisation and automation of work proceed, so access to occupations of the middle and higher levels increasingly demands formal educational qualifications.' Very similar expressions are to be found at several points in the writings of Floud and Halsey (1958, pp. 169–70; 1961 pp. 1–2) and other contemporaries. What is characteristic in their work is the stress on the increase in educational and skill levels, and the need for formal entry qualifications for jobs. That is to say, they are concentrating on the increased need for formal educational credentials, rather than on the changing demand created by the evolving occupational structure.

It may seem inconsistent to state that the 'LSE school' was very much concerned with the occupational requirements of industrial society, and yet to claim that Glass *et al.* discount them. The explanation lies in the way in which this crucial process was interpreted. The LSE emphasis was on the change in job *content*, in the need for new levels of education and training. But there is an alternative emphasis which was more popular at that time among American sociologists, and this is the creation of completely new occupations and the *expansion in numbers* of existing non-manual employment opportunities: it is this latter feature which occupational transition encapsulates. For modernisation writers like W. E. Moore or Bendix, or the advocates of the Convergence Thesis, a key element of industrialisation is the increase in the numbers and proportions of white collar jobs which change the 'shape' of the occupational structure from a pyramid to a diamond.

Had the 'American' approach been adopted by the English sociologists, they would have seen that just as the level and availability of education could vary, so too could the level and availability of middle-class jobs. This in turn means that social mobility can change even if educational levels and distribution remain constant. But influenced as they were by the Glass mobility study, subsequent writers in England operated with the mistaken assumption of a stable occupational structure (see Payne *et al.*, 1977a).

Little and Westergaard's minor classic (1964) was both a turning point and yet also a typical product of this LSE credentialist view of social mobility. It is a turning point because it demonstrated that the 1944 Education Act had only achieved very limited success in reducing class differentials in educational attainment. Although more children were obtaining qualifications, and there had been some improvement in educational achievement by working-class children over the comparable pre-war generation, the barriers had *changed* rather than been removed. This article was the death-knell of the early Fabian optimism.

But nevertheless, it was still *typical* of the LSE tradition in its assumptions that credentials were replacing job experience as the basis for career selection and development, and also that social mobility for the unqualified children of the working classes was becoming increasingly limited. In fact, neither of these two assumptions was supported by any empirical evidence in the paper. They were presented as established sociological facts about industrial society which required almost no discussion. Indeed, Little and Westergaard went on to propose that the rise in the proportion of educated middle-class children would choke off the chances of working-class children succeeding in later life: there was a straightforward counter-balance to the rise of social mobility through education by a decrease in social mobility through late career promotion. This conclusion was predicated on the statement that rates of social mobility were not only low but practically stable.

At that time (and up to the present day, as Payne (1986) indicates), the dominant conception of social mobility was that Britain was essentially an immobile society. The results of the 1949 LSE survey showed basically that middle-class sons grew up to follow their middle-class fathers, while the sons of the working class grew up to be manual workers like *their* fathers. The chances of a labourer's son becoming a factory manager were virtually nil: any movements up or down the occupational scale between the two generations were small ones. For Glass and his co-authors, education was a key factor in determining the distribution of a relatively fixed supply of middle-class jobs: if all children had equal access to schooling, then these jobs would go to the most able; to the most capable of doing them, rather than to those coming from a privileged family background but who were themselves comparatively less able. More working-class children would be upwardly mobile, so *displacing* the less able middle-class children who would be downwardly mobile into manual occupations.

Little and Westergaard drew on Glass's *Social Mobility in Britain* to argue that there had been no increase in social mobility because the younger cohorts in that study are no more mobile than the older. Therefore, the new educated class would displace the older class of persons whose careers had been built on service, experience and proven performance at work. This conclusion was based on two false premises. The first of these was that mobility rates are low and stable. The evidence presented in Chapters 4 and 5 show that mobility rates are not as low nor as stable as Glass's results were taken to indicate. There is no need to restate the case here, although it may be worthwhile to observe that mobility for the respondents's most recent job also changes with time.[2] The rejection of this basic premise of Little and Westergaard alone destroys the ground for asserting that increased education *blocks* the working classes' alternative routes of access to good jobs, because as we have seen, the supply of 'good jobs' has been increasing and this has enabled there to be greater upward mobility. Little and Westergaard assumed mobility was a zero-sum game and thus that new winners would mean new losers. However, in an expanding universe of middle-class jobs, there might be more and more winners without cost to the original winners.

The second premise in Little and Westergaard's work was that social mobility is dependent on educational qualifications. This is an eminently more plausible premise. After all, the evidence of professionalisation, the growth of new occupational specialisms requiring long and particular training, and the increased technicality of knowledge in established fields, all point to the need for access to good jobs being via the educational route. And as far as these specific social changes are concerned, the importance of education is beyond reasonable doubt. However, these changes do not apply to *all* jobs, or necessarily to a majority of jobs, despite the impression that most academics (who were raised and are still working within the educational system) may have. This point can be demonstrated by looking at the education of the upper middle class (UMC), the class which *par excellence* is the creation of modern society.

THE EDUCATION OF THE UPPER MIDDLE (OR 'LIEUTENANT') CLASS

The first stage of the analysis is to look at those people who were born into upper-middle class families, to see how they were educated, what qualifications they achieved, and how these relate to their subsequent mobility. The second stage is a more general one, a consideration of the educational experience of those *not* born in the UMC but who have been upwardly mobile into that class during their own lifetimes. In each case, it is possible to regard education as type of schooling received, and as level of qualifications obtained. Both are of interest, although obviously the system of education – selective, comprehensive, private – determines access to qualifications. In Table 6.1, the high proportion of Scots attending comprehensive schools is of note: 30.3 per cent in column (a).

The Scottish system anticipated the English by several decades, but without any apparent reduction to the class differentials in output of qualified manpower. Men with UMC origins were more likely to attend private secondary education (29.7 per cent in column (b)) than the sample as a whole (4.6 per cent in column (a)), or, to put it another way, a son of the UMC was six and a half times more likely to receive a private education than was any child taken at random within the population (column (c)). This still leaves 70 per cent of UMC children who take their chances in the state system; however, an examination of the outcome of this shows that they are not in fact risking much. Thirty-

Education and Mobility

Table 6.1 Type of secondary schooling

School type*	(a) All males %	(b) Men born in 'UMC'	(c) Ratio (b) to (a)
Private	4.6	29.7	6.5
Selective (Grammar and Direct Grant in England)	19.2	32.7	1.7
Comprehensive	30.3	20.8	0.7
Junior Secondary (Secondary Modern in England)	37.1	11.1	0.3
Other Scottish	8.0	1.8	0.2
Other English or n.e.c.	0.9	4.0	4.4
TOTALS	100 n=4289	100 n=226	

*'Private' includes the fee-paying day schools (so prominent in Edinburgh). 'Selective' includes those attending 'omnibus' schools who had to pass an examination to enter them, while the remaining pupils are allocated to the 'comprehensive' category. Junior Secondary includes the pre-war equivalents. Further details of the Scottish education system can be found in Ford, Payne and Robertson (1975) and Ulas (1983). The author is grateful to Graeme Ford for his research into the history of Scottish schools and for the preparation of some of the data presented in this section.

two per cent of them were educated within fully selective state schools, the Scottish equivalent of Grammar Schools, and this was nearly twice as many as the average for the entire sample.

Of course, it follows from this that the UMC child was generally able to avoid the junior secondary schools, and in fact only 11 per cent of them attended these schools which catered for over 37 per cent of the population at large. It is of some significance that *as many as* 11 per cent of these privileged children did in fact end up in the lowest educational category; the consequences of this for their subsequent careers is taken up below.

The lieutenant class is, then, notably successful in mobilising its status to secure direct educational privilege for its progeny. Sixty-two per cent of them had either private or selective education as against 34 per cent for class II, the next highest occupational group.

How does this pattern of schooling relate to social mobility? Table 6.2 shows that those men born in the UMC and retaining their class position – column (a) – do in fact show a higher degree of educational privilege than any other group. In all, 44 per cent of them received private education, almost ten times more than the average for the sample, while a further 34 per cent went to state selective schools.

Table 6.2 Type of secondary schooling and social mobility of men born into UMC families

School type	(a) Men retaining their UMC position %	(b) Ratio of (a) to sample proportions	(c) Men downwardly mobile from UMC %	(d) Ratio of (c) to sample proportions
Private	44.2	9.6	19.1	4.2
Selective	33.7	1.8	32.1	1.7
Comprehensive	13.7	0.5	26.0	0.9
Junior Secondary	4.2	0.1	16.0	0.4
Other Scottish	—	—	3.1	0.4
Other English or n.e.c.	4.2	4.7	3.8	4.2
TOTALS	100 n=95		100 n=131	

A further point, which does not emerge from the figures presented, is the fact that one group within the lieutenant class, the self-employed higher professionals, shows the highest level use of private education of any group in the study. No fewer than 79 per cent of those self-recruited, self-employed professionals went to private schools.

It must be remembered, however, that the majority of those with UMC origins do not themselves maintain their UMC status, in fact three in every five move out of the class. Focusing then on these UMC 'drop-outs' (column (c)), it seems that they are not quite as educationally privileged as the UMC self-recruiters, but they remain a very privileged group indeed as compared with the population at large. They are four times more likely to have had private education and almost twice as likely to have gone to selective state schools. It would appear then that having the right background and the right schooling is no automatic guarantee of the maintenance of one's parental status, even if the combination is a considerable advantage.

The alternative index of education is qualification levels, rather than type of school attended. This is shown in Table 6.3:

Table 6.3 Destination of those with UMC origins by educational success

	Downward self-recruiters	Downward mobile to middle class	Downward mobile to working class	TOTALS
% high qualifications, i.e. either high school success (Highers or better), and/or high FE success (HNC or better)	58.3	37.4	4.3	100 n=139
% low qualifications (i.e. neither high school success nor high FE success)	20.4	47.6	32.0	100 n=103

In this table, secondary and post-secondary education has been combined for simplicity. In fact, although the education system is organised in separate tiers, possession or non-possession of qualifications can be regarded as a single social outcome. The details of the process – for instance, whether secondary or post-secondary sub-systems are the major blocks to access – remain of interest but at a lower level. The advantage of the unified approach is that it prevents a narrow and incomplete view of education which omits further and higher education from the total picture, as did most of the early writing (see Girod *et al.*, 1977). The unified approach does raise technical difficulties in establishing equivalences between different systems of qualifications. Obviously an A-level ranks above an O-level, but does the latter compare with an ONC or 3rd level City and Guilds? The present categories are very broad, but examination of other cut-off points shows the same basic pattern in the relationship between mobility and educational qualifications.

In Table 6.3, 96 per cent of those persons of UMC background who attain educational success (first row) in fact maintain some level of middle-class identity, with no fewer than 58 per cent being recruited back into the UMC class itself. While *lack* of educational success does increase the likelihood of downward mobility for the sons of this class, the second row of Table 6.3 shows that 20 per cent of these born in this class and having neither 'high' school success nor compensatory 'high' further education were nevertheless able to secure jobs in the UMC, while a further 48 per cent were able to maintain some kind of middle-class status. As a means of securing the transmission of intergenerational privilege, educational success appears to form a sufficient but not a necessary condition.

EDUCATING THE INCOMERS

The analysis so far has dealt with flows *out* from UMC origins. The next stage is to look at *inflows*, that is, from which social origins do the present members of the UMC class come, and what levels of education have they achieved? To what extent is the education system the gatekeeper regulating access to this privileged social stratum? Table 6.4 is the equivalent to the earlier Table 6.1.

The incomers to the UMC (column (*b*)) have a pattern of education which is somewhat different from that for individuals with UMC origins. The use of private schools is far less, although still two and a

Table 6.4 Type of secondary schooling: inflows

School type	(a) All males in Sample %	(b) Men upwardly mobile into UMC %	(c) Ratio (b) to (a)
Private	4.6	12.0	2.6
Selective	19.2	38.4	2.0
Comprehensive	30.3	27.2	0.9
Junior Secondary	37.1	18.2	0.5
Other Scottish	8.0	2.2	0.3
Other English or n.e.c.	0.9	2.0	2.2
TOTALS	100 n=4289	100 n=357	

half times the average, while the incidence of state selective education is somewhat higher. Taken together they amount to 50 per cent, which is double the average figure but far less than we saw for the UMC self-recruiters (Table 6.1). Most significantly, 18 per cent of the incomers have only junior secondary education, while 27 per cent went to comprehensive schools, or in other words, about half those who were upwardly mobile into the UMC had not attended a privileged type of school.

The qualifications of the present members of the lieutenant class are shown in Table 6.5, discriminating between those from different class backgrounds.

Table 6.5 Inflow to UMC by level of educational Qualification*

Class of Origin	Qualification level of Incomers		Totals n
	Low	High	
II	30.1	69.9	93
III	42.4	57.6	66
IV	57.1	42.9	35
V	65.8	34.2	79
VI	65.9	34.1	44
VII	56.2	43.8	48
TOTALS	50.4	49.6	365

*High/Low as in Table 6.3

The first, and perhaps rather surprising fact to observe is the large number of current members of the UMC with modest or non-existent educational attainment. In Table 6.5, half of the UMC fall into this 'low' success category. In no sense then can education be seen as necessary for entry to the UMC. The data presented earlier on outflows *from* the UMC might have tempted one to conclude that education and advantageous class background could be viewed as *alternative* resources, either of which being generally sufficient to secure transmission of pivilege. As a corollary of this, one might expect that the further a person's origins was from the UMC, the greater would be his dependence on education as a means of securing upward social mobility. The reverse in fact holds true. The long-distance upwardly mobile are considerably less well qualified on average than those from classes proximate to the UMC, and there appears to be a fairly neat inverse relationship between class of origin and education for those upwardly mobile into the top class. On the other hand, what this table does not reveal is that those sons of working-class parents who do obtain high educational qualification are almost always upwardly mobile: nine in every ten of such children subsequently entered the middle class.

To summarise this brief review of education and the UMC, high levels of qualifications generally ensure upward mobility of safeguard against downward mobility. But there is still a very considerable amount of upward mobility and status maintenance without formal qualifications, particularly in the managerial and senior supervisory categories.

There are simpler ways of challenging Little and Westergaard's thesis than the method which has been chosen here, as witness Goldthorpe (1977). However, it is important to explore the shortcomings of their argument in the way chosen, because it highlights more clearly the need for a basic reconceptualisation than would a simple disproof of the thesis by the presentation of more recent data. What has been at the heart of the exercise is an attempt to indicate not that education and mobility are uneasy bedfellows – which after all Jencks and others have already argued – but why they make so poor a pair.

EDUCATION AND OCCUPATIONS

One dimension of this should already be clear; the rapid expansion of occupational opportunity has created a demand for competent manpower, not just qualified manpower. To put it another way, the occupational demand has expanded faster than the educational supply. In the SMS sample, 64 per cent of men had no kind of school exam pass whatsoever. A further 18 per cent had only qualifications of a level lower than O-grades – in English terms, lower than CSE. In post-school education, nearly half had no further training beyond 'Watching Nelly': of the remaining half, four in five had served basic apprenticeships of whom about half had additionally obtained City and Guilds-type qualifications below the standard of ONC. Nor is the

Figure 6.1 A diagrammatic representation of education and occupations

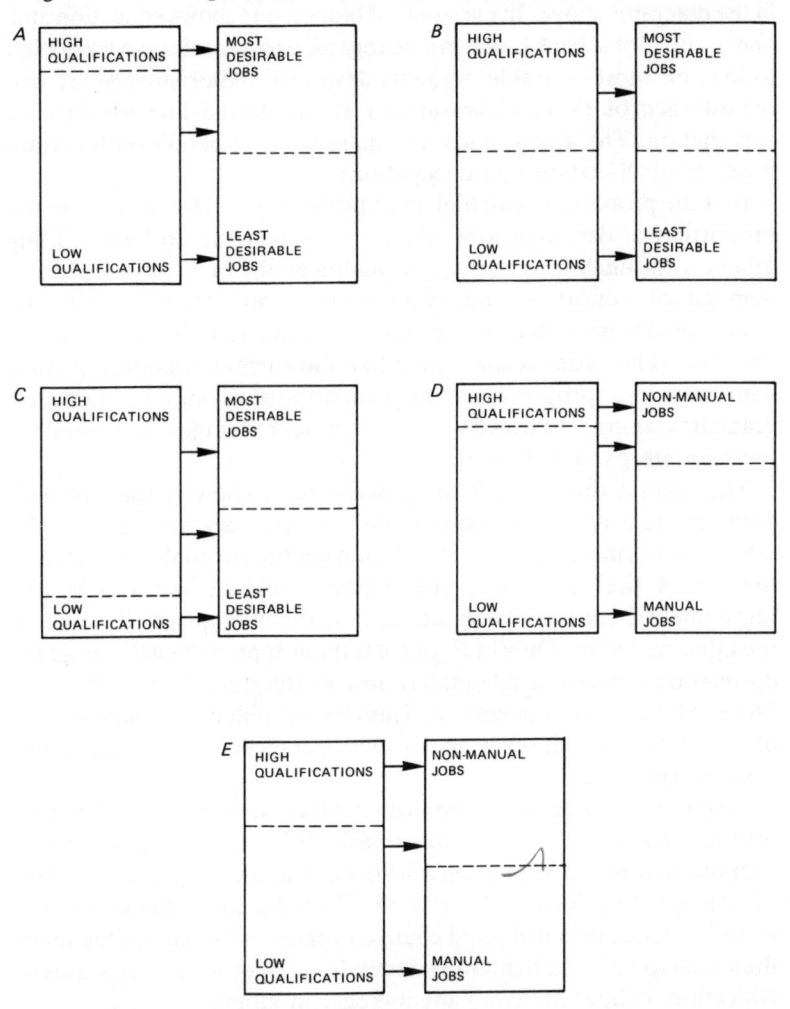

pattern of low standards of qualifications merely explained by the fact that the sample includes men of all ages: if one compares older men with those educated post-war, only about 11 per cent of the former had better than O-grade equivalent compared with 19 per cent of the younger men.

As a result of this poverty of qualifications, the association between education and occupation is a paradoxical one. Education generally guarantees a good job, but a lack of education (the more common condition) has not acted as a barrier to occupational success as shown in the diagrams above. In each pair of blocks, one shows education and one occupations: each block can be regarded as a continuum from high to low, or 'most desirable' to 'least desirable'. Alternatively, we can regard each block as dichotomised at the dotted line for ease of explanation. The arrows show the main flows of people with certain levels of qualification into occupations.

In A the proportion with high qualifications is much smaller than the proportion of desirable jobs: the shortfall is made up by recruiting others with much lower levels of qualification. In B the supply and demand of education and occupations is in balance. In C the educational supply exceeds the capacity of the desirable job sector to absorb it. This latter is something like the current American picture with a very large proportion of the population receiving education, and graduates taking jobs which would be considered somewhat menial for their counterparts in Britain.

The second thing which these three pairs show is that the link between education and occupation can be very strong, but the *association* as measured by a correlation coefficient could appear to be low. In A the value of a correlation would be reduced by the recruitment from the low qualified: in C the over qualified would be the effective factor. Only in B, or something approaching it, would the correlational measure adequately reflect the underlying link which Floud, Halsey *et al.*, recognised. This raises problems for path analysis or any method which relies on correlational techniques for diachronic comparisons.

To put this another way, even when educational provision was low, selection had to be made on *some* basis. It is perfectly reasonable to suppose that the *sorts* of people who were selected at an earlier time *without* qualifications might now be selected *with* qualifications: this would produce no substantial change in rates of mobility. One might then wish to talk of a tightening dependence of occupational status on education without implying any increase in mobility.

It is clearly important to make this conceptual distinction between the extent to which education is *linked* to occupation, by which we mean the extent to which high education *guarantees access* to a top job, and the extent to which education *explains* occupation – that is, the strength of the association between these two factors. Obviously, where there is a relatively low degree of educational provision the 'link' may be high and the 'association' low, as we saw in diagram A. The same goes for diagram D which is meant to represent the relevant proportions in Britain during the earlier part of this century. In contrast, diagram E shows something like the current situation in Britain today. Here, we know that the supply of good jobs has been growing, so that quite separate speculation might be that the link could remain strong while the association weakened. In other words, the relative balance of educational supply and occupational demand is crucial in understanding the second half of the class background-education-occupational attainment equation.

However, only the first half of this equation combining class background, educational experience and occupational attainment has received even moderate attention from the earlier writers. Generally speaking, they implied that the second half of the equation was not problematic, i.e. that the association between formal education and achieved status is a close one. In fact the two links in the chain are analytically separate and must be so considered in any explanation. Educational reform changed both the rules of access for the working class *and* also promoted an increase in the output of qualifications. It must be an open question whether the relationship between educational success and occupational status remains constant during the double change which comprised the shift from an earlier, mainly elitist, system to a more popular and accessible education. Even if one assumes that there has been an improvement in both access and outcome, it does not follow that there will be a proportionate rise in mobility.

This is another way of expressing the earlier point that education may be a sufficient condition for access to good jobs, but not a necessary one. The distinction between the two is particularly relevant for analyses which use correlational measures (most recently Raffe, 1981) where the increase in associational values is implicitly taken as meaning that the sufficient conditional relationship has become a necessary conditional relationship. Raffe does not properly come to terms with this distinction and therefore confuses the increased *supply* of qualified manpower with the nature of the intrinsic relationship between qualification and occupation. To put it another way, Raffe is really saying that at a very general level those with more education *tend* to be found in more desirable jobs. This is true, but it is neither a very precise statement nor very enlightening about *why* education and jobs are sometimes associated.

In other words, as long as education is restricted to the few who are also privileged in most other respects, the exact role of education in determining achieved status must remain somewhat opaque. It is possible that what appears as a tight link between the possession of education and occupational success is only partially valid, and that as the education base expands this fact will become apparent. Alternatively, there may be an interaction between class of origin and education such that education is less efficacious for the 'new' educated classes.

EDUCATION AND THE ELITE

This raises an interesting point about recruitment to top jobs which can be developed before continuing with the main line of argument about the demand side of the education–occupation relationship. In Chapter 4, it was argued that the upper middle class is different from the 'true' elite. To what extent do they share educational experience, and can the position of the elite be seen as a result of their education?

It is almost an article of faith in British sociology that the English Public Schools (not to mention Oxbridge) are the key to the cohesion and solidarity of the ruling class. Some writers make even more extensive claims: for example, Rex (1974, p. 215) writes:

> One thing is clear is that the maintenance of the old ruling class as a sociological entity depends upon the preservation of a separate form of education where that class's values can be fostered and maintained. Not merely must the actual office-holders within the various institutions be educated and indoctrinated; so also must a wider class who constitute a kind of reservoir from which new supplies of suitably trained talent can flow in the future, but who serve also to give the existing 'Establishment' officers a sense of legitimacy and support.

However, not only does the Scottish lieutenant class not share in educational tradition to the same degree: it do not seem to have *any* coherent educational tradition. Where then is the argument for cohesion, solidarity, value-orientation and resocialisation of new recruits thought to be so necessary for the operation of the class system?

To put this another way, if the elite and the lieutenant class do *not* share the same educational experience, this should, extending Rex's logic, produce a *lack* of cohesion, solidarity, value orientation and resocialisation, leading to conflict between the two strata. The extent

Education and Mobility

to which each experiences a different schooling can be seen by comparing Tables 6.2 and 6.4 above with Table 6.6 below.

Table 6.6 Types of schooling of elite groups in various studies*

1951–7	Labour MPs	52.1% GS	
		19.6% PS	
	Tory MPs	23.2% GS	
		75.5% PS	(Guttsman, p. 35)
1971	Directors of major firms	27.2% GS	
		64.3% PS	(Whitley, p. 70: for list of firms,
	Directors of City Financial Institutions	16.4% GS	see Whitley, p. 66)
		79.8% PS	
1900–7	Company Chairman (% for known cases)	13% GS (approx)	(Stanworth & Giddens, p. 84;
		78.3% PS	for type of firm, see p. 81. 'the public schools more than held their own over the period', p. 89)
1966–7	Higher Civil Service entrants	44% LEA Schools	
		54% non LEA Schools	(Kelsall, p. 176)
1960–2	Bishops	N/A GS	
		85% PS	(Thomson, p. 202)

*The references are all to Stanworth and Giddens (eds) (1974). The reader is cautioned that each study has its own definitions of elites and school types which may not be strictly comparable. Urry and Wakeford (1973) contains further data, but mainly for the 1950s and early 1960s: see, however, pp. 213–42 for items such as 83 per cent of the Army elite in 1959 had been public school educated. GS = Grammar School, PS = Public School.

Three things are clear from this. While the UMC has about 40 per cent of its members educated at 'Grammar School', the various elites generally have smaller proportions with such education. Secondly, whereas the UMC has a further 20 per cent of its members with a private education, the elites' figures (Labour MPs excepted) run at 54 per cent, 64 per cent, 95 per cent, 79 per cent, or 85 per cent; this is the most important difference. Finally, over 40 per cent of the UMC have attended neither type of privileged education: among the economic elite at least, this figure must be around only 5 per cent to 10 per cent.

Kendrick *et al.* (1982b, p. 23) have objected to an earlier version of this argument on two grounds. The 'upper middle class' as defined here includes occupational categories which by no stretch of the imagination can be described as 'upper middle class', and by taking the upper 12 per cent of categories on the Hope–Goldthorpe scale, the class has been made too large. Unfortunately, no details are given of the first criticism, but in general the Scottish UMC is very similar to that used as class I by Goldthorpe. It is true that some specific occupations are given an exaggerated eminence – masseurs, managers of football clubs, and coal merchants – but Kendrick *et al.* may not have appreciated that these were included mainly as owners or managers of large operations (see Appendix below) and make up very little of class I.

The idea of an upper middle class of a fairly large size is not unusual. In addition to the evidence about the size of elites and their neighbouring class already presented, other authors such as Wright (1978, p. 63) – who by coincidence comes up with a figure of 12 per cent for the American managerial UMC (plus 6 per cent for the small employer class) – and King (1981, p. 81) – in his adaptation of Brown's data showing 12.4 per cent senior managers and professionals, plus 2.6 per cent for employers and proprietors – have come up with similar estimates. In fact, the size criticism seems to arise from a strange piece of tautology: Kendrick *et al.* say that by making the UMC 12 per cent when the fee paying education sector is only 4.5 per cent, the analysis must 'bias the account towards stressing the "openness" of Scottish society' (1982b, p. 23).

But this is to prejudge the relationship between education and class status. The size of the UMC was decided before the level of fee paying was known. Kendrick *et al.* seem to imply that only if two variables are of the same size can a fair comparison be made, or worse, that the UMC are in some way defined by their access to privileged education. But these are empirical questions, and have to be considered in the light of the other evidence about elites and the rest of the middle class and other forms of privileged education. This evidence clearly suggests a marked difference between the elite and the upper middle class in terms of both education and background, which raises the question of why is there no inter-strata conflict?

The evidence given is *compatible* with the view that the members of the elite share an educational experience which serves to bind them together. However, if Rex means by a 'wider class' of supporters that the UMC also share in the educational arrangements of the elite, then there would seem to be little support for this position. Certainly the UMC as a whole cannot be included, with only one in five participating in private schooling. Again, with such different traditions and over 40 per cent of its members with relatively poor education, it seems improbable that the members of the UMC share an ethic which depends on secondary education. It has already been noted that those who must travel furthest to gain access to the UMC, and who are therefore least likely to share background values, are very unlikely to experience the socialising derived from privileged education. Again, only about 30 per cent of the sons of the UMC had private education, and of these about a third were downwardly mobile, so private education is not such a significant or effective method of conferring occupational advantage to one's offspring as one might believe.

Allowing for some simplification, the composition of any group depends on its ability to self-recruit; the nature of its intake from other groups; and the rate of expansion (or contraction) of the group. Consider the typical view of an elite: it recruits from its own sons; it takes in only a small number of 'outsiders' who are supposed to be from the class most like itself – i.e. a homogeneous intake in the sense of being both similar to the elite and internally consistent as an intake; and the rate of expansion is presumably very low. In consequence, there is no *need* for major resocialisation of the intake. But what happens if expansion is more rapid, or if self-recruitment weakens, or if an intake is less homogeneous? Presumably the need for a mechanism to adjust the newcomers to the values of the group is greater, unless social cohesion is to decline.

Now it has already been shown that the UMC as a whole is expanding, has fairly low rates of self-recruitment and has no unified secondary education experience. This can be expanded by treating each of its four constituent occupational categories separately. Only the self-employed professionals are anything like the 'typical elite'. In the absence of any strong growth in the numbers, such a group can dominate successive generations by maintaining high levels of self-recruitment and by filling any shortfall by highly selective recruitment from those other sectors of society most like itself. Because the incomers are already somewhat like the 'host' group, and because the 'hosts' outnumber the new recruits, cultural continuity is assured. And yet the self-employed professionals are the UMC category which have the highest levels of privileged education. The other categories with more rapid growth, and larger, more heterogeneous intakes, have no strong single educational character (indeed, there are considerable difference in the expansion rates and type of recruitment between the three categories themselves).

It would seem to follow from this that privileged education is not a significant factor in binding the several constitutions of the UMC to the elite, and that the public school should not be regarded as providing a *necessary* socialising force (even for the elite?). It would be an equally adequate explanation of the SMS findings for the UMC to say that the most secure groups, who can hand on their position of advantage, are incidentally able to purchase the badge of privileged education. As a commodity, the schools 'hidden' (or half-hidden?) curriculum is geared to attract the custom of the paying parent. The outcome may be a heightening of consciousness for its pupils, and the foundation of networks which can be activated later in careers – but the education is dependent on the client (the elite?), not the other way around.

If this speculative proposition is accepted, then it becomes necessary to look elsewhere for the supposed mechanisms of socialisation which operate for both elite and UMC. Socialisation through university (i.e. a later and separate part of the education 'system' (see Watson, 1964)), occupation, or even an absence of a mechanism seem likely answers. One plausible explanation to be found in Nichols (1969): selective promotion by employers of individuals who are competent and show a minimal commitment to 'a-political' capitalist values. In other words, a low level belief in adequate levels of efficiency and personal career goals at work, and material comfort in the domestic life, is sufficient to sustain much of modern capitalism, particularly for the lieutenant class. There is no need for schools to teach such values in a positive sense: the values have become part of general currency.

The traditional view, which laid at Rex's door, that privileged education is a requirement for individual entry and a prerequisite for system maintenance, may be mistaken. It may equally well be that the 'elite' are merely confirmed in their line of succession by an education which is appropriate. A shared experience of public school education may help the cohesion of the elite, but that is a more limited argument. It certainly cannot be true that the lieutenant class as a whole is caught up in this education system, and so, by the traditional view, it must be isolated from the elite. This might help to explain the former's subordinate position and lack of progress to the ranks of the elite, but it suggests an important disjunction in the class structure, and leaves unanswered the question of why the UMC accept their position and are seen (on a common-sense basis) to be as committed in their support of the system as are the elite.

EDUCATION AND INDUSTRIAL SECTOR

In arguing first that mobility to the upper middle class did not seem to be education-dependent, and in contrasting elite experiences with those of their lieutenants, the basic case has been that education has been given an exaggerated place in the sociological schema. This is not to argue, however, that it is totally unimportant, and this final section can be seen as something of an attempt to find a new position for education, one in which it is better integrated with the occupational or demand side of the process. Earlier in this chapter, Little and Westergaard were quoted as identifying professionalisation, bureaucratisation and automation as causes for increased demand for formal qualifications. But not only are each of these forces separate, the extent of their influence is likely to vary from occupation to occupation, and industrial sector to industrial sector. In other words, the conditions within industrial groupings which produced the mobility trends discussed in the previous chapter may also determine what entry qualifications are necessary for a career in any given industry, or in any given occupational grouping. In particular, the industrial rates of mobility may reflect rules of recruitment which in practice are largely education rules, so that the overall rate of mobility is the outcome of a complex of changes in several specific education–industry relationships.

To explore this, it is necessary to return to the data on first jobs, so that any effects due to historical periods and intragenerational mobility can be controlled. Rather than using moving averages, either pre-war and post-war groupings, four fixed cohorts approximating to each decade covered by the study will be used. As the previous chapter showed, the latter are a reasonably satisfactory representation of the trends at different periods, although that of the 1940s is less good in this respect. Once again the constraints of sample size will dictate the use of fairly broad categories and an indirect approach to problems with variables successively included and excluded from the analysis, in order to maintain viable numbers.

A useful starting point is to examine the relationship between mobility and education in each of the industrial sectors discussed in the previous chapter, as shown in Table 6.7.

Table 6.7 Proportion of upmobiles: men intergenerationally mobile from manual origins to non-manual destinations who had 'high qualifications'

Industry	1930s	1940s	1950s	1960s
Old staples	50.0	45.5	20.8	50.0
Light manufacturing	41.7	28.6	63.6	42.9
Basic services	16.7	12.8	26.8	38.7
New services	34.8	29.7	48.8	40.4
Whole sample*	13.8	17.0	28.2	31.7

* i.e. those with high qualifications in the cohort (excluding primary industry) whatever their mobility.

The bottom row shows qualification levels rising during the whole period in these four industries (excluding agriculture and fishing) as a whole. However, even in the 1960s, only about one in three had this level of education. If we use this row as a base, then mobility can be seen to be associated with education, because thirteen out of the sixteen cell values are higher than the appropriate column base figure. The cell values are not particularly high: in only one case out of sixteen is the value more than half, so that a strong argument that mobility is dependent on qualifications must be rejected because in fact a majority of the upwardly mobile have low qualifications.

If we can turn to the row patterns, it is interesting to see that there is no clear tendency for mobility to become more associated with qualifications. Even if the 1940s are discounted because that decade encompasses the war and its after effects, there is little additional evidence of monotonic trends. The best that can be said in search for trends is that values for the 1940s tend to lower (presumably the war effect of accelerating young men into jobs), while the 1960s' values tend to be slightly higher than the 1930s'. No trends are common to all four industry groupings which have radically different profiles, with basic services being notably lower than the others across the whole period. This is the only grouping in which the 1960s is clearly higher than earlier years.

If education is not strongly associated with upward occupational mobility is it more clearly related to immobility or downward mobility? Again, there are few obvious patterns in the data.

Table 6.8 Proportions of mobile groups with 'high qualifications'

Industry	1930–39 n=841			1940–49 n=859			1950–59 n=891			1960–69 n=795		
	a*	b	c	a	b	c	a	b	c	a	b	c
Old staples	22.2	15.8	6.0	40.0	21.7	6.6	46.0	35.7	22.2	56.3	14.3	18.4
Light industry	40.0	19.0	3.1	50.0	6.1	3.4	60.0	17.2	14.9	71.4	29.2	7.5
Basic services	44.4	11.9	2.6	50.0	29.1	6.9	50.0	28.8	14.9	47.1	22.4	7.9
New services	69.0	4.8	3.3	52.0	0.0	10.3	73.1	33.3	8.1	71.9	36.1	17.9

*a = immobile non-manual; b = downwardly mobile; c = immobile manual

If occupational achievement was increasingly dependent on qualification then those who remain in the non-manual sector should be better qualified at each cohort. This holds for manufacture but is less true for services. If the same occupation/qualification relationship is true, then those who 'fail' – i.e. are downwardly mobile, or remain 'trapped' in manual occupations – should show the converse; declining levels of qualifications. This does not hold true. In manufacturing and basic services, the post-war levels for the immobiles are higher than pre-war, as is the 1960 level in new services. Again, the downwardly mobile cells show surprisingly high values, particularly post-war, although the picture is less clear cut. To uphold the tightening link argument, we would not just expect high and rising qualification levels for the mobile and the non-manual immobiles, but low and decreasing levels for the downwardly mobile and manual immobiles. Instead, if there is a single statement which can encompass Tables 6.7 and 6.8, it must be that over and above the many fluctuations, there is a tendency for all four mobility categories to increase their qualification levels. In other words, more people have educational qualifications but this provides a poor guide to their occupational or mobility outcomes.

On the other hand, the evidence so far has been presented as percentages of mobility groups, without regard for the relative size of these or the industrial groups. If we express the data in terms of cohort percentages, regarding high occupation/high qualification and low occupation/low qualification cases as predictive 'successes' for the tightening bond thesis, and high/low combinations as failures, then the findings look more favourable. Overall, the hypothesis scores 79.9 per cent 'successes', which on the face of it seems quite good. However, the best possible fit in the data depends on the structure of the categories: for example, in all there are 860 non-manual posts but only 641 men with high qualifications, so that there must be at least 219 low qualifications men in high occupational statuses. Conversely, even if all the 641 highly qualified cases were allocated to the manual class and the whole of the non-manual class filled with the lowly qualified, there would still be room for 1360 lowly qualified cases in the manual class. Expressed as a percentage of all predictions (i.e. the number of cases in the analysis) this gives a best possible fit for upper limit score of 92.3 per cent, and a worse possible score of 47.5 per cent. As a score somewhere between the two, 75.9 per cent does not look quite so impressive as it would if the upper limit were 100 per cent and lower limit 0 per cent.

The same approach can be used to disaggregate these results into trends and industrial components. First, the cohort pattern shows up some interesting period effects.

Table 6.9 Percentage correct predictions of association between qualifications and occupational status on the basis of the tightening link hypothesis

	1930s	1940s	1950s	1960s
Actual successes (%)	82.6	75.8	72.4	72.3
Upper limit (%)	91.4	89.4	98.6	89.1
Lower limit (%)	63.7	55.4	42.2	25.6
Successes standardised*	68.2	60.0	53.5	73.5

*expressed as % improvement on lower limit (i.e. upper limit = 100% improvement)

The standardised measure provides a means of comparing observations at various times and locations, controlling for the occupational and educational distributions. Having calculated the theoretical upper and lower limits for a given distribution, as outlined above, the range which the observed value could take is the difference between the upper and lower limits. For example, Table 6.9 shows that in the 1930s the range was 91.4 per cent − 63.7 per cent = 27.7 per cent. The observed value can then be expressed as an improvement on the lower limit: in this case 82.6 per cent was 18.9 percentage points 'better' than 63.7 per cent. The 18.9 percentage points can be expressed as a proportion of the 27.7 percentage points of the range (this can be done directly because both are percentages calculated from the same base). If this new proportion is expressed as a percentage, where the range (27.7) = 100 per cent, the standardised measure has new limits of 0 per cent and 100 per cent, and each 1 per cent represents a unit of improvement on the original lower limit. Whereas a value of 100 per cent occurs when the original upper limit or best possible fit is achieved, a value of 0 per cent occurs when the original lower limit is achieved, but in this latter case there would have to be a completely inverse relationship between the two variables, analogous to a correlation coefficient of −1. At 50 per cent, the standardised measure reflects a situation of no association, analogous to perfect mobility, where the cell values are proportional to the marginals. Even at 100 per cent, this does not mean that there are no failures in prediction, only that as many successes as possible with that distribution of occupations and education have been achieved. In a case like the new services in the 1950s, the combination of a shortage of qualified manpower and a large demand for non-manual occupations resulted in many unqualified men doing non-manual work, with a standardised measure score of 100 per cent.

If the bond were tightening, one would expect each successive cohort to provide more 'successes'. In fact this does not occur in either the basic or standardised figures. In the former, the earliest period shows the tightest link, with the other three showing a lower and relatively stable percentage. The standardised indicator, however, shows that, given the size of the categories, the 1960s had a closer link. What is more marked is the drop in the lower limit across the period with the sharpest fall in the last cohort. This is produced chiefly by the structural shift in occupations from manual to non-manual: over the first thirty years, this rises from 22.4 per cent to 29.6 per cent, and then jumps to 42.7 per cent in the last decade. High qualifications, meanwhile, increase from 14 per cent to 30 per cent, over thirty years and only increase to 31.7 per cent in the final decade. The largest increase in the supply of qualified manpower is between the 1940s (17 per cent) and the 1950s (29.6 per cent), a change which does not seem to be strongly reflected in Table 6.9.

The essential characteristic of this mode of analysis is that it makes full allowance for a known structure of occupation and of education. The structure of occupations is a statement (albeit imperfect) about demand for certain levels of labour (manual and non-manual), while the educational data are a statement about the supply of men qualified to carry out such labour. It will be recalled that 'qualified' in this sense means having passed Highers of HND, or better. Obviously one could draw the definition lower (e.g. 'O' levels) or even higher, or with a larger data set include graduations of qualification level. The choice of definition here is both pragmatic, because a dichotomy is a more manageable level of analysis, and logical, because if there is a tightening link it should show up for this level of qualification: after all, if the highest school leaving qualification were to be put poorly related to occupational destination, that is indeed a strong piece of evidence against the link thesis.

What Table 6.9 tells us is that, allowing for the ways both of these change over four decades, it is only the 1960s (on the standardised measure) that show any sign of the link tightening. In other words, the link is a feature of comparatively recent times, and generated more by the changes in the occupational structure (the relative growth of the non-manual sector) than by changes in the supply of qualified manpower (the increase in the numbers of men with 'high qualifications').

While this may stand as an adequate summary, it is worth examining the differences between our four industrial groupings. Table 6.10 expresses the data from Tables 6.7 and 6.8 in this latter mode of analysis.

Table 6.10 Inter-industry variations in prediction rate (%) of the tightening link thesis

	Old staples	Light manufacturing	Old services	New services
Actual successes	77.7	82.7	76.2	66.5
Upper limit	98.8	97.2	94.1	73.3
Lower limit	62.6	64.7	61.1	13.4
Standardised success	41.7	55.4	45.8	88.6

Although each sector has a different character, it is the new services sector which is most clearly distinctive, with a poorer absolute successes score but a higher standardised score. This is a reflection of its particular occupational and educational profile. Its non-manual sector is large: at 70 per cent this is twice the size of each of the other groupings. So too is its proportion of highly qualified manpower at 43 per cent. In calculating the upper limit for the link, the result is a low score because of the greater relative shortage of qualified men to fill the large non-manual category. In calculating the lower limit, many more low-qualified men are 'displaced' from the manual sector when the larger group of highly qualified men are allocated to it, so that the former are counted as failures and produce a lower success count.

Again, if the trends within the four groupings are examined, there is little coherence over time even if one ignores the 1940s as 'deviant'. This lack of coherence is evidence of either differences between the industries and/or differences in the forty-year period, as argued in the previous chapter. Even so, on the basic prediction rates, there is a tendency (albeit with exceptions) for the success rate to fall. On the standardised score, all except the new services hold their level or increase, if one takes the oldest and youngest cohorts: only in the 1960s do all four take a value in excess of 50 per cent. One could, therefore,

Table 6.11 Inter-industrial variation in prediction rate of the tightening link

	Industry	1930–9	1940–9	1950–9	1960–9
Raw success score	Old staples	86.6	83.0	66.3	74.7
	Light manufacturing	85.7	85.1	81.1	77.8
	Basic services	82.2	75.2	71.7	75.0
	New services	74.1	57.0	60.9	63.9
Standardised success score	Old staples	38.8	45.0	35.9	54.2
	Light manufacturing	56.1	68.7	61.7	61.4
	Basic services	58.1	39.7	34.8	58.4
	New services	94.8	91.4	100.0	74.5

cautiously argue from Table 6.11 for some kind of generalised change which affected all industries (even if some are more affected than others) with the 1960s being in some way different from earlier periods. Similarly, one could maintain that the industries *also* show distinctive profiles, with new services the most distinctive over the whole period.

If the overall pattern is conceived of as merely the product of these separate profiles, then the size of the four industrial groupings becomes a significant issue. In terms of total manpower, basic services with 1153 men is about twice the size of each of the other three. However, it is a declining sector, so that in the 1930s it was over 43 per cent of the total while in the 1960s it was only 37 per cent. Old staples declined from 22.8 per cent to 14 per cent, light manufacturing showed marginal growth, while the new services grew from 15.4 per cent to 29 per cent. The effect of those changes is obviously to imprint more of the new services type of profile on to the overall pattern. It will be noticed that the dominant influences throughout remain what is normally taken as the tertiary sector.

In fact this is more true than may be immediately apparent. Although absolute size is important, it is the level of qualification and non-manual opportunity that structures the link predictions. In the 1930s, basic services contained 29 per cent of the qualified, while new services held 38 per cent: by the 1960s this had changed to 24 per cent and 48 per cent, while old staples' share had declined 5 per cent to

Education and Mobility 151

about 12 per cent, and light manufacturing had not changed. A similar picture appears for jobs, with the new services increasing from 38 per cent to 53 per cent of all non-manual jobs. Thus the opportunity for the high qualification/high occupation status association is increasingly concentrated in the new services, while the opportunity for low qualification/low occupational status is concentrated mainly on secondary industry, although this is an increasingly small sector. The occupational/industrial transition is again shown to work both within industries and between industries.

Before leaving this analysis, there is one other observation to make which refers to the model outlined in an earlier part of this chapter. In Figure 6.1, it was argued in general that one needed to look at changes in *both* occupational and educational distributions, and in particular that the balance between the two could show a strong link *and* a strong association. The data on the industrial grouping in specific periods (such as the old staples for most of the forty years, and light manufacturing in the 1960s) showed cases where such a balance existed but in which the connection between education and occupation was poor. We must therefore add a rider to the earlier discussion and note that Figure 6.1 and its attendant discussion oversimplified the real world, because some other process of job allocation must be at work to explain the relatively high levels of displacement that have been found. Both in these particular cases and indeed in most others, the 'failures' of prediction have been concentrated, if not exclusively located, among the non-manual immobiles and the upwardly mobile although not necessarily for the same reasons.

The analysis of the last few pages has concentrated on the tightening bond thesis per se, which may have obscured, as it were, the reverse side of the coin. That is to say, the same data also point towards a possible explanation of the changes in mobility over time discussed in the previous chapter. It will be recalled that one conclusion was that non-manual job opportunities were increasingly concentrated in the new service sector, a sector which throughout the period had recruited a relatively high proportion of sons of non-manual workers. In addition to this, we now know that for most of the period, seven out of ten of such recruits had high levels of education (cols (*a*), Table 6.8) and while upwardly mobile recruits were less qualified, they were better qualified than average (Table 6.7). Tables 6.10 and 6.11 also show the new services to have the highest association of occupation and education, both overall and in each cohort.

The pattern of recruitment is not black and white, but compared with other sectors, the new services seem to use qualifications as a 'rule' of selection; their non-manual jobs tending on the whole to require advanced technical knowledge. Heavy recruitment from non-manual backgrounds may be a by-product of the fact that it is men from these backgrounds who have better access to educational success. The way in which expanded secondary education opportunities have been largely filled by the children of the middle classes is well documented, so that in the 1960s the advantaged position of such people, together with the dominance of the new services sector, combined to *reduce* upward mobility chances.

SOME CONCLUDING REMARKS

The preceding discussion has not used the word mobility a great deal because it has taken all categories of mobility together, whether upward or downward, or present or absent. This has enabled us to argue not only that upward mobility is not closely connected with high educational achievement, but that this can be seen as a natural outcome of the fact that education and occupation have not been closely related. The thrust of the argument has been this latter idea.

The reasons that have been adduced for this have been variations on the theme that a satisfactory explanation must be sought in terms of both the increasing supply of qualified manpower and the growth of non-manual employment. As we have seen, the growing importance of the new services industries has been particularly influential, but it remains for the forty years in question only a minority grouping. Its full influence is only beginning to be felt in the 1960s, while the style of closer connection between education and occupation has been slow to develop in the more traditional industrial sectors.

It must be acknowledged that these comments are based on one particular operationalisation of the question. To take the highest school-leaving qualification, rather than some lower measure, reduces the proportion defined as qualified, while operating with a manual/non-manual dichotomy includes classes III and IV in the higher occupational category, some of whose members might reasonably be expected to be less well qualified. In fact this criticism is not entirely warranted. Class III *is* relatively unqualified (about four in every five) but IV is only slightly lower in its qualification level that class II, which in turn is marginally *more* qualified than class I. Even if this criticism is accepted, and the analysis has unintentionally been set up in such a way that the two variables are 'unbalanced', it would still be the case that some kind of connection – increasing over time, and across all industries – should be manifest if there were a tightening link. But on the contrary, this has not been the case. This is not to say that the analysis could not in principle be extended to include other and more complex levels of both qualification and occupation.

Having examined the industrial effects in terms of the whole of the non-manual class, it is useful to comment briefly on the upper middle class in particular. It is not necessary to repeat the analysis just completed on the larger group for the latter, to indicate how the two sets of findings fit together. The account of the upper middle class showed in some detail how the present numbers of that class had experienced schooling. These different experiences reflect the underlying structure of the industrial sectors, with a higher proportion of the new services upper middle class group being more qualified than the UMC in the other sectors (72.3 per cent compared with about 50 per cent). In the case of the first jobs, the difference is more pronounced but with light manufacturing perhaps showing a higher level of qualification because of its increasingly technological base. Taken together, the two sections show in different ways how the connection between education and occupation – and thereby with mobility – is a complex one. When Little and Westergaard wrote of the increase in 'professionalisation, bureaucratisation and automation' they were perhaps more correct than they realised, because it is precisely in those economic activities that these processes have thrived – most notably in the new services (and to lesser extent in light manufacturing) – and that there is most of the little evidence of a tightening link. The overall pattern is also determined by the different performances of these sectors with the growth in size of the new services sector clearly the most dominant effect. None the less, given the recency of such developments, and the distribution between the four industrial groupings among, say, the present upper middle class, it is easy to see why the lieutenant class is less qualified than Little and Westergaard imply.

If these lieutenants do not require school qualification to achieve their occupational status, they presumably were able to mobilise some other kind of skill, experience, or ascriptive quality. In the same way, the education of the elite seems to depend less on technical qualification than on some basic advantage which *inter alia* allows for the purchase of a distinctive education which in turn reinforces the separateness of the elite. But whereas the elite share some kind of educational experience which may help to bind them together, the upper middle class, and by implication the rest of the non-manual class, do not share a common educational culture. This may well help to explain the manifest lack of a middle, or upper middle, class consciousness.

In the light of the data presented in this chapter, the early hopes of the LSE Fabians seem somewhat misplaced. Ironically, the two major reports of the Nuffield Study, those of Halsey *et al.* (1980) and Goldthorpe *et al.* (1980a), symbolise that fact. One deals with class inequalities of access to education, but despite its title of 'Origins and Destinations', deals not at all with occupational or class destinations. The other deals with mobility but ignores education. Although neither addresses the problem, a *de facto* separation of family background and education, and of family background and occupational destination, is brought about by the publication of two separate volumes. While this chapter has implicitly given support for such separation, it has not rejected all notions of the connection. Indeed, it was observed above that at the level of a sufficient condition, qualification and both mobility and status maintenance are associated. However, the nature of the association has been shown to depend primarily on the underlying occupational and industrial processes of modern society.

7 Careers, Cohorts and Classes

Intragenerational or 'career' mobility which compares first jobs with those held at a later stage in people's lives, is not only interesting in its own right but in the present account it serves two functions. First, it helps to amplify the trend analysis in Chapter 5, which used mobility to 'first' job in order to examine historical changes independent of career effects. Second, career mobility can be treated as part of the work experience of a generation, so providing a perspective on ideas such as deskilling or labour markets which have been used to cenceptualise employment processes.

Whereas some occupations are filled by people at the beginning of their working lives, others stand at the top of a series of previous occupational positions. Labouring and many other types of manual work are examples of the former, while managerial or senior administrative jobs in bureaucracies illustrate the latter. Some people start in one type and then move on.

Career mobility will therefore operate in various ways within the occupational hierarchy, so that the amount of ultimate intergenerational mobility 'disguised' by an analysis of first jobs is not a constant. For some people, the amount of further mobility is greater than others because they have embarked on a 'career' rather than just taken a job. Again, older men will have already achieved more career mobility than younger men. And if mobility *to* first job changes over time due to occupational transition, there is every possibility that mobility *from* first job, i.e. the subsequent process of obtaining further jobs, also changes historically. The latter point provides the basis for Little and Westergaard's suggestion that as credentialism increases, occupational achievement by work experience and promotion decreases so producing a 'counterbalance' with the result that overall mobility does not change.

Having effectively dealt with the counterbalance thesis in Chapter 6, there is no need to dwell on it again here. However, it is worth commenting on Goldthorpe's treatment of the idea (1980a, pp. 54–7) as it is a good example of how difficult it is to sort out exactly what happens. Goldthorpe concludes (p. 57) that the 1972 survey results are:

contrary to the counter-balance thesis in indicating that, over recent decades, an increase in direct entry to the higher levels of the class structure has occurred without there being any apparent decline in the chances of access via indirect routes.

His evidence for this is given in his figure 2.2, and is based on a comparison between men born 1908–27 and 1928–47 (and a subsidiary set of men born 1928–37). The essence of his figure 2.2 has been presented here as Table 7.1, which shows on the left-hand side increases in direct entry, although direct entry to classes I and II from class I and II origins (i.e. self-recruitment) shows a larger increase than all the others put together.

The evidence for indirect flows on the right-hand side of the table show a *lower* rate in four of the five possible kinds of mobility, with self-recruitment again having the largest difference. This would seem to contradict Goldthorpe's statement that there has been no decline in use of indirect routes.

There are two reasons for this. Golthorpe has chosen to express the use of indirect routes as *chances* of access, so that he is actually saying that, for *those who start work in a lower-level occupation*, the probability of regaining advantage does not change significantly. In other words, he is talking about 'counter-mobility' (i.e. experiencing *first* downward and *then* upward mobility), not indirect access (experiencing *only* upward mobility later in the career) or counterbalance (the *relationship* between direct mobility and indirect access). He deals with counter-mobility on p. 55, and then summarises on p. 57 following figure 2.2, so running the two concepts together. More specifically, he is confusing counter-mobility to classes I and II with direct and indirect access to non-manual occupations.

The other reason for the inconsistency between Goldthorpe's results and his commentary is his confusion of changes in a process over a historical period and the stage of development reached by particular cohorts. 'Indirect mobility' is indicated by movement to the job at time of interview, and younger men have progressed less far in their careers than older men. Thus other things being equal, older cohorts would show *more* indirect entry than younger cohorts; in Goldthorpe's terms, the chances of counter-mobility should *decrease* from older to younger cohorts. But as Table 7.1 shows, although the older cohort does indeed have more indirect mobility, the amounts of difference are not very great, while Goldthorpe indicates that his probability of counter-mobility remains at just under 50 per cent.

Table 7.1 Goldthorpe's data on counterbalance: outflow percentages*

From origin in classes	Direct entry to				Indirect entry to			
	Classes I & II		Classes III IV & V		Classes I & II		Classes III IV & V	
	Old cohort	Young cohort	Old cohort	Young cohort	Old cohort	Young cohort	Old cohort	Young cohort
I & II	23	38	n/a	n/a	36	27	n/a	n/a
III, IV, V	6	11	13	15	23	22	22	18
VI, VII	3	6	8	9	13	13	20	17

*SOURCE: Goldthorpe, 1980a, fig. 2.2, pp. 56–7. Classes as Goldthorpe *not* SMS.

In fact, if one calculates *all* chances of counter-mobility by including Goldthorpe's classes III, IV and V, the probability *increases* from about 50 per cent to 55 per cent for the men aged 35 and over (the subsidiary set). If we accept that these men do indeed have completed careers, then the comparison between them and the oldest set, in showing an increase in counter-mobility, lends support to the idea of increased indirect mobility coinciding with increased direct mobility. It therefore seems plausible to suggest that early career indirect entry may be actually *increasing* in such a was as nearly to balance later career progression. Goldthorpe may after all be correct in his conclusion, but not for the reasons which he gives.

DIRECT AND INDIRECT MOBILITY

In the analysis of trends in Chapter 5, it was necessary to control for career effect, and so take a job in the early career for all respondents. First job was chosen as the best available because it covered a longer period, marks the change from background and education to employment, and first job influences subsequent career development. The point was made at the time that this is only one index of mobility, and an incomplete one: there is more mobility to come due to career progression. The idea of direct and indirect entry can be used to estimate the size of this effect on the inflow rates used in earlier analysis.

For ease of explanation, the first information on entry routes is presented in Figure 7.1 for the whole sample, using the manual/non-manual dichotomy. Between first and current jobs, the non-manual sector has grown as a result of career development and occupational transition by about 20 per cent overall. This has drawn in 24 per cent of indirect entrants, slightly more from manual origins than from non-manual (the extra 4 per cent to balance indirect downward movement which we note is a relatively small factor). In round terms, mobility to first job accounts for nearly half of all mobility as measured to current job. The pattern of direct recruitment to non-manual first jobs – very roughly half and half from manual and non-manual origins – is repeated for the indirect recruitment. To be more precise, 53 per cent of non-manual first jobs go to the sons of non-manual fathers, compared with 49 per cent of current jobs. The difference is small, indicating a slight tendency for the sons of manual workers to 'catch up' on the sons of non-manual workers by career achievement.

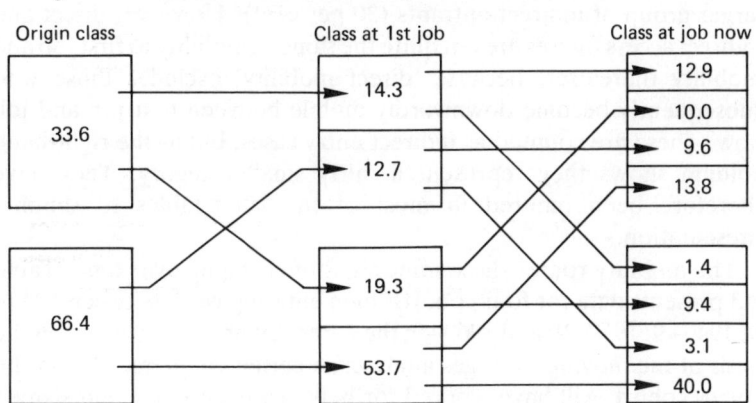

Figure 7.1 Direct and indirect entry to non-manual work: n = 4027

Origin class	Class at 1st job	Class at job now
33.6	14.3	12.9
	12.7	10.0
		9.6
		13.8
66.4	19.3	1.4
	53.7	9.4
		3.1
		40.0

In looking at cohorts, we can also examine inflows; because the data will be used in several ways, summaries in tabular form will be presented in preference to diagrams. Thus Table 7.2 corresponds to Figure 7.1 (with rounding of percentages to whole numbers for ease of comparison).

The outflow figures show that, respondent for respondent, non-manual sons are more than twice as likely to obtain non-manual jobs by direct access as sons of manual sons and also have a 50 per cent better chance of indirect access. The inflow figures show that the two groups make up a slightly more even proportion of direct entrants (28

Table 7.2 Direct and indirect entry to manual and non-manual classes

Origin class	% mobility	Direct to Non-manual	Direct to Manual	Indirect to Non-manual	Indirect to Manual
Non-manual	Gross	13	9	10	1
	outflow	38	28	30	4
	inflow	28	17	22	3
	N	519	378	401	55
Manual	Gross	10	40	14	3
	outflow	14	60	21	5
	inflow	21	74	30	6
	N	385	1610	554	124

per cent to 21 per cent) and that the sons of manual workers are the larger group of indirect entrants (30 per cent). However, direct and indirect access figures are not quite the same as mobility to first job and mobility thereafter, because 'direct mobility' excludes those who subsequently become downwardly mobile between first job and job now. These are counted as indirect entry cases, but as the right-hand column shows they represent a fairly small category. They have therefore been omitted in most of the later tables to simplify presentation.

The mobility routes show some signs of changing over time. Table 7.3 presents data for four cohorts: men entering work between 1930–9; 1940–9; 1950–9; and 1960–9; the dates having been selected on the basis of the moving averages analyses in earlier chapters. Men in the '1950s cohort' will have worked for between twenty-five and sixteen years: the youngest men would have left school aged 15 and been 31 years old at interview. Most men leaving school at that age enter manual work, and will have had sixteen years in which to make their achievements. It is reasonable to suggest that *most but not all* of this cohort's career mobility, at least in terms of crossing the manual/non-manual line, will have been completed. The same cannot be said for men entering work in the 1960s (and in particular the later years) who clearly lack their span of career achievement.

These figures show how difficult it is to talk about trends: the 1960s display very considerable variation from the other cohorts, while we

Table 7.3 Direct and indirect entry to non-manual occupation in four cohorts (date of first job)

Origin class	% mobility	Direct entry				Indirect entry			
		1930s	1940s	1950s	1960s	1930s	1940s	1950s	1960s
Non-manual	Gross	10	10	12	19	14	10	10	6
	outflow	30	34	37	48	42	35	33	16
	inflow	22	20	24	42	31	21	22	14
	N	94	92	112	221	132	96	99	74
Manual	Gross	5	10	10	12	15	18	16	8
	outflow	8	15	15	19	22	26	23	13
	inflow	12	21	22	26	35	37	32	17
	N	52	97	99	137	147	170	148	89

also know that the 1940s' cohorts includes the Second World War and its immediate post-war disruption. Proceeding cautiously, one can observe that direct entry mobility rates rise throughout for both classes of origin. The direct relative (outflow) chances at beginning and end of the period are much more in favour of the non-manual sons (about four times better in the 1930s and two and a half times in the 1960s, as against just over twice in the 1940s and 1960s). The middle two cohorts also show more similarity on inflow. Perhaps the best summary of direct entry is that, while the non-manual sons made steady gains in mobility for the three decades, the sons of manual workers to some extent closed the gap by the 1940s, held on in the 1950s, but despite increasing their mobility further were left behind in the 1960s by a surge of non-manual access by the sons of the non-manual class.

The indirect entry figures are rather different. Leaving aside the 1960s for the moment, there is decline in indirect entry by the sons of non-manual workers (although little difference between the 1940s and 1950s), while the sons of manual workers did marginally better in the 1940s but have a similar pattern for the 1930s and the 1950s. At the beginning of the period, the non-manual sons were twice as likely as manual sons to enter non-manual work; by the 1950s that differential had been halved and the inflow measure shows about a third of all non-manual jobs going to indirect entrants with manual backgrounds. The manual entrants seem to have retained most of their indirect entry while gaining on direct entry. The non-manual entrants have gained on direct entry and relinquished some of their indirect access.

Where do the 1960s come into this? It is too early to tell whether the indirect access patterns are simply a result of incomplete careers or of a more basic change in the recruitment pattern. Certainly direct access is at its highest, so the extent to which there is room for indirect access may be reduced unless the non-manual class has grown enough to balance this. One way of looking at this is to consider three 'job points'; first job, job ten years later and job at time of interview, which helps to focus on the career effect.

MOBILITY IN CAREER STAGES

The generally rising proportions obtaining non-manual work at first job and ten years after starting work are clear from columns (*a*) and (*b*) of Table 7.4.

Table 7.4 Percentage gross mobility/immobility, non-manual occupational destinations

Cohort	Origin	(a) 1st Job	(b) 10 Yr. Job	(c) Job now	(b)−(a)	(c)−(b)
1930s	Non-manual	10.7	13.9	23.2	3.2	9.3
N = 976	Manual	7.6	11.3	20.4	3.7	9.1
1940s	Non-manual	10.9	16.5	20.2	5.6	3.7
N = 930	Manual	13.4	18.3	28.7	4.9	10.4
1950s	Non-manual	12.2	17.4	22.1	5.2	4.7
N = 954	Manual	13.1	19.2	25.9	6.1	6.7
1960s	Non-manual	21.7 (20.6)	24.3 (23.9)	25.3	2.6 (2.3)	1.0 (1.4)
N = 1167	Manual	15.9 (15.1)	18.7 (20.2)	19.4	2.8 (5.1)	0.7 (−0.6)

If we look at the *differences* between first job and job ten years later (the two fixed points for each cohort, as opposed to the variable career length to job at time of interview) two main features stand out. On the one hand, the percentages from both origins obtaining non-manual jobs in the opening decade of their careers show a slight increase, except for the 1960s. But men entering work after the mid-1960s had not worked a full ten years by the time of interview, so this dip is not unexpected. Indeed, if we take men who fall into the first half of that cohort (starting work between 1960 and 1964 – the numbers in brackets in Table 7.4) then there is less of a fall.

On the other hand, the differences between men with manual and with non-manual backgrounds in each of the four cohorts is very small (less than 1 per cent), and both origins show similar upward trends. This suggests that the expansion of non-manual opportunity continues to work ten years into the career rather than all opportunity being increasingly concentrated into initial employment. If anything, the opportunities for career mobility are increasing and this applied to men of both class origin.

The third feature of early career achievement is that men with non-manual origins in the 1960s represent a distinctive new level of entry to non-manual employment: 21.7 per cent at first job and 24.3 per cent after ten years (columns (*a*) and (*b*)). The sons of manual workers, however, seem to display a continuation of earlier trends by increasing their achievement by 1 or 2 per cent (at least for those starting work in the first half of the 1960s), whereas the non-manual sons jump by several percentage points – up by almost 10 per cent at first job. This particular category will require further consideration.

Turning next to the variable section of careers between 'ten-year job' and job at time of interview, we see no uniform direction of change even in the three cohorts in which careers have had time to 'mature'. Nor do the two origin groups even show moves in the same direction between cohorts (e.g. 1930s and 1940s; and 1950s). It seems, therefore, that mobility after the first ten years of work varies according to which cohort one is in and what origins one has, so that the process of occupational attainment has not been systematic since 1930. For the sons of non-manual workers, there is already a higher proportion in non-manual work in the 1960s cohort than in any earlier cohort. This fact tends to reinforce the impression gained from the other cohorts that while the sons of manual workers who started work in the 1940s, and to a lesser extent in the 1950s, did relatively well compared with the sons of non-manual workers, any advantage gained since the 1930s has been lost in the 1960s.

How does this amplify the conclusions drawn in Chapter 5 on the basis of first jobs? For the 1930s' cohort, the continuing process of mobility moves men from manual and non-manual origins upward in parallel by about 9 per cent: the first job analysis has apparently sliced off the first part of a uniform process in which the first ten years of career accounts for about a quarter of total mobility, i.e. roughly in proportion with the period's share of the full career. In the next cohort (the one affected by the Second World War), the later career seems to show less movement. Sons of non-manual workers peak earlier and lower than in the previous cohort, while their manual counterparts continue to hold on to their relative advantage set by their success on developing much as in the previous cohort. Compared with eventual full mobility, the first job mobility pattern tends slightly to overestimate non-manual attainment relative to manual attainment. In the 1950s' cohort – and now we are approaching the point where 'full career mobility' may not be achieved – the two origin groups move more in concert once again. There may be more mobility yet to come but the first job picture seems to be carried through. As we have established that even the 'ten-year job' data on the last cohort is incomplete, there is little to be said about the 1960s, except, of course, that *for the time being* the first job figures necessarily correspond quite closely to the other later measures of mobility. It is, on the other hand, interesting to speculate that if the 1950s pattern of career achievement is projected on to the 1960s' cohort, then there is a further 5 per cent overall mobility for each of the two origin groups to achieve. This would give a final figure of at least three-quarters of non-manual sons and nearly half of the manual sons entering non-manual employment by the end of their careers.

Thus while first job mobility cannot give a precise picture of eventual mobility, both the access and the stages of mobility analysis confirm the general pattern earlier identified in trends of recruitment. That is to say, there is no evidence that what is happening at first job is counteracted by a different process in later career. *Therefore, we can use recruitment patterns for men starting work as a good indicator of whether mobility as a whole is increasing or decreasing.* It follows that the conclusions in Chapter 5 can be taken with greater confidence because a potential hidden countereffect has been eliminated. Alternatively, it must be remembered that this is a statement of the 'broad brush' position: career mobility does modify the details of mobility gained from first job analysis. One would need to proceed with caution before generalising from some of the more localised or specific points at first job to total mobility.

We can also now comment on whether indirect mobility is changing over time, although both the 1950s' cohort (to some extent) and the 1960s' cohort (to a great extent) have truncated career spans. Indirect movement to non-manual occupations by the sons of non-manual workers seems to be decreasing slightly; if there were even a little more movement yet to come in the 1950s' cohort, this would be enough to halt any talk of a trend. Similarly, among the sons of manual workers, there would be no decrease. It can therefore be stated that the increase in direct entry is not yet offset by a decrease in later career mobility. However, the 1960s' cohort shows such an abrupt change that it may be an early indication of a structural change in that decade.

Finally, what do these patterns imply for the experience of mobile and immobile people? If one takes the older men now in non-manual employment, perhaps a fifth have come from manual origins, plus another two-thirds who, whatever their backgrounds, have 'worked their way up' in their own careers. That is to say only about one in five are straight second-generation non-manual. Among the younger men (who may in due course be joined by others who have worked their way up), the direct entrants from manual origins are a quarter, but the

Careers, Cohorts and Classes 165

indirect access of those with even some work life experience of employment is down to one-third. The direct second-generation non-manual entrants make up two in every five of the younger non-manual workers. If this continues, fewer incumbents of the non-manual class will have lived part of their lives in a manual working-class environment, as background and/or career. As we shall see, this is a product of the emerging structure of employment opportunities.

INDUSTRIAL SECTORS AND MOBILITY ROUTES

On the evidence from Chapter 5, different mobility routes are to be expected in the various industrial sectors, and this is borne out by Table 7.5 which deals with the three-quarters of the sample who have always worked in a single industrial sector.

Primary industry has virtually no upward mobility at first job and a very low flow to job now. The main route is indirect entry for the sons of non-manual workers, which accounts for one-third of the sector and two-thirds of the available non-manual positions. This is two or three times greater than any other sector. The indirect flow for sons of manual workers is also considerable, and although generally lower than the rest of the sample on gross and inflow measures, on outflow comes closer to the other sectors.

The direct entry patterns for old staples, light manufacturing and basic services are very similar, but less so for indirect entry. Old staples have lower rates of indirect recruitment from non-manual origins, while basic services have higher rates of indirect recruitment from manual origins. Old staples have a high proportion of non-manual employees recruited from manual origins (i.e. total inflow = 65 per cent).

Finally, the new services have distinctive recruitment routes for men with non-manual origins. This group makes up half the inflow through direct access and altogether 85 per cent end up in non-manual work. Even the sons of manual workers have distinctively high rates of access at first job; their indirect access is more typical of the other sectors, except that as a proportion of all employees this group must be relatively small.

The five sectors have a range of non-manual proportions, from 9 per cent to 63 per cent at first job, and 27 per cent to 81 per cent at job now. Old staples, light manufacturing and basic services expand by about 12 per cent, new services by 19 per cent and primary industry by 40 per

Table 7.5 Entry to non-manual employment by origin class: five industrial sectors

Class of origin	% Mobility	Direct entry					Indirect entry				
		Ag. & Fish	Old staples	Light manuf.	Basic servs.	New servs.	Ag. & Fish	Old staples	Light manuf.	Basic servs.	New servs.
Manual	Gross	7	6	9	10	40	34	3	8	9	10
	Outflow	11	32	34	31	74	54	17	27	28	19
	Inflow	14	23	25	22	50	69	12	20	21	13
	N	22	34	100	178	239	110	18	80	163	60
Non-manual	Gross	1	7	9	8	19	8	11	12	17	11
	Outflow	1	8	12	12	43	22	14	17	25	24
	Inflow	1	24	24	19	24	16	41	31	38	13
	N	1	36	95	153	113	26	62	126	303	64

cent. This does not explain the recruitment patterns of the two origin classes: for example, in primary industry both origin groups are overwhelmingly recruited after first job, but in old staples and basic services manual workers also enter non-manual work to a very marked extent by the indirect route. Similarly, basic services and light manufacturing have almost indentical 'profiles' of opportunity, but whereas in the former two out of three sons of manual workers use the indirect route, in the latter indirect and direct entry are almost in balance. These results indicate different career structure for the non-manual work available in each sector.

This suggests a slight modification of the conclusions about trends in earlier chapters. First, very little was said then about primary industry; we now see that such mobility as it contains does not show up at first job, and its non-manual incumbents will typically achieve their position later in life having worked in a manual capacity. Second, the three sectors of old staples, light manufacturing, and basic services show broadly similar rates of career mobility, so that conclusions based on their first job patterns apply in principle to later mobility, in that their characteristics are carried on through the career. However, old staples tends to have less indirect access for the sons of non-manual workers, so that relatively speaking there is more upward career mobility in that sector than the other two.

Third, the new services' indirect access shows less of the sharp class differential at direct entry but since this is not a reversal of that position, but rather a roughly equal increase to the proportions at first job, the conclusions drawn from the first job pattern do not require substantial re-evaluation.

Indeed, the basic observations generally hold true. There is no substantial evidence that career mobility works to remove the sectoral effects evident at first job. Rather, the structural pattern established by recruitment of men beginning work seems to remain with them for the rest of their careers. Their mobility is dependent on the mix of industries in the society at any given time, both on entry and in subsequent careers.

However, this is to relate sectoral figures for the whole sample to a trend analysis for cohorts. To be more accurate, we also need to compare cohorts within each sector, although once again the numbers in some of the cells become very small. To overcome this, Table 7.6 concentrates on gross mobility rates. On the whole, these figures confirm the earlier statements made on the basis of separate cohort and sector analyses. The distinctiveness of the 1960s, on both direct

Table 7.6 Access to non-manual occupations by cohort, sector and origin class: percentage of movement in each cohort/sector*

Industry Sector	Origin Class	Direct Entry					Indirect Entry				
		All	1930s	1940s	1950s	1960s	All	1930s	1940s	1950s	1960
Primary N=269	Non-manual	6	4	9	4	7	34	46	34	32	20
	Manual	1	0	0	2	0	8	5	10	11	7
Old staples N=459	Non-manual	7	4	6	5	13	3	4	3	4	2
	Manual	7	2	7	8	13	11	10	16	11	7
Light manu. N=946	Non-manual	10	8	9	8	14	7	6	8	10	5
	Manual	9	6	10	10	10	12	18	15	13	2
Basic services N=1589	Non-manual	10	7	8	10	13	9	14	9	9	6
	Manual	9	7	10	8	10	17	18	22	18	10
New services N=477	Non-manual	48	34	21	38	53	11	15	14	11	7
	Manual	19	8	23	24	22	12	17	16	13	5
All N=3740	Non-manual	13	9	9	12	19	10	13	11	10	6
	Manual	10	5	10	10	12	14	16	18	15	7

* i.e. Cells do not total to 100% because non-movers are excluded: e.g. in primary industry, 49% (6 + 34 + 1 + 8) moved into non-manual, and 51% (not shown) became manual workers.   Cohort numbers 898, 860, 886 and 1096.

and indirect access, applies to all sectors except possibly to the small primary sector for direct entry. Direct entry tends to rise across the board, except for the sons of non-manual workers in the new services in the 1940s, a deviant pattern that has no immediate explanation. The middle of the period shows that manual sons in all sectors except the primary closed the gap between their chances and those of the non-manual sons of direct access to non-manual work. However, in new services and light manufacturing, the position of manual sons has not improved for indirect access. The statements about the sectors also hold true, although one notices a slight increase in upward mobility may be creeping into the recent years of primary industry, while the basic services' higher proportions of indirect access by manual sons is more obvious in the late cohorts.

It is interesting to note how these patterns are associated with levels of education. The original counterbalance model assumed that direct access would be by means of qualifications, and indirect access – by job experience and promotion – would therefore be reduced. It is true that direct access is more closely associated with education: overall, two-thirds of direct entrants had more than minimum school leaving age (MSLA) experience of secondary education, compared with less than one-third of the indirect entrants. But this still allows one-third of direct entrants to have only basic education, and one in three of the indirect entrants had post-basic secondary education in addition to their career experience to help them achieve mobility.

In all industrial sectors, regardless of class or origin, the direct entrants were better qualified than indirect entrants. However, whereas 77 per cent of direct entrants among non-manual sons were educated beyond the minimum, only 52 per cent of the sons of manual workers were, while the indirect entrant figures were 40 per cent and 17 per cent. The higher qualifications of non-manual sons apply to all sectors and routes of access. Thus while there *is* a relationship between direct and indirect access, there is also a strong class of origin effect, and the nature of the former is not so strong as might have been expected from the Little and Westergaard formulation.

In primary and old staple industries, minimum education was the most common (60 per cent) for both classes of origin whatever the form of entry, but in new services over 90 per cent of direct entrants and nearly 50 per cent of indirect entrants had more than MSLA education. Light manufacturing came next with 61 per cent and 32 per cent, followed by basic services with 52 per cent and 21 per cent. It follows that while there are access and origin effects, there is also a sectoral effect at work, most notably in the two extremes of the sectoral range, primary and new services industries.

In comparison, the cohorts offer a rather confused picture. Both the 1930s and the 1960s have high levels of education for direct entrants (71 per cent and 76 per cent) but the levels are lower in the 1940s and 1950s (58 per cent and 55 per cent). On the other hand, the levels for indirect entry are at about 30 per cent for all cohorts except the 1950s which is only 15 per cent. Two historical 'events' seem to be intervening here. First, the 1940s' cohorts has had both its education and its direct entry to work dislocated by the war and its aftermath: therefore, its direct access is low but that leaves a core of qualified men who later became indirect entrants to non-manual work. On the other hand, the 1950s' cohort reflects a generally lower level of educational achievement. This has been attributed to a particular feature of the Scottish educational system at that time – a 'consolidated' examination certificate in which all subjects had to be passed at one attempt. Contemporary comment noted how this leaving certificate was unattractive to the sons of manual workers since, if they failed, they were then too old to obtain apprenticeships. Indeed, the pressure to change this system grew rapidly during the 1950s until a disaggregated qualification was introduced, with an immediate result that many more children began staying on at school after minimum school leaving age (see Ford et al., 1975).

These educational patterns do not resemble Little and Westergaard's expectation of a simple counterbalance of more educated direct entrance and less uneducated indirect entrance. There are continued origin, route and sector effects, together with concrete historical variation. On the one hand, there is the continued association of origin and education, and the expansion of education, so that even indirect access shows more education. On the other, the fit of education and occupation is not as close as other commentators have previously believed.

Because our major interest has been to establish links with Chapter 5, the account so far has dealt with manual/non-manual patterns. The logic of the analysis can be extended to any other structure of classes: Goldthorpe, as we saw, uses three occupational classes. Two complications follow, however: the numbers in each cell become increasingly small, and the direct/indirect patterns change because the more classes, the more routes of indirect access are created, and the higher becomes the proportion of movements that are classified as indirect.

Given these limitations, and with the main patterns of career effects on access to non-manual occupations established, there is not a high priority to further elaboration of the cohort/sector/class line of analysis. Of rather more interest is to use career mobility as a tool for investigating other areas where previously no use has been made of mobility rates. In the opening chapters, Braverman's deskilling thesis and the segmented labour market model were introduced as areas of debate to which analysis of occupational, as against social, mobility could contribute. Both are also areas in which the manual working class can be differentiated and given more attention than in the earlier parts of this study.

THE DESKILLING THESIS

Braverman's account of deskilling deals with several levels of occupation but the core case is that of skilled manual work. In British terms, this can be equated to SEG 9 (see Chapter 3), jobs requiring the completion of an apprenticeship for entry: in the present study, the equivalent is occupational class V. If one is to seek evidence of deskilling, it will be in changes involving this stratum (see Lee, 1981, p. 63).

Following Braverman, we might expect, first, that the number and proportion of skilled manual workers would decline. Second, formerly skilled labourers would be displaced into 'less skilled' (semi- and unskilled manual) occupations (creating downward mobility). Third, the employer would be able to substitute less skilled labour for skilled labour in that occupation (i.e. creating upward career mobility for the former). Fourth (and not directly accessible from the mobility data), skilled workers should find themselves doing less skilled work under the same occupational title. The 'distance' between skilled and less skilled occupations is reduced so that it becomes 'easier' for individuals to move between the two categories. This should be visible in the career histories of skilled workers who have been exposed to deskilling in their lifetimes: the flow out of skilled occupations into less skilled ones should increase with time, as should the counterflow of men with lower levels of skills into 'skilled' work. The increase in levels of deskilling over time is a result of the increasing pressures for profit maximisation under capitalism, but there should also be a higher rate of deskilling among older men who have been 'at risk' of being deskilled longer and have old skills which are increasingly irrelevant.

In a parallel, but less direct, way intergenerational mobility between skilled and less skilled classes should also increase. This is because the skilled class has its essential social differences removed: deskilling erodes income, work status, and any cause of separate identity due to possession of craft skills. It is therefore to be expected that any social advantage or informal mechanisms of controlling entry to occupations for the next generation will similarly be eroded. Sons will be less likely to follow fathers into skilled work, while the sons of less skilled workers will be better able to compete for jobs whose skill content has been reduced and which are no longer perceived as anything 'special'. The same argument can be made for the proletarianisation of routine white collar workers, although given the small numbers of these in the present study, this is not developed here.

The evidence for the first of these propositions, that the scale of skilled employment is being reduced, is substantial. As the time-series in Chapter 3 showed, SEG 9 has decreased between 1921 and 1971 from 38 per cent to 33 per cent of male occupations. The difference between fathers' and sons' generations in the mobility tables in Chapter 4 was about 8 per cent, while, at least post-Second World War, the proportion of men in the SMS sample starting work as apprentices has declined from just over 40 per cent to around 35 per cent.

However, even this substantial evidence is not sufficient to carry complete conviction. On the one hand, the decline in skilled manual recruitment is concentrated in the post-war period, and may well reflect only a temporary *increase* in recruitment due to the Second World War. On the other hand, the deskilling thesis calls not only for a reduction in skilled employment but also an increase in less skilled manual work. In fact the reverse is true: as Figure 7.2 shows, recruitment to the latter category falls from around 45 per cent to 25 per cent.

The decline in less skilled employment as a first job is one of the largest effects in the study. Figure 7.2 also shows the complexity of skilled manual recruitment. Its initial small dip in the curve and its subsequent peak coincide with the war and the post-war adjustment, when, after fewer young men had served apprenticeships between 1939 and 1945, there was an effort to step up training in the late 1940s. From that high point in the years 1946–50, the recruitment of skilled men has dropped about 5 per cent or 6 per cent (although the proportion of successive cohorts still in skilled work at the time of interview does not fall).

These proportions of skilled and less skilled workers are, of course,

Figure 7.2 Moving averages for five-year cohorts (year of entry): proportions entering skilled and less skilled manual first jobs

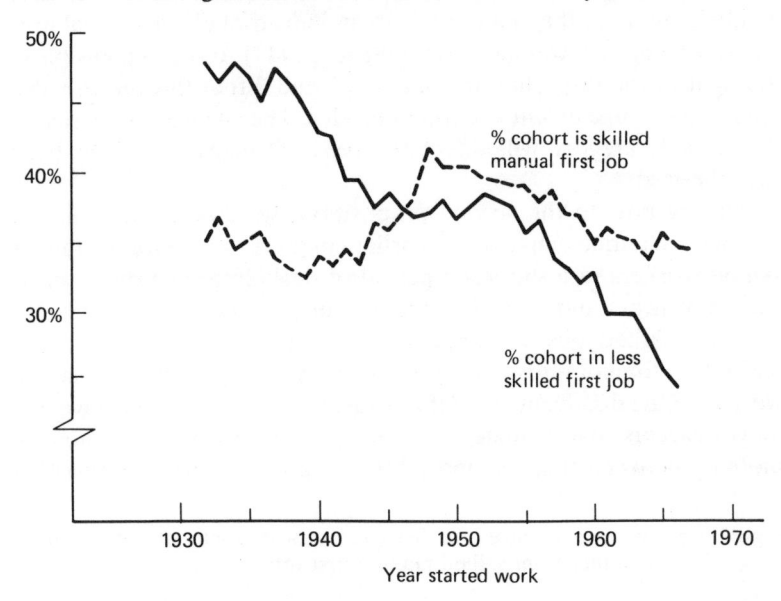

[Graph showing two lines from 1930 to 1970. Solid line labeled "% cohort in less skilled first job" starts near 48% in 1930, declines to around 30% by 1970. Dashed line labeled "% cohort is skilled manual first job" stays around 33-38% throughout. X-axis: "Year started work".]

not only the results of recruitment policies dealing with manual labour but also arise from the recruitment of non-manual workers. A substantial part of the decline in less skilled work as a proportion of the whole is produced by this latter effect: for example, in both 1944–8 and 1956–60 the absolute number of men entering less skilled work at first job was the same, but in the former case they made up 37.2 per cent of the total and in the latter only 32.8 per cent (although over the whole period there is also a big drop in absolute numbers, about 215 to 150 in the respective five-year cohorts). In other words, the 'decline' of manual work is partly due to long-term shift in employment patterns which has expanded the requirement for non-manual labour from about 18 per cent of starting jobs to 35 per cent. The fact that *skilled* manual work continues to recruit at a relatively high level shows a marked continued demand for such labour because the overall market is so dominated by the shift to non-manual work.

However, this decrease is not necessarily due to deskilling in Braverman's sense. An alternative explanation has already been suggested, namely, that some industrial sectors are in decline, so removing job opportunities. Between 1961 and 1971, the main loss of skilled manual jobs was in the old staples, transport and distribution, and while this was balanced to some extent by new opportunities in several other sectors, the net effect was a drop of 100 000. Kendrick *et al.* attribute more than half of this to an industrial effect, with almost all gains being in newer industries (1982b, p. 117). It seems plausible in the light of the discussion in Chapters 2 and 3 that this process also operated to some extent in earlier decades. The changes in the size of the skilled category will affect the other changes that have been hypothesised.

Turning now to the second proposition, we can use the moving average technique employed in earlier chapters to explore the fate of skilled workers in a supposed period of deskilling. Figure 7.3 deals with downward mobility, i.e. those skilled workers displaced into other less skilled jobs. The upper line shows mobility between first job and job at time of interview for men starting work as skilled manual workers. One disadvantage of this measure is that older men have had longer careers than younger men, so a line (the lower one showing mobility between first job and job ten years later) has been plotted

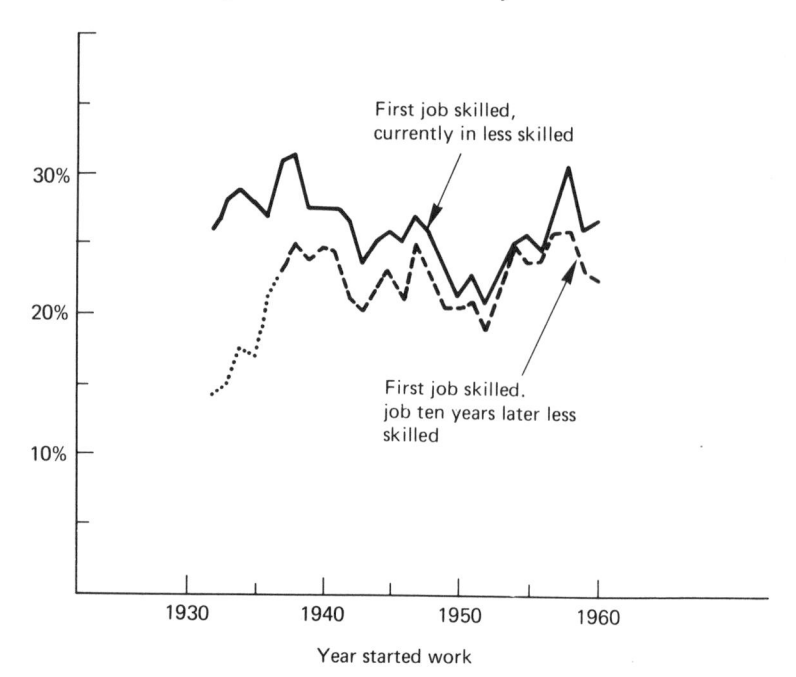

Figure 7.3 Moving averages for five-year cohorts (year of entry) career mobility from skilled manual first job

which controls for this career differential. Unfortunately, for technical reasons, in coding those of the latter jobs which fell during the war years, there is not much that can be said about the early part of the data and the line is therefore shown only by dots.

Men whose job after ten years coincided with war service had their last civilian job recorded instead. This truncates the 'ten years' and therefore underestimates the actual mobility to be expected. Professional armed forces personnel (i.e. those not called up or 'volunteered') were coded to military occupations. Again, only men who have completed ten years of work are included in the graphs in this section, the dates in the time-series indicating year of first employment.

Two main impressions stand out from Figure 7.3. First, the two measures are very similar which shows that downward mobility, if experienced, is experienced in the first ten years of work and not much thereafter. If we are observing deskilling, it affects only young workers which seems somewhat improbable. If we retain the deskilling explanation, we have isolated it as a problem of young men (throughout the period) which would be a new finding. A simpler explanation might be that the 'drop-out' from skilled work reflects 'failed' apprenticeships or career changes made by young men who discover other job opportunities more to their liking.

The second conclusion to be drawn from Figure 7.3 is that there is no marked trend in the data. The vast majority of the points plotted in both lines fall within a 5 or 6 per cent band. There is no sign of any rising trend which is not what one would expect from the logic of Braverman's analysis of valorisation: the process of extracting increasing surplus value from labour should be an intensifying one. Interestingly, the absence of trend contrasts with general patterns of mobility which show distinct patterns throughout the period (e.g. Chapter 5).

A parallel analysis of *upward* mobility for men starting employment as semi-or unskilled manual workers into skilled work is made in Figure 7.4.

In this case, the upper line is the job after ten years' work and latest occupation is the lower line. Once again, there is not much difference between the lines although slightly more than in Figure 7.3: the conclusion again is that most mobility is completed within the first decade of work. The fact that the lower line is the mobility to latest job suggests that some men starting in less-skilled jobs may experience upward mobility in early life which is late followed by downward mobility, but the effect is very small. More important is the lack of any

Figure 7.4 Moving averages for five-year cohorts (year of entry) career mobility from semi- or unskilled manual first job

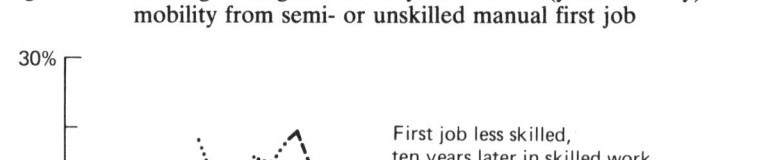

rising trend of entry by men who started without skills into skilled work: although the lines fluctuate, they hold to an average at near 15 per cent, with only two or three percentage points variation.

On the evidence of Figures 7.3 and 7.4, we would conclude that skilled workers are not, as a general category, being displaced into less skilled work, nor are they being supplanted by men who have lower levels of skills. Among young men, during a period which has seen little change in these patterns, about one in four move into less skilled work while about one in six move in the reverse direction. In absolute terms, there is no increase in these figures, so that there are no grounds for arguing that deskilling is being accelerated among men starting work between 1930 and 1960.

Nor is there significant increase in movement after 10 years of work. If deskilling were only a continuing process (i.e. not an accelerating one over the period) we would expect that older men with longer careers would be more deskilled because they had been 'at risk' for longer, and might be in precisely those older occupations most likely to be supplanted by new technologies. However, mobility between ten-year job and current job is very small indeed. Furthermore, there is little to indicate that recruitment to skilled work among young men is doing more than decline slowly, and that is largely due to sectoral shift. If skilled craft labour were being eliminated, then one would expect a more marked fall, especially as the non-manual sector was expanding and so depressing the proportion of all work which was manual. The evidence in terms of changes within manual work is contrary to the four propositions at the start of this section.

An analysis of movements at a higher level in the occupational hierarchy is complicated by the alternative models of deskilling that one may adopt. At times, Braverman concentrates exclusively on craft labour, while at others, he deals with routine white collar work. Later contributors to the debate, such as Crompton and Jones (1984), have extended the deskilling argument to middle range and arguably senior white collar work like computer programmers, accountants and managers. There are thus three possible outcomes for mobility. If we see the entire labour force being equally deskilled, then there should be no change in mobility. If we see deskilling at its most extreme among skilled manual workers, we would expect an increasing distance between manual and non-manual work. Third, if we argue that the lower ranges of white collar work are more susceptible to deskilling than other white collar work, we might expect higher flows between the former and manual work.

Figure 7.5 shows percentages of men starting employment as 'lower non-manual', i.e. including routine clerical work (but not shop assistants who, for reasons of their Hope–Goldthorpe scale score, are allocated to the 'less-skilled' category), supervisors, self-employed artisans and technicians. There is little difference in flows from lower non-manual to skilled manual between employment after ten years

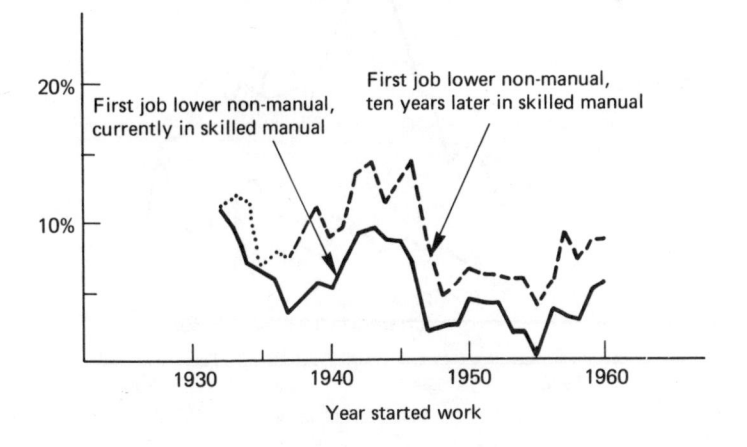

Figure 7.5 Moving averages for five-year cohorts (year of entry) career mobility from lower range non-manual first jobs

and later in the career. The transfer into non-manual work for both indicators is mainly less than 10 per cent, except for an early career peak for men who started work during the war. There is little evidence of any simple trend. This is indicative of a view that the most easily proletarianised portion of non-manual employment has not been deskilled *relative* to skilled manual labour. Either the deskilling effect is in some way contained, or the two types of work have been 'equally' deskilled so that the social distance between them remains constant.

A rather different picture emerges from an analysis of the proportions of men starting work in skilled manual employment and then moving upward (Figure 7.6). In the 1930s, between 5 and 10 per cent of men starting in skilled manual work moved upward. For men who began work in the 1950s, the figure was between 10 and 15 per cent. Although the short-term fluctuations are considerable, there seems to be a rising trend. However, the line showing career mobility to current job displays much more movement. Its peak during the early 1940s is probably another manifestation of wartime labour substitution and its after effects. Furness has commented on how dilutees were integrated into production by allocating them a very restricted part of the productive process, under a greatly expanded system of supervision by workers who under other conditions would themselves be supervised (Furness, 1981). If we 'flatten' this peak the result would be another

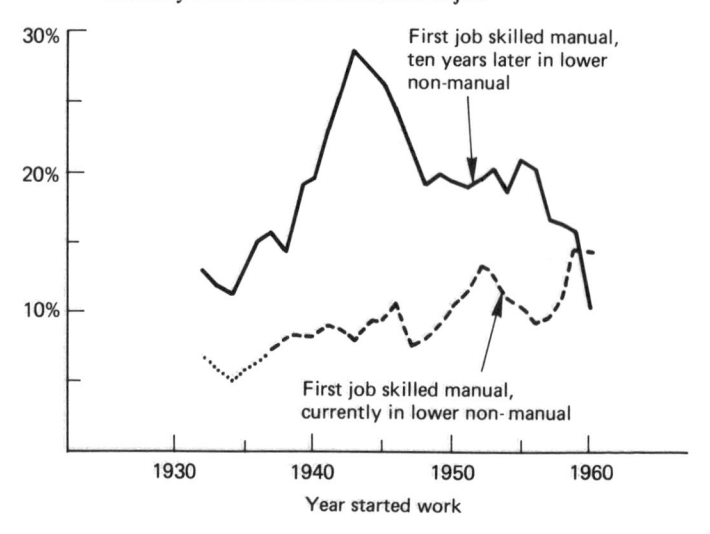

Figure 7.6 Moving averages for five-year cohorts (year of entry) career mobility from skilled manual first job

rising trend (the last few years excepted) broadly parallel to the ten-year job but about 10 per cent higher, rather more than in the previous three graphs. The abrupt decline in the late 1950s is probably a product of the lack of career development among younger men noted in the earlier part of this chapter, although if this is so, it is a feature of manual/non-manual movements.

Following the logic used earlier, classes are becoming more similar if there are more moves between them. One could therefore argue that lower non-manual work and skilled manual work are becoming slightly more like each other, or in other words, it is not skilled manual work that is being deskilled but rather lower non-manual work. This is not really what Braverman claimed. Nor do we need a deskilling explanation to account for the time-series. First, the up-grading of the skill levels thesis and the expansion of the non-manual sector would lead one to expect the same pattern of results. Second, Stewart *et al.* (1980) show how a substantial proportion of recruits to routine white collar work are drawn late in their careers from skilled manual work as a result of employer policy towards long-service employees. And third, the occupational classes used in the present analyses are seen as career-related: supervisors and self-employed artisans would normally be expected to spend their early working years in manual employment. All three explanations call for high rates of mobility between skilled manual and lower non-manual occupations.

Indeed, taking the results in all four of the time-series figures, a more satisfactory explanation can be found in the argument of sectoral shift used in earlier chapters. As economic activity moves from one industrial sector to another, new kinds of skills are required. Without going into great details, skilled employment has declined in old staples, light manufacturing and basic services, the three sectors in which it is chiefly found. However, the sharper declines have been in old staples and basic services, reflecting the decline of textiles, coal and shipbuilding and metals on the one hand, and in particular transport, communication and distribution on the other. The old staples can be regarded as in absolute decline whereas basic services arguably reflect changes in technology and organisation which require fewer workers with traditional skills.

Among the less skilled, primary industry is a more significant factor because its labour is overwhelmingly concentrated in this type of employment and its labour force is reduced by half in the period in question. The old staples also show very substantial decline, but light manufacturing maintains a relatively stable position. Basic services show falls throughout the period, but the new services are a small source of such employment and changes very little.

Sectoral analyses therefore suggests that while in the case of primary industry and old staples the requirement for manual labour may be reduced by new technology, the main effect is a simple decline in the size of the sector as an employer. Basic services remain a major employer but new technology displaces labour, while light manufacturing and new services show less sign of such changes. Thus only some parts of the economy come anywhere near Braverman's prediction, and much of manufacturing, from which he draws most of his craft work examples, fails to conform to his expectations.

The underlying sectoral shift, together with the evidence on mobility, must be regarded as challenging the deskilling thesis, in as far as that thesis can be tested using mobility data in this way. The levels of career transfer as proportions of origin in occupations remain fairly stable (e.g. Figures 7.3 and 7.4) even though the origin occupations change in size: the total net effect is to reduce transfers between skilled and less skilled work, as the origin categories (and notably the less skilled) contract proportionately. Therefore, both in terms of career movements and in terms of recruitment patterns (Figure 7.2) there is little sign of deskilling, and none of any accelerating trend – which would be expected if significant advantages were accruing to the employers from the degradation of labour.

It could be argued that with about one-quarter of all those starting skilled manual work dropping into less-skilled work, and about a sixth of those starting less skilled moving in the reverse direction, there is evidence of deskilling. It is not possible to say for certain whether this is the case, but if it is, one is left with a problem. Why is it that these adjustments take place so early in the career (see Figures 7.3, 7.4 and 7.5)? The only case where there is noticeable late career mobility is out of skilled labour into the lower reaches of non-manual work, which include supervisory positions, technician posts and self-employment, all offering better pay and popularly rated as more desirable jobs.

Common sense suggests that it would be older men with older skills who would be least adaptable and employable in new technologies. However, if these levels of movement are taken as evidence of deskilling, then we have isolated the deskilling of *workers* as a process predominantly concentrated among the young. A simpler explanation is that employers want to recruit as large a number of apprentices as they can (allowing for cyclical effects) because this provides cheap labour while at the same time pacifying the trade unions. When the apprenticeships are completed, some workers are discarded as they are no longer a source of cheap labour. This, together with a not unexpected opting for different jobs by young men who 'chose wrong' on leaving school, would explain the resorting processes observed.

This absence of deskilling effect in these data is none the less quite compatible with certain models of deskilling. The Crompton critique has already been noted: it could be that, despite the arguments to the contrary, there really is an effect that is so contained *within* skilled work that it remains invisible to a structural analysis. Certainly there has been a degradation in the work tasks of many skilled workers, and minor changes in status hierarchies have resulted. However, that does not invalidate this kind of analysis because such changes should result in mobility effects which do not appear.

A second argument would be that work which might in the past have been done by skilled men is now done by unskilled men or by unskilled *women* in new processes. Again, the data presented here do not touch on such an argument. If it is true, it would be the case not that male *workers* were deskilled, but that *work* was deskilled (and possibly that female workers were deskilled). However, this does not result in a decline in opportunity for men: the proportion in less skilled labour declines as we saw in Figure 7.2, as new non-manual opportunities change the character of the labour market.

This leads to a third and perhaps the most important point about deskilling. The nature of work itself may be degraded without producing any significant labour market effects. As Braverman argues, reduction in autonomy and greater alienation from the product are an essential part of labour degradation. However, while in humanistic sense the *work situation* may worsen, this need not be automatically reflected in the *market situation* of the workers because other market forces counterbalance any potential deterioration. This would be the case if, as we have seen, the trend of occupational transition towards non-manual labour changes the overall opportunity structure. Furthermore, the potential of trade unions to intervene against attempts to degrade market situation is considerable.

The central dynamic in such an explanation is the capacity of capital to modify itself in several different ways at once. The introduction of new technologies of production (both sociological and scientific), together with the concentration of capital and the growth of large-scale enterprises, generates a fundamental shift in the kinds of labour required by modern capitalism. This 'long wave' or systemic transition (Lee, 1981, p. 61) takes the sting out of deskilling. There is no logical incompatibility degradation of work tasks on the one hand, and the upgrading of labour on the other: the two processes impinge on different people at different times in the same society.

OCCUPATIONAL MOBILITY AND LABOUR MARKETS

The idea of differential impact of such processes also applies to labour markets. Career mobility is constrained by segmentation of employment opportunities. As was observed earlier, the SMS data do not provide an adequate coverage of blacks, women, the very young and old, or the handicapped, the groups which have typically been seen as the secondary labour force. It is possible, however, to examine the employment experience of those members of the sample who form the lowest skill level (class VII), and to compare their 'careers' with those of more skilled workers. This should indicate how far unskilled male manual workers are part of the segmentation effect, or, in other words, where the boundaries of labour market segments may be (and hence the relative scale of primary and secondary markets). Employment histories and changes of employer also provide information about the extent to which internal labour markets operate. These segments can be seen as operating in addition to the 'segments' of occupation, cohort, sector and origin already identified.

If there is a dual market in Scotland, there are two main requirements to be met. First, the two segments would have to be shown to be different; for example, on job turnover, unemployment, and income. Second, there would have to be very little exchange between the two segments: that is to say there would be virtually no career movement from one to the other. Without these preconditions there is no dichotomy in the labour market worth explaining.

Dealing first with the question of unemployment, the share borne by the unskilled is much greater than the group's proportion in the labour force. At the time of the interview, less than one in three of those found to be unemployed were from the non-manual sector, which makes up about 46 per cent of the population. Among the skilled and semi-skilled, the proportions were about equal at about 40 per cent. But the unskilled had 29.5 per cent of the unemployed, despite being on 14.2 per cent of the workforce. To put it another way, the unskilled sector had more of its members out of work than the non-manual sector, which is three times bigger. Almost one in five of the unskilled men in the sample were out of a job compared with 8.5 per cent of the sample as a whole.

However, this insecurity is not so clearly reflected in the number of jobs making up the employment histories of unskilled workers. On average, an unskilled worker had held 6.7 jobs, compared with 6.2 for other manual workers and 4.9 for non-manual jobs. For cases that were second generation unskilled, the average was a little higher at 7.1 jobs. At the same time, some of the unskilled did show up disproportionately among cases with very high numbers of jobs. Fifteen per cent had more than ten jobs compared with 12 per cent and 8 per cent for other manual and non-manual workers. And 8 per cent had more than fifteen jobs compared with about half that proportion for the other classes. These findings support the usual view that job turnover is higher for unskilled workers, but not to the extent that one might have expected. Perhaps it is only the female and youth part of the sector that shows the sharper contrast with non-manual adult males. Turning to levels of income, the Scottish data match the information generally available through official statistical reports, such as the New Earning Survey. However, the SMS survey was a protracted one, undertaken during a period of rapid inflation, so there are some obvious drawbacks about discussing its income data. The absolute values are already largely irrelevant, while even the relative position can only be a very crude indicator of the state of earnings over one part of a period of considerable change.

The ratio of mean gross earnings for unskilled, skilled and non-manual workers was 1:1.14:1.36. In 1975 pounds, twice as many unskilled workers (17.1 per cent) were earning less than £38 in comparison with the other categories. Up to the middle range of up to £58, the unskilled/non-manual ratio in cumulative percentages is still 2 to 1. At the top of the range, only 3 per cent of unskilled workers were making over £77, compared with 12 per cent of skilled workers and 28.8 per cent of the non-manual class. Unskilled work is therefore not synonymous with low pay but it does carry a much higher chance of a low wage. Even within the unskilled category, some are more disadvantaged than others (see Payne and Ford, 1983 for more details).

On the questions of unemployment, job turnover and earnings, it would seem that the unskilled are relatively disadvantaged, but it remains unclear whether their world of work is *fundamentally* different from the other sector or sectors. The SMS evidence is at best a weak support for the predicted characteristics of a secondary sector. If attention is focused on other, more skilled manual workers, one might equally well argue for a *triadic* labour market model.

This leaves the second major prerequisite of the dual labour market thesis, the requirement that the two sectors are relatively closed, so that movement from one to the other is not common. We can examine this by seeing if people change their employment from one sector to another during their careers, for example, between their first and last jobs.

Table 7.7 Mobility between first and present job for adult males born 1909–48

| | | Respondent's job now | | | |
		Non-manual	Skilled & semi-skilled	Unskilled manual	Totals
Respondent's first job	Non-manual	84.5 (45.6)	10.7 (6.9)	4.8 (8.3)	1039 (25.1)
	Skilled and semi-skilled	34.9 (46.1)	49.5 (77.9)	15.6 (65.3)	2540 (61.3)
	Unskilled	28.2 (8.3)	43.4 (15.2)	28.4 (26.4)	564 (13.6)
	TOTALS	N = 1924 (46.6)	N = 1613 (38.9)	N = 606 (14.6)	4143 (100)

Most strikingly, the third row of Table 7.7 shows that of those who started work as unskilled manual workers 28.2 per cent are now non-manual workers and 43.4 per cent are doing manual work requiring some degree of skill. Only 28.4 are still in the same sector as they started, so that nearly three in every four have moved out of the unskilled manual sector during their careers. Again, as the right hand column shows, those presently in unskilled employment come from a range of occupational starting points. Nearly two-thirds are from the skilled and semi-skilled category and only just one-quarter started their working lives as unskilled workers. Part of this exchange may be an artefact of the categorisation of jobs to 'semi-skilled' as opposed to 'unskilled', but the levels of exchange are so high that it seems implausible to explain them away as mere products of occupational classification.

These results do not support the thesis of a dual labour market because such large numbers are moving between the major sectors during their working lives and are therefore selling their labour in what are supposed to be two exclusive markets. The only area where some degree of closure is evident is in the top row, which shows that 84.5 per cent of men starting in non-manual work were still doing the same type of work at the time of interview. But even here, more men move into non-manual work than start in it, so the non-manual sector cannot be regarded as 'closed'. What is true is that the movements are chiefly in one direction: into the non-manual sector but not out of it.

Taken overall, unskilled manual workers do not seem to constitute a secondary labour force, confined to some identifiable separate labour market. Nor is it possible to identify any sub-sectors using the levels of analysis that have sufficed to differentiate findings elsewhere in this study. Controlling for age (i.e. using the four cohorts) does not substantially alter the inter-group *differences* in rates of unemployment, number of jobs or income, although it does have an effect on the rates themselves.

However, the five industrial sectors do demonstrate some differences in number of previous jobs held by their workforce (past unemployment cannot be compared and the quality of the income data does not warrant detailed usage).

Primary industry tends to have lower rates of job turnover with one-third having had fewer than three jobs. New services are also relatively stable. One presumably reflects the pattern of family, small business, and local employment in agriculture and fishing, while the other suggests the greater stability and continuity of public and large commercial institutions. In addition, it may arise from the specify of technical knowledge skills which discourage job transfer, and also the relative youth of employees in this sector. It is interesting that the conventional notion of a career does not appear to be manifested in these figures for the new services, as Table 7.8 shows.

Table 7.8 Number of previous jobs by current industrial sector

Industrial sector	Number of previous jobs					Totals
	1 and 2	3 and 4	5 and 6	7 – 10	>10	
Primary	37.4	31.2	12.9	12.7	5.8	7.4
Old staples	12.2	41.9	23.8	15.9	6.2	12.8
Light manuf.	11.6	38.2	24.4	16.8	9.0	24.6
Basic servs.	12.4	38.0	23.7	15.8	10.1	41.5
New services	25.3	40.2	18.1	12.7	3.7	13.6
All	15.8	38.3	22.4	15.3	8.2	4373

While each sector logically can have primary and secondary labour markets within it, the association of low turnover and the service sector, and higher turnover and light manufacturing – two expanding sectors in the 1960s – perhaps helps to explain why the idea of segmented labour markets may have become popular when it did. The underlying structure of sectoral shift has changed the circumstances of employment in the direction of segmentation. Certainly the association between industry and the labour market has been recognised in the literature, although the relative size of sectors does not seem to have attracted attention. For example, Loveridge and Mok (1979) have suggested that oil, chemicals, public utilities and metals comprise a primary segment, while textiles, leather goods, glassware and foods are a secondary sector. This seems a relatively unlikely grouping as far as the evidence for male employment goes: although the first does have 14.4 per cent unskilled manual workers, as against 19.3 per cent, this is not very different from the residual rate of 13.9 per cent.

A second dimension of labour market theory on which the same data-set can shed some interesting if indirect light is the idea of the internal labour market. While nothing can be said about whether employees have changed employers, we can tell if they have changed industrial sectors, which measure can be taken as a crude idicator of employer change. If there is an internal labour market system, then the better jobs go to men in the company who by definition are already in the same sector. Only menial jobs would be filled from outside by men either from in or outside the sector. Menial jobs, or those lower in the occupational hierarchy, should therefore show more sign of inter-sector changes of employment. In general this is so, with the non-manual and skilled occupational classes having around three-quarters of its current manpower drawn from earlier jobs in the same sector, but only 60 per cent for class VII. The routine non-manual class is one exception to high sectoral recruitment among the non-manual classes: it too falls below 60 per cent. As might be expected, older men are more likely to have changed sector: 42 per cent in the oldest cohort compared with 29 per cent and 28 per cent for the two youngest cohorts. This is not simply a matter of chronological exposure to risk but reflects the decline of primary and old staples sectors as sources of employment which displaced some of their labour force. Compared with flows of *mobility* between class VII and other classes (three-quarters leaving the former) *movement between sectors* is low, at about one-third (and possibly falling). Sectors may therefore constitute 'better' market segments than skill levels.

One final piece of information about career mobility concerns the way respondents found their current jobs. Offered a choice of 'ways in which the job was found', 15 per cent said promotion and a further 5 per cent gave some other reason connected with a move within their employing organisation. Together, these can be seen as reflecting an internal labour market: the figure of 20 per cent being somewhat lower than the unweighted average of 66 per cent for same industry sector. The figure of 20 per cent does not vary much by cohort, except that the men who started work in the 1960s are three or four percentage points lower on the promotion category (but slightly higher on other employer reasons).

Promotion was notably low in primary industry (8 per cent) and high in the new services (21 per cent), while at 11 per cent only old staples had much variation from the norm for 'other internal ways'. In class terms, manual occupations all score low on promotion, while class I in particular scores high with two in five of its members promoted; twice the rate for other non-manuals and eight times that for the manuals. These figures may be taken as suggesting to a small degree an internal labour market, but there is no sign of it expanding among younger workers, and it does not seem to be associated with newer manufacturing or anything other than the upper parts of the new services. Within the limits of the analysis possible, here the conclusion must be an agnostic one.

Career mobility is a very important part of total mobility. Although in this chapter it has been presented in terms of other arguments, which may have given an impression that as a process in its own right it was less significant, that is not the case. On average, there is as much mobility in the course of careers as there is in intergenerational terms to first job. Unfortunately, because of variable career length, it is more difficult to be precise about this or to talk about trends.

What has been shown is that, by and large, the picture of mobility in terms of changes and sectors is similar whatever the point in career that is under analysis. This is important because it justifies the attention paid earlier to first job trends as mobility indicators. The *level* of mobility changes as careers develop but the *structure* holds true. If anything is changing it is the increase in access, particularly by the direct route, to non-manual employment which shows up as increasingly high rates of non-manual self-recruitment and upward mobility in early career. Younger men in the non-manual class are twice as likely never to have directly experienced the manual working class (as family or own employment) as older men. The sons of non-manual workers not only have a better chance of getting non-manual jobs, but the analysis of career mobility shows that they get them earlier in their careers as well.

However, this is not yet accompanied by a decrease in indirect access. Whether educated or not, the flows into non-manual jobs after initial employment remain high, although the youthfulness of the youngest cohort makes this a tentative conclusion. There is no sign of a counterbalance effect.

Career mobility has also been used to show that the deskilling argument has not produced the labour substitution that would be expected following Braverman's thesis. To the extent that there is a 'deskilling', it can be explained by sectoral shift (hardly a managerial strategy) and the resorting of young workers in their early careers – which equally needs no elaborate theory to explain it. We have also seen that, in so far as unskilled male workers can be regarded as part of a secondary labour force, the evidence for a dual labour market is rather thin. It must be conceded that a failure to locate segmentation may simply reflect a failure of operationalisation, but the author's view is that a substantial phenomenon should be sufficiently robust to survive the methods used in this chapter. Certainly a sector effect was visible on these terms, so that rather than abandoning segmented labour market models it is necessary to argue for modification towards a sectoral rather than a simple skill level approach. In this chapter, as in earlier ones, we find that a model of segmentation – whether of labour markets or mobility – based on skill or class alone is less satisfactory than one combining *several* dimensions of segmentation, most notably the industrial sector.

8 Mobility and Social Class

Mobility studies are often criticised for being merely historical, which is to say that they describe the processes affecting past stages in careers. However, while this may not predict future trends, it is precisely these past processes which create today's patterns. A class consists of men aged 65 with fifty years experience of employment, as well as the newest recruits in their teens. Indeed, perhaps a more substantial criticism of mobility studies would be that they have *not* been historical enough, because they have not been grounded in the economic changes that have led to the emergence of modern society.

In Scotland, the combination of a conservative tradition of capital export on the part of the capitalist class, a weak home consumer market due to low wage levels, a reliance on declining export markets which previously had seen little competition, and the relative physical isolation of the country, delayed the introduction of new technology and new products until after the Second World War. As a result, the type of employment available was decidedly less 'modern' than in England as a whole until relatively recent years. It is within this framework of occupational opportunities that the men in the Scottish Mobility Study began their careers.

Whatever their intentions, their employment depended on industrial expansion and contraction, and the demand for labour to fill particular types of job. To put it in Weberian terms, the market on which they sold their labour was determined both by the supply of sellers *and* the demand of industrial buyers, while their individual capacities to sell were further constrained by the family backgrounds from which they came. Their various class situations on first entering the labour market went a long way to deciding subsequent life chances: once in employment, only a limited range of other occupations will be typically available, i.e. the chances of further mobility are restricted. The demand side of the market relationship has been largely ignored in more recent class analyses.

This is one of the reasons why it is important to link mobility analysis, with its inevitable interest in class, to historical locations and theories of social change. The expansion and contraction of sectors and occupations is more complex than generally accepted by both Marxist and post-industrial society theorists. While there is, in the broadest terms, a growth of white collar work, we saw in Chapters 3 and 5 how the components of that growth change at different rates, go into reverse, or fluctuate according to contemporary sectoral shifts. Only by taking these into account can we explain mobility and class patterns.

Thus within a general tendency to expand the numbers of non-manual jobs across all sectors, some sectors increase their employment of managers and professionals, while others relied on semi-professionals and higher technicians. The organisation and technical processes of sectors differ, and so do their mixes of labour. At the same time, the relative size of the sectors is crucial, with the new services increasingly dominating the market for new non-manual employments. Around 1960, this latter sectoral shift effect seems to have replaced the wider up-grading of skills as the dominant factor in early career mobility prospects.

It has also been possible to identify the effects of global events like the war and the Depression. Interestingly, mobility for young men is not closed off by recession or industrial decline, although it tends to be greater in days of expansion. Nor does the creation of non-manual jobs per se automatically increase mobility, although the two are commonly associated. While we have been emphasising the demand side, supply is also determined by what we have loosely called the rules of recruitment. If we wish to describe mobility, we can do so with a fair degree of accuracy by using occupation and sectors as variables and treating the *net* effect of any changes in recruitment rules as zero. That is not to say the rules never change or cannot make a difference, but rather that in the present analysis they have been given a lower status in the argument and less attention because several rule changes seem either small or cancel one another out.

In particular, credentialism as a process of recruitment seems to be a much more limited and later phenomenon than usually believed. Many men who have been upwardly mobile over a long distance have few or no formal qualifications, and a substantial proportion of upper middle class sons have been downwardly mobile despite a successful education. This situation seems to be changing, as overall levels of qualified manpower rise and the new employment opportunities are increasingly concentrated in the service sector where qualifications have always been a more relevant factor.

Although Scotland does have a very different education system, it seems unlikely that this finding is uniquely Scottish. Indeed, despite the emphasis on specifically Scottish historical conditions, the general model – if not the exact detail of the findings – should be applicable to any other modern industrial society including England. Whereas recent comparative analyses have seen forms of government such as Social Democracy as causes of differences in national rates of mobility, the logic of the present study is that a comparison of economic structures would be a more fruitful method. The relative size, and the time of growth, of sectors may prove a better explanation of national differences.

For example, England and Wales have a labour force which is slightly more non-manual than Scotland's, although the differences, particularly in the manufacturing sector, have been diminishing. One would therefore expect not just broad similarities but that the differences in mobility would be located in the sectors which also differ. The South East of England, with its concentration of services is likely to be less like Scotland than the North which has shared much of the Scottish experience over a longer period.

Despite the early emphasis on the disadvantages of Scotland's economy and the levelling off of mobility chances, the other overriding finding must be the high levels of occupational fluidity, which are shared by England and Wales. The apparent paradox is partly caused by taking different measures of mobility, and partly by the fact that more than one process seems to be taking place. On the one hand, the manual/non-manual divide is not being reduced (certainly at first job) and the manual working class tends to be increasingly self-recruited. This is associated with decreasing downward mobility from the non-manual class and no improvement in relative mobility rates. On the other hand, those sons of manual workers who do escape (and in absolute terms this is a substantial number) may do so by obtaining access over a long distance in the occupational hierarchy, while movements *within* both the manual and non-manual classes are considerable. If one's theoretical concern leads to a class dichotomy, then the former is important, whereas an interest in smaller classes or status groups will direct attention to the higher level of occupational fluidity over seven classes.

Whichever may be the case, it will still be necessary to reconceptualise the basic models of class structure as they apply to modern Britain. High levels of occupational fluidity need to be theorised into existing frameworks. The convenient models of threshold, buffer zone, and increasing constriction, do not deal with a real world in which a third or more of the members of the middle classes come from outside.

This is particularly true for the upper middle class of managers and professionals who have been singled out by a number of writers as the key feature of modern society. The evidence suggests that this is a relatively open class, whose members are not as yet secure in passing their advantages to their sons or successful in exercising closure. The sharpest disjunction in the study is between this class and the elite rather than between the upper middle class and the rest of society. How the upper middle class can exercise its powers and capitalise on its position is not yet clear, given its transient membership. The mobility factor means that simple positional or functional arguments do not work because there is an interaction between the structure of inequality and the actor's own past experiences.

Some of these findings reinforce recent conclusions about mobility in England and Wales, derived from a more traditional framework. This is to be expected because the occupational emphasis in the Scottish study does not abandon the basic tools of mobility and class analysis. On the contrary, it has been possible to offer *explanations* of mobility rates, couched in terms of advanced capitalism or post-industrial society, rather than ascribing rates of mobility to generalised workings of class politics. In other words, we have been able to go beyond mobility to see how occupational and sectoral transition lie at the heart of any understanding of modern society, and how mobility itself needs to be cast in such a historical framework before we can come to grips with the dynamics of social class.

Appendix Methodological Details

THE RECREATION OF SOCIO-ECONOMIC GROUP TIME-SERIES

The generation of the time-series is onerous rather than difficult, requiring great arithmetical care. It took several man-weeks of work for the author to devise the method and produce the figures, and almost as long for a colleague, John Mackenzie, to replicate the process using the same procedures (incidentally producing identical totals). The prefaces to the reports and, later, the classifications of occupations give a great deal of guidance about modifications of definitions (the 1961 Census General Report (HMSO, 1968a, pp. 184–93) is particularly useful). The author also discussed his time-series with personnel at Titchfield and Edinburgh who had long experience of occupational coding, to mutual agreement on the interpretations made. The essence of the comparability problem lies in the changes to classifications in 1951 (1921 and 1931 are very similar) and again in 1961 (1961 and 1971 are also very similar at an occupational level). The method adopted was to take each entry in the early tables and to search for its closest equivalent in the *Classification of Occupations, 1970* (HMSO, 1971b). In the vast majority of cases the same titles occurred in both; for example 'rivetter' can be found in both, even if the specific work tasks have evolved in the interim (code 146 in 1921 and code 021 in 1971). The 1921 rivetter can then be allocated to the same SEG as his 1971 equivalent by consulting the SEG listings at the rear of the *Classification of Occupations, 1970*. Fortunately, the earlier *published* tables use a more detailed listing of occupations than do modern reports; 1921 has over 900 occupational categories, reducing to 600 in 1951 and around 200 in 1961. Thus the data are presented in greater precision for the tables requiring modification, with over 900 row entries in an occupational table running to nearly forty foolscap pages for the national level count. (See HMSO (1921), *Census of Scotland 1921. Occupation and Industries Report*, pp. 12–50). This wealth of information for the early years makes it easier to identify equivalents and to aggregate accurately into the 1970 SEGs.

One limitation to this process concerned managers. The tables do not distinguish between managers of large and small operations. This distinction in the later tables was therefore abandoned to maintain comparability at the expense of detail. The result may be to inflate the number of 'real' managers with wide responsibilities (which would bias the evidence against the line of argument proposed above by the author). After 1921, tables show managerial status cross-tabulated against occupation, so that there is a check against any person exercising managerial functions being omitted because the word 'manager' was not part of their main job title.

The same cross-referencing is possible for foremen and supervisors from

1931 on, while 'working on own account' is a concept used throughout (SEG 12 in 1971). SEG 11, unskilled manual work, consists of jobs insufficiently specified to warrant a title: it is possible that amalgamating 'labourers' and 'other workers' may, with the reclassification of 1951 and 1961, produce some artefactual error in the boundaries between unskilled and semi-skilled manual workers (SEG 10).

In all cases, the data refer to the population in or seeking work. This condition, which later Censuses refer to as 'economically active' excludes those in full-time education or who are retired, but includes the unemployed. It is thus not responsive to short-term cyclical changes in employment such as the Depression of 1931, except to the extent that people may record themselves as workers in an occupation which in fact is a temporary expedient job, taken because they are unemployed in their main occupation. The time-series, in other words, refers to an amalgam of characteristics of the labour force and the occupational opportunities, rather than to one or the other. Clearly the time-series must be used with caution. But at the level of SEGs (i.e. in practice subdivision into fourteen categories) the degree of precision required is not as great as if one used many more categories. Surprisingly, few occupations per se are added or subtracted from the listings: 'crofter-fishermen' and 'crofter-farmers' were amalgamated in 1961 into 'crofters', for instance, and 'computer programmer' was added in 1951. It is this continuity, together with the greater detail of the earlier reports, which provides the solid basis for the development of the time-series.

One critic has objected to this kind of analysis, arguing that the changes in categorisation between censuses makes it impossible to reconstruct a valid time-series, and (more surprisingly) that the whole enterprise of testing occupational transition in the Britain of this century is misguided. Jones (1977) invokes Mitchell and H. Jones's comment on the changes between 1951 and 1961 as evidence that a time-series cannot be established 'even between fairly large aggregates of occupational codes'. However, the original statement runs to several tightly argued pages (Mitchell and H. Jones, 1971, pp. 184-93) the main thrust of which is that direct comparison of the 1951 and 1961 Census class tables is not possible. Indeed, the General Report of the 1961 Census contains a comparison based on a reclassification, which indicates that the census statisticians themselves were satisfied that a time-series was feasible, provided it was not based on a simplistic reading of the basic occupational tables with different systems of classification.

In the second place, the quotation used by Jones refers to a table which lists 260 occupational aggregates organised into about 70 larger aggregates, which in turn are aggregated into 29 even larger occupational blocks. In this context, what do 'fairly large aggregates of occupational codes' (Mitchell and Jones, 1971, p. 36) mean: the 260, the 70, or the 29? The same section refers to some of the occupational units (the 260) as 'larger', so it is not at all clear that the Report is referring even to the 29 occupational orders. Jones has made two errors of interpretation here: the size of grouping which can be compared is much smaller than he implies, and neither Mitchell and Jones, nor the General Report, are referring to the much larger 14 SEG's which are used here.

However, the data refer to women who by the census definition are employed full-time. Part-timers are excluded, and information is not available to quantify this extra labour: one estimate based on tables 1 and 24 of the *1961*

Appendix Methodological Details

Census Scotland Occupational Report shows about 85 per cent of women in paid employment listing themselves as full time. Women out of paid work under-register themselves as unemployed: it is possible that they also under-list themselves as economically active (i.e. looking for work) in the census returns. Unfortunately, as more women have taken paid employment towards the end of our time-series, this potential error factor would have a differential effect during the fifty years. The present analysis is, of course, not unique in suffering from this defect, although by reporting men and women separately one source of confusion is contained. Implicit in this analysis is the idea that a woman in paid work takes on an independent occupational identity, i.e. that she should not be classified as belonging to her husband's occupational category. This seems self-evident for purposes of labour market analysis, but is more problematic when occupational categories are presented as classes.

Unfortunately, the very complex changes that underlie the 1981 Census classification make it impossible to present a straightforward comparison between 1971 and 1981. One partial source can be found in the rather different set of categories used by Elias (1985). In general terms, a preliminary analysis of the UK data seems to suggest that managerial, professional, supervisory and highly technical occupations continue to increase for males, while skilled and other manual occupations, together with clerical and sales work, decline. For women, the increases are similar, but there is no decline in clerical or sales occupations (Elias, 1985, pp. 20–1). At the crudest level, it seems likely that the continuation of our time-series would show 'more of the same'.

THE CLASS CATEGORIES

The analysis of movements is based on a class system consisting of seven broad categories, as indicated in Table A.1.

Table A.1 The Scottish Mobility Study class schema

Class	Cats	Composition	Size
I	1–4	Professionals, large managers and proprietors, senior supervisory staff	13.5
II	5–8	Semi professionals, technicians, small managers, small proprietors	13.4
III	9–10 12–13	Lower technicians, self-employed artisans, supervisors of manual workers	13.4
IV	14	Routine non-manual workers	7.7
V	11:15–16	Skilled manual employees	20.7
VI	17–18	Semi-skilled manual employees	16.3
VII	19–20	Unskilled manual employees	14.1

Appendix Methodological Details

Each of the 124 occupational groups of the Hope–Goldthorpe Scale was amalgamated into one of twenty categories on the basis of their scale scores and employment status. The latter was seen as central to the construction of the scale, so that with the exception of 2.7 per cent of cases, managers were not merged with employees, or supervisors with the self-employed, and so on. Then the twenty categories were taken in sequential blocks according to their mean scale value.

This created a scale which was based on the simple premise that employment status was central to the ranking exercise, and which retains the basic ranking of the Hope–Goldthorpe scale. It avoids most of the arbitrary disjunctions and combinations in Goldthorpe's class schema. Further details can be found in Payne *et al.*, 1976, or from the author.

THE SCOTTISH MOBILITY STUDY SAMPLE

The Scottish Mobility Study was based on a sample of male Scots aged 20 to 64 and resident in Scotland in 1975. The sample (which was designed in consultation with Graham Kalton) covered the whole of the country, except for Orkney, Shetland, and the Outer Isles, i.e. 98.7 per cent of the population. Sixty-eight urban and landward areas with electorates of over 6000 were treated as a continuous systematic random sample, yielding 68.8 per cent of the total. In 'rural' areas, a cluster sample of seventy-three units of approximately twenty-five names was drawn, having been stratified by county. The effect of a probability proportionate to size sample was that 'rural' often meant small market towns.

The overall completion rate was 81.9 per cent, calculated as follows:

Original draw		17 022
Less females	9090	
Less males too old	1257	
Less males too young	315	
	10 662	
Less dead at 1 April 1974	123	
Less moved before 1 April 1974	215	
(no replacement available)	338	
Less allowance for above against non-contacts (24.1% of 217)	52	
Total discards, etc.	11 052	
Total possible interviews:		5970
Not interviewed:		
Moved, failed to locate	264 (4.4%)	
Non-contacts (assumed to be right age, etc.)	165 (2.8%)	
Interviewed but appropriated by market research agency	75 (1.3%)	

Too ill	48 (0.8%)
Refusals	513 (8.6%)
Other incomplete	18 (0.3%)
	1083
Interviewed	4887
	= 81.9%

The response rate exceeded 70 per cent in every constituency, although central Glasgow was marginally less well represented than elsewhere. The fieldwork was carried out in Summer 1974 and Spring 1975, with great care taken over briefing, editing and coding (done twice, separately, in all cases). Fuller details are available from the author on request. The dataset consisting of 4887 respondent records is available from the ESRC Data Archive, University of Essex, or the Research Centre for the Social Science, University of Edinburgh.

Notes

4 Occupational Fluidity and Class Structure

1. Log-linear analyses of the SMS data using various combinations of classes and cohorts by Anderson (1976) and Ulas (1983) show similar results to those of Hauser *et al.* (1975a, 1975b), namely, that once structural change has been accounted for, a satisfactory model can be fitted without requiring a term to allow for changes in mobility rates.

5 Trends in Occupational Mobility

1. Secondary industry consists of SIC (HMSO, 1968b) standard orders 3–19 (basically manufacturers of food; drink; tobacco; chemicals; metals; mechanical, electrical instruments and engineering; shipbuilding; vehicles; metal goods; textiles; clothing; construction materials; timber; paper and printing). Tertiary industry consists of standard orders 20–7 (basically construction; utilities; transport and communication; distribution; finance and commerce; professional and scientific services; public administration and defence).
2. The staples are taken as SIC minimal list headings 101–9, 261–3, 311–23, 370, 411–29 and 481–9. The remaining manufacturing industries 'light industry' – are 211–499, excluding the staples.

   The knowledge industries are minimal list headings 860–906, while 'basic services' (i.e. construction, transport, distribution and public utilities) are 500–832. Other primary industry is omitted.

6 Education and Mobility

1. Many of the ideas in this chapter stem from long conversations with Graeme Ford and Marion Ulas, both of whom have written on aspects of the mobility data and education (Ulas, 1983; Ford *et al.*, 1975; Payne *et al.*, 1979).
2. In other words, the trend data in the previous chapter refer to first jobs, and jobs ten years after starting work. As an indication of the pattern for the respondents' latest jobs, the upward mobility rates over seven classes for the four ten-year birth cohorts from 1909 were 35.6 per cent, 42.3 per cent, 49.0 per cent and 44.8 per cent. Downward mobility was 37.9 per cent, 28.3 per cent, 26.0 per cent and 24.4 per cent respectively. This point is developed in the next chapter.

Bibliography

ANDERSON, A. (1976) *A Loglinear Model of Changing Mobility Rates in the Scottish Mobility Study.* Working Paper no. 10, SMS, University of Aberdeen (unpub).
ANDERSON, M. (1974) 'Sociological Research Activity in Scotland', paper read at the British Association Meeting (Section N), University of Stirling, Sept.
BAIN, G. *et al.* (1972) 'The Labour Force', in Halsey, A. H. (ed.), *Trends in British Society since 1900.* London: Macmillan.
BECHHOFER, F. (1969) 'Occupations', in Stacy, M. (ed.), *Comparability in Social Research.* London: Heinemann.
BLAU, P. and DUNCAN, O. (1967) *The American Occupational Structure.* New York: Wiley.
BOTTOMORE, T. (1965) *Classes in Modern Society.* London: Allen & Unwin.
BRAVERMAN, H. (1974) *Labour and Monopoly Capitalism.* New York: Monthly Press Review.
BROWN, A. J. (1969) 'Some English Thoughts on the Scottish Economy', *Scottish Journal of Political Economy*, Nov.
BROWN, G. (1975) *The Red Paper on Scotland.* Edinburgh: EUSBP.
BROWN, R. K. (1978) 'Work', in P. Abrams (ed.) *Work, Urbanism and Inequality.* London: Weidenfeld & Nicolson.
BRYDEN, J. (1979) 'Core-Periphery, Problems – the Scottish Case', in Seers, D. *et al.* (eds) q.v.
BUCHANAN, K. (1968) 'The Revolt Against Satellisation in Scotland and Wales', *Monthly Review*, vol. 19.
BUDGE, I. and URWIN, D. (1966) *Scottish Political Behaviour.* London: Longmans.
BURNHAM, J. (1945) *The Managerial Revolution.* Harmondsworth: Penguin.
BUTTERWORTH, E. and WEIR, D. (eds) (1984) *The New Sociology of Modern Britain.* London: Fontana.
CAIRNCROSS, A. K. (ed.) (1954) *The Scottish Economy.* Cambridge: Cambridge University Press.
CAMPBELL, R. M. (1965) *Scotland Since 1707.* Oxford: Oxford University Press.
CHAPMAN, A. D. (1984) 'Patterns of Occupational Mobility Amongst Men and Women in Scotland, 1930–1970', PhD Thesis, CNAA, Plymouth Polytechnic.
COLE, G. D. H. and POSTGATE, R. (1961) *The Common People.* London: Methuen.
CROMPTON, R. (1980) 'Class Mobility and Modern Britain', *Sociology*, vol. 14, no. 1.
CROMPTON, R. and JONES, G. (1984) *White Collar Proletariate.* London: Macmillan.

Bibliography

CROSLAND, A. (1956) *The Future of Socialism*. London: Cape.
CRUICKSHANK, K. and McMANUS, C. (1976) 'Getting into Medicine', *New Society*, 15 Jan.
DAHRENDORF, R. (1964) 'Recent Changes in the Class Structure of European Societies', *Daedalus*, vol. 93, Winter.
DEAN, P. and COLE, W. (1962) *British Economic Growth 1968-1959*. Cambridge: Cambridge University Press.
DICKSON, T. (ed.) (1980) *Scottish Capitalism*. London: Lawrence & Wishart.
ELIAS, P. (1985) 'Changes in Occupational Structure, 1971-1981', paper read at Edinburgh Survey Methodology Group Seminar, Edinburgh, Feb.
ERIKSON, C. (1972) *Invisible Immigrants*. London: Weidenfeld & Nicolson.
FIRN, J. (1975) 'External Control and Regional Policy', in G. Brown (ed.) q.v.
FLOUD, J. and HALSEY, A. (1958) 'The Sociology of Education', *Current Sociology*, vol. 7, no. 3.
FLOUD, J. and HALSEY, A. (1961) 'Introduction', in A. H. Halsey, J. Floud and L. A. Anderson, *Education, Economy and Society*. London: Collier-Macmillan.
FORD, G., PAYNE, G. and ROBERTSON, C. (1975) 'Education and Mobility in Scotland: The Institutional Framework of the Schools', paper read at SSRC Internal Seminar on Mobility, University of Aberdeen, Sept.
FURNESS, K. (1981) 'Workplace, Community and the "Crisis" of Clydeside's Political Economy during the First World War', paper presented at BSA (Scotland) Conference, Aberdeen, March (xerox).
GALBRAITH, J. K. (1967) *The New Industrial State*. London: Hamish Hamilton.
GARNSEY, E. (1975) 'Occupational Structure in Industrial Societies', *Sociology*, vol. 3, no. 3.
GIDDENS, A. (1974) 'Elites in the British Class Structure', in Stanworth, P. and Giddens, A. q.v.
GIDDENS, A. and MACKENZIE (eds) (1982) *Social Class and the Division of Labour*. London: Cambridge University Press.
GIROD, D. V. *et al.* (1977) 'The Other Road: the role of vocational training in the process of achievement', paper presented at the ISA Research Conference on Social Stratification, Dublin, April (xerox).
GLASS, D.V. (ed.) (1954) *Social Mobility in Britain*. London: Routledge & Kegan Paul.
GLYNN, S. and OXBORROW, J. (1976) *Interwar Britain*. London: Allen & Unwin.
GOLDTHORPE, J. (1980a) *Social Mobility and Class Structure in Modern Britain*. Oxford: Oxford University Press (with C. Llewellyn and C. Payne).
GOLDTHORPE, J. (1980b) 'Reply to Crompton', *Sociology*, vol. 14, no. 1, Feb.
GOLDTHORPE, J. (1982) 'On the Service Class', in Giddens, A. and Mackenzie, G. (eds) q.v.
GRAY, J., MACPHERSON, A. and RAFFE, D. (1982) *Reconstruction of Secondary Education*. London: Routledge & Kegan Paul.
HALSEY, A. H. *et al.* (1980) *Origins and Destinations*. Oxford: Oxford University Press.

Bibliography

HANHAM, H. J. (1969) *Scottish Nationalism*. London: Faber.
HARGEAVE, A. (1971) 'Economy and Industry', in Glen, D. (ed.) *Whither Scotland*. London: Gollancz.
HARVIE, C. (1977) *Scotland and Nationalism*. London: Allen & Unwin.
HAUSER, R. et al. (1975a) 'Temporal Change in Occupational Mobility', *ASR*, vol. 40, June.
HAUSER, R. et al. (1975b) 'Structural Change in Occupational Mobility Among Men in the US', *ASR*, vol. 40, Oct.
HECHTER, M. (1975) *Internal Colonialism*. London: Routledge & Kegan Paul.
HIGHET, J. (1960) *The Scottish Churches*. London: Skeffington.
HMSO (1921) and (1931), (1951a), (1961) *Census of Scotland, 1921. Occupations and Industries Report*. Edinburgh: HMSO.
HMSO (1951b) *Census of Scotland, 1951: General Report*. vol. III. Edinburgh: HMSO.
HMSO (1966) *Gazetteer of Place Names*. Sample Census. Edinburgh: HMSO.
HMSO (1967) *Scottish Administration* (rev. edn). Edinburgh: HMSO.
HMSO (1968a) *Census of Great Britain, 1961. General Report*. London: HMSO.
HMSO (1968b) *Standard Industrial Classification*. London: HMSO.
HMSO (1971a) *Census of Great Britain, 1971, General Report*. vol. 1. London: HMSO.
HMSO (1971b) *The Classification of Occupations, 1970*. London: HMSO.
HMSO (1971c) *Census of Great Britain. Economic Activity. Tables Pt. IV*. London: HMSO.
HMSO (1971d) *British Labour Statistics Historical Abstract 1886–1968*. London: Department of Employment.
HMSO (1980) *People in Britain*, OPCS/GRO. London: HMSO.
HOBSBAWM, E. (1969) *Industry and Empire*, Harmondsworth, Penguin.
HOPE, K. (1984) *As Others See Us*. London: Cambridge University Press.
HOPE, K. and GOLDTHORPE, J. (1974) *The Social Grading of Occupations*. Oxford: Oxford University Press.
HUNT, A. (ed.) (1977) *Class and Class Structure*. London: Lawrence & Wishart.
JACKSON, F. T. (1968) *The Enterprising Scot*. Edinburgh: Edinburgh University Press.
JOHNSON, T. et al. (1971) *The Structure and Growth of the Scottish Economy*. London: Collins.
JONES, T. (1977) 'Occupational Transition in Advanced Industrial Societies – A Reply', *Sociological Review*, vol. 25, no. 2.
KELLAS, J. (1968) *Modern Scotland*. London: Pall Mall.
KELLY, A. (1976) *Family Background, Subject Specialisation and Occupational Recruitment of Scottish University Students*. Edinburgh: Centre for Educational Sociology (xerox).
KENDRICK, S. (1986) 'Occupational Change in Modern Scotland', in McCrone, D. (1986) (ed.), *The Scottish Government Yearbook 1986*. Edinburgh: University of Edinburgh.
KENDRICK, S. and McCRONE, D. (1981) 'The National Level of Analysis', paper read at BSA Scotland Conference, Aberdeen, March.

KENDRICK, S., McCRONE, D. and BECHHOFER, F. (1982a) *Education and Social Mobility*. Working Paper No. 3, Social Structure of Modern Scotland Project, University of Edinburgh (xerox).
KENDRICK, S., McCRONE, D. and BECHHOFER, F. (1982b) *Industrial and Occupational Structure*. Working Paper No. 2, Social Structure of Modern Scotland Project, University of Edinburgh (xerox).
KENDRICK, S., McCRONE, D. and BECHHOFER, F. (1983) 'Scotland is British', paper read at BSA Conference, Cardiff, April (xerox).
KENT, R. (1980) 'A Survey of Empirical Sociological Research on Scotland', paper read BA Conference, Stirling, April.
KERR, A. J. C. (1962) *Schools of Scotland*. Glasgow: MacLellan.
KING, R. *et al.* (1981) *The Middle Class*. London: Longmans.
LEE, C. H. (1979) *British Regional Employment Statistics 1841–1971*. Cambridge: Cambridge University Press.
LEE, D. (1981) 'Skill, Craft and Class', *Sociology*, vol. 15, no. 1.
LEE, G. (1981) *Who Gets to the Top?* Aldershot: Gower.
LENMAN, B. (1977) *An Economic History of Modern Scotland*. London: Batsford.
LENSKI, G. E. (1966) *Power and Privilege*. New York: McGraw-Hill.
LESSER, C. E. V. and SILVEY, H. (1950) 'Scottish Industries during the Inter-War Period', *The Manchester School of Economic and Social Studies*, vol. XVIII, May.
LITTLE, A. and WESTERGAARD, J. (1964) 'The Trends of Class Differentials in Education Opportunity in England and Wales', *BJS*, vol. 15.
LOVERIDGE, R. and MOK, A. (1979) *Theories of Labour Market Segmentation* The Hague, Martinus Nijhoff.
LYTHE, S. *The Economy of Scotland in its European Setting 1550–1625*. Edinburgh: Oliver & Boyd.
MACKAY, G. (1973) 'Scotland', in Broady, M. (ed.), *Marginal Regions: Essays in Social Planning*. London: Bedford Square Press.
MACPHERSON, A. (1958) *Eleven Year Olds Grow Up*. London: University of London Press.
McCRONE, D. (1965) *Scotland's Economic Progress 1951–1960*. London: Allen & Unwin.
McEWAN, J. (1975) 'Highland Landlordism', in Brown, G. (ed.) q.v.
MARSHALL, T. H. (1965) *Class, Citizenship and Social Development*. New York: Doubleday, Anchor Press.
MAXWELL, J. (1969) *Sixteen Years On*. London: University of London Press.
MILIBAND, R. (1969) *The State in Capitalist Society*. London: Weidenfeld & Nicolson.
MILLER, S. M. (1960) 'Comparative Social Mobility', *Current Sociology*, vol. 9.
MILLS, C. W. (1963) 'A Marx for the Managers', in Horowitz, I. L. (ed.), *Power, Politics and People*. London: Oxford University Press.
MITCHELL, B. and JONES, H. (1971) *Second Abstract of British Historical Statistics*. Cambridge: Cambridge University Press.
MOORE, W. E. (1974) *Social Change*. Englewood Cliffs, N.J.: Prentice Hall, (1963, 1974).

MORTON, J. (1975) 'Two Scotlands', *New Society*, 10 April.
NAIRN, T. (1977) *The Break Up of Britain*. London: New Left Books.
NICHOLS, T. (1969) *Ownership, Control and Ideology*. London: Allen & Unwin.
NOBLE, T. (1980) *Modern Britain* (2nd edn) London: Batsford.
OFFE, C. (1976) *Industry and Inequality*. London: Edward Arnold.
PAGE, E. (1978) 'Michael Hechter's Internal Colonialism Thesis: Some Theoretical & Methodological Problems', *European Journal of Political Research*, vol. 6.
PAHL, R. and WINKLER, J. (1974) 'The Economic Elite', in Stanworth, P. and Giddens, A. q.v.
PARKIN, F. (1971) *Class Inequality and Political Order*. London: MacGibbon & Kee.
PARSLER, R. (ed.) (1980) *Capitalism, Class and Politics in Scotland*. Aldershot: Gower.
PATON, M. J. (1968) *The Claim of Scotland*. London: Allen & Unwin.
PAYNE, G. (1973) 'Typologies of Middle Class Mobility', *Sociology*, vol. 7, no. 3.
PAYNE, G. (1977a) 'Occupation Transition in Advanced Industrial Societies', *Sociological Review*, vol. 25, no. 1.
PAYNE, G. (1977b) 'Understanding Occupational Transition', *Sociological Review*, vol. 25, no. 2.
PAYNE, G. (1986) *Mobility and Change in Modern Society*. London: Macmillan.
PAYNE, G., FORD, G. and ROBERTSON, C. (1975) 'Social Mobility in a Scottish Context', paper at SSRC International Seminar on Occupational Mobility, Aberdeen, Sept.
PAYNE, G., FORD, G. and ROBERTSON, C. (1976) 'Changes in Occupational Mobility in Scotland', *Scottish Journal of Sociology*, vol. 1, no. 1.
PAYNE, G. and FORD, G. (1977a) 'Social Mobility in the Upper Echelons', BSA Conference, Sheffield, March.
PAYNE, G. and FORD, G. (1977b) 'The Lieutenant Class', *New Society*, vol. 41, no. 772.
PAYNE, G. and FORD, G. (1977c) 'Occupational Mobility and Educational Process in Scotland', paper presented to ISA Research Conference on Social Stratification, Dublin, April.
PAYNE, G. *et al.* (1979) *Education and Social Mobility*. SIP Occasional Papers No. 8, Edinburgh.
PAYNE, G. *et al.* (1980) 'Occupational Change and Social Mobility in Scotland since the First World War', in Gaskin, M. (ed.), *The Political Economy of Tolerable Survival*. London: Croom Helm.
PAYNE, G. and FORD, G. (1983) 'The Occupational Dimension', in Brown, G. (ed.), *Scotland: The Real Divide*. Edinburgh: Mainstream Press.
PAYNE, G. *et al.* (1983a) 'Trends in Female Social Mobility', in Gamarnikow, E. *et al.* (eds) *Gender, Class and Work*. London: Heinemann.
PAYNE, G. *et al.* (1983b) 'Employment and Mobility in Peripheral Regions', paper read at BSA Conference, Cardiff, April (xerox).
PELLING, H. (1963) *A History of British Trade Unionism*. Harmondsworth: Penguin.

POLLARD, G. (1972) *The Development of the British Economy 1914-67* (2nd edn) London: Edward Arnold.
POULANTZAS, N. (1973) *Political Power and Social Classes*. London: New Left Books.
RAFFE, D. (1981) *Education, the Tightening Bond and Social Mobility*, BSA Conference, Aberystwyth, April.
RALLINGS, C. and LEE, A. N. (1980) 'Politics of the Periphery: The Case of Cornwall', ECPR Conference, Brussels.
REX, J. (1974) 'Capitalism, Elites and the Ruling Class', in Stanworth P. and Giddens, A. q.v.
RICHMOND, A. (1969) 'Migration in Industrial Societies', in Jackson, J. A., *Migration*. Cambridge: Cambridge University Press.
RIDGE, J. (1974) *Mobility in Britain Reconsidered*. Oxford: Oxford University Press.
ROUTH, G. (1965) *Occupations and Pay in Great Britain 1906-60*. Cambridge: Cambridge University Press.
ROUTH, G. (1980) *Occupation and Pay in Great Britain* (2nd edn). London: Macmillan.
SCASE, R. (1976) 'A Review of "Class in a Capitalist Society"', *Sociology*, vol. 10, no. 3.
SCOTT, J. & HUGHES, M. (1975) 'Ownership and Control in a Satellite Economy', *Economy*, vol. 10, no. 3.
SCOTT, J. and HUGHES, M. (1980) *The Anatomy of Scottish Capitalism*. London: Croom Helm.
SEERS, D., SCHAFFER, B. and KILJUNEN, M. (eds) (1979) *Underdeveloped Europe*. Hassocks: Harvester Press.
SLAVEN, A. (1975) *The Development of the West of Scotland 1750-1960*. London: Routledge & Kegan Paul.
SMOUT, C. (1963) *Scottish Trade on the Eve of Union 1660-1707*. Edinburgh: Oliver & Boyd.
SOROKIN, P. (1927) *Social Mobility*. New York: Harper & Row.
STANWORTH, P. and GIDDENS, A. (eds) (1974) *Elites and Power in British Society*. London: Cambridge University Press.
STEVENSON, J. (1977) *Social Conditions in Britain Between the Wars*. Harmondsworth: Penguin.
STEWART, A. *et al.* (1980) *Social Stratification and Occupations*. London: Macmillan.
THOMAS, B. (1973) *Migration and Economic Growth* (2nd edn). Cambridge: Cambridge University Press.
TOOTHILL (1961) *Toothill Report* (Inquiry into the Scottish Economy), Scottish Council. Edinburgh: HMSO.
UHLENBERG, P. (1973) 'Non-Economic Determinants of Non-Migrant', *Rural Sociology*, vol. 38, no. 3.
ULAS, M. (1983) 'Trends in Education, Class and Mobility: The Experience of Scottish Males 1925-1975', unpub. M. Phil thesis, Plymouth Polytechnic.
URRY, J. and WAKEFORD, J. (1973) *Power in Britain*. London: Heinemann.
WADE, N. A. (1939) *Post-Primary Education in the Primary Schools of Scotland* London: University of London Press.

WATSON, W. (1964) 'Social Mobility and Social Class in Industrial Communities', in Gluckman, M. (ed.), *Closed Systems and Open Minds*. Edinburgh: Oliver & Boyd.
WESTERGAARD, J. and RESLER, H. (1977) *Class in a Capitalist Society*. Harmondsworth: Penguin.
WRIGHT, E. O. (1978) *Class, Crisis and the State*. London: New Left Books.

Author Index

Abrams, P. 199
Anderson, A. 198, 199
Anderson, L. A. 200
Anderson, M. 11, 199

Bain, G. 36, 199
Bechhofer, F. 36, 199. 202
Bell, D. 114
Bendix, R. 126
Blau, P. 32, 122, 199
Bottomore, T. 61, 78, 79, 82, 83, 87, 199
Braverman, H. 46, 47, 58, 171, 173, 175, 177, 179, 180, 181, 188, 199
Brown, A. J. 33, 199
Brown, G. 199
Brown, R. K. xi, 36, 140, 199
Bryden, J. 9, 199
Buchanan, K. 9, 199
Budge, J. 199
Burnham, J. 80, 199
Butterworth, E. 8, 199

Cairncross, A. K. 12, 199
Calder, A. 99
Campbell, R. M. 15, 16, 199
Carter, M. xi
Chapman, A. D. 5, 199
Cole, G. D. H. 99, 199
Cole, W. 52, 200
Crompton, R. 93, 177, 181, 199
Crosland, A. 80, 200
Cruikshank, K. 84, 200

Dahrendorf, R. 81, 82, 200
Deane, P. 52, 200
Dickson, T. 9, 33, 200
Duncan, O. 32, 122, 199

Elias, P. 195, 200
Erikson, C. 32, 200

Firn, J. 24, 200
Floud, J. 124, 125, 136, 200
Ford, G. xi, 11, 129, 170, 183, 198, 200, 203
Furness, K. 178, 200

Galbraith, J. K. 80, 200
Gamarnikow, E. 203
Garnsey, E. 38, 200
Gaskin, M. 203
Giddens, A. 5, 78, 79, 88, 89, 122, 139, 200, 204
Girod, R. 131, 200
Glass, D. V. 60, 61, 68, 73, 74, 80, 89, 94, 124, 125, 126, 127, 200
Glen, D. 201
Gluckman, M. 205
Glynn, S. 18, 19, 22, 200
Goldthorpe, J. M. 6, 34, 36, 55, 60, 61, 62, 78, 81, 82, 88, 93, 94, 134, 140, 154, 155, 156, 157, 158, 170, 177, 196, 200, 201
Gray, J. 124, 200

Halsey, A. H. 31, 122, 124, 125, 136, 154, 200
Hanham, H. J. 10, 11, 16, 201
Hargreave, A. 25, 201
Harvie, C. 15, 19, 23, 24, 201
Hauser, R. 198, 201
Hechter, M. 9, 201
Highet, J. 11, 201
HMSO 11, 12, 13, 30, 36, 193, 198, 201, 204
Hobsbawm, E. 17, 18, 19, 22, 201
Hope, K. 36, 55, 60, 94, 124, 140, 177, 196, 201
Horowitz, I. 202
Hughes, M. 16, 24, 204
Hunt, A. 4, 80, 201

Jackson, F. T. 16, 201
Jencks, C. 134
Johnson, T. 52, 201
Jones, G. 177, 199
Jones, H. 194, 202
Jones, T. 26, 29, 198, 201

Kalton, G. 196
Kellas, J. 10, 11, 30, 201
Kelly, A. 84, 201
Kenrick, S. 9, 10, 20, 21, 26, 28, 30, 33, 37, 53, 54, 124, 140, 174, 201, 202

Author Index

Kent, R. 11, 202
Kerr, A. J. C. 202
Kiljunen, M. 204
King, R. 140, 202

Lee, A. 9, 204
Lee, C. H. 202
Lee, D. 20, 171, 181, 202
Lee, G. 79, 202
Lenski, G. E. 82, 202
Lenman, B. 15, 16, 17, 20, 33, 202
Leser, C. E. V. 29, 98, 202
Little, A. 124, 125, 126, 127, 128, 134, 143, 153, 155, 169, 170, 202
Loveridge, R. 186, 202
Lythe, S. 14, 202

McCrone, D. 9, 19, 201, 202
McEwan, J. 14, 202
Mackay, G. 12, 202
Mackenzie, J. 193, 202
McManus, C. 84, 200
Macpherson, A. 124, 200, 202
Marshall, T. H. 122, 202
Maxwell, J. 124, 202
Miliband, R. 78, 79, 80, 82, 83, 87, 202
Miller, S. M. 80, 81, 202
Mills, C. W. 85, 202
Mitchell, B. 194, 202
Mok, A. 186, 202
Moore, R. xi
Moore, W. E. 35, 36, 40, 45, 52, 52, 115, 118, 126, 202
Morton, J. 12, 203

Nairn, T. 9, 203
Nichols, T. 79, 142, 203
Noble, T. 8, 203

Offe, C. 203
Oxborrow, J. 19, 22, 200

Page, E. 9, 203
Pahl, R. 78, 203
Parkin, F. 5, 61, 75, 76, 77, 89, 122, 203
Parsler, R. 11, 203
Paton, M. 10, 203

Payne, G. xi, 2, 3, 5, 12, 20, 32, 37, 38, 53, 61, 108, 126, 127, 129, 183, 196, 198, 200, 203
Payne, J. xi
Pelling, H. 99, 203
Petrie, C. 162
Pollard, G. 22, 204
Postgate, R. 99, 199
Poulantzas, N. 4, 80, 204

Raffe, D. 122, 137, 200, 204
Rallings, C. 9, 204
Renner, K. 81,
Resler, H. 8, 74, 79, 85, 205
Rex, J. 138, 141, 142, 204
Richmond, A. 32, 204
Ridge, J. 122, 204
Robertson, C. xi, 129, 200, 203
Routh, G. 36, 204

Scaffer, B. 204
Scase, R. 61, 204
Scott, J. 16, 24, 204
Seers, D. 204
Silvey, H. 29, 98, 202
Slaven, A. 15, 18, 20, 23, 24, 204
Smout, C. 14, 204
Sorokin, P. 61, 89, 204
Stanworth, P. 88, 139, 204
Stevenson, J. 22, 204
Stewart, A. 179, 204

Thomas, B. 32, 204

Uhlenberg, P. 32, 204
Ulas, M. 129, 198, 204
Urry, J. 79, 139, 204
Urwin, D. 199

Wade, N. A. 16, 204
Wakeford, J. 79, 139, 204
Watson, W. 32, 142, 205
Weir, D. 8, 199
Westergaard, J. 8, 61, 74, 79, 85, 124, 125, 126, 127, 128, 134, 143, 153, 155, 169, 170, 202, 205
Winkler, J. 78, 203
Wright, E. O. 4, 140, 205

Subject Index

Aberdeen xi, 12, 17
  see also Scottish Mobility Study
accountants 177
Act of Union 11, 14, 33
administration and defence industries 26, 27, 28, 58
administrators, senior 65
AEI 22
agriculture 17, 25, 26, 27, 28, 29, 108, 185
  see also under workers
apprenticeship 42, 45, 94, 134, 170, 171, 172, 175, 181
Argyll Motor Co. 19
armed forces 1, 36, 63, 99
  see also defence
ascription 122
association
  index of trade 11
Australia 17, 30
automation 125, 143, 153
average, moving 94–115, 175, 177

banking 4, 11, 15, 16, 17, 22
BATs 22
BBC 11
Bishops 139
Blackwoods Magazine 17
Border counties 12
bourgoisie 4, 81, 82
Bowater 22
'branch plant' syndome 24, 29
British Journal of Sociology xii
British Maternity Study 124
buffer zone 74, 75, 76, 89, 103, 191
businessmen, small 67, 68, 81
building industry 26, 27, 28, 98
bureaucratisation 125, 143, 153

Canada 30
capital 8, 10, 15, 17, 22, 24, 58, 82, 84, 86, 88, 98, 181, 189
  capital formation 52
Capital 20
capitalism 110, 171
  advanced 2, 9, 192
  modern capitalism 142

monopoly 4
  world 9, 33
capitalist society 9, 80, 81, 87
career 5, 25, 27, 35, 64, 68, 69, 71, 88, 89, 93, 94, 97, 100, 124, 127, 142, 155, 158, 161
career mobility 160
Catholicism 11
cattle breeding 11
census 9, 25, 27, 28, 29, 35, 36, 37, 38, 55, 193, 194, 195
Centre for Educational Sociology 124
charities 11
chemicals industry 15, 98, 112, 186, 198
China 15
Cinema 19
civil servants 11, 83
class
  action 62
  analysis 192
  boundaries 60, 90
  conflict 4
  consciousness 71
  dichotomy 191
  differentials 124, 126
  formation 62, 71, 74, 90
  hierarchy 6, 78
  inequality 122
  mobility 1–3, 6
  politics 192
  position 31, 90
  relations 4
  structure 60–1, 68, 73, 74–8, 89, 124, 191, 198
  system 61, 62
  theory 4
Class in a Capitalist Society 74
class, capitalist 17, 24, 189
  intermediate 58
  lieutenant 82–3, 86–9, 128–30, 138, 142, 153
  manual 5, 58, 60, 63, 64, 68, 70, 72, 74–6, 80
  middle 71, 74, 76, 80, 87–8, 116–17, 125, 127
  mew middle 4, 58, 78
  non-manual 5, 60, 63, 68, 71, 90, 106, 107, 161

208

Subject Index

class, capitalist – *continued*
  occupational 4
  professional/managerial 5, 80, 90, 122
  ruling 9, 79, 83, 87, 138
  semi-skilled 70
  service 62, 78, 81, 82
  skilled manual 63, 68
  unskilled 70
  upper 80, 87
  upper middle 58, 68, 73, 77, 123, 124, 128–32, 134, 138–43, 153, 154, 191, 192
  working 69, 71, 72, 74, 76, 80, 125, 127, 137
class I (upper middle class) 63, 64, 65, 66, 67, 69, 70, 72, 73, 75, 76, 101, 102, 103, 104, 105, 107, 112, 113, 114, 115, 116, 117, 123, 140, 152, 156, 157, 187, 195
class II (semi-professional and technicians) 64, 65, 66, 67, 68, 72, 73, 75, 76, 85, 86, 101, 102, 103, 104, 105, 106, 107, 112, 113, 114, 115, 116, 117, 120, 130, 133, 152, 156, 157, 195
class III (supervisors) 64, 65, 66, 68, 69, 72, 75, 76, 86, 101, 102, 103, 104, 105, 106, 107, 112, 113, 114, 115, 116, 120, 133, 152, 157, 158, 195
class IV (routine white collar) 64, 65, 66, 69, 72, 73, 75, 76, 101, 102, 103, 104, 105, 106, 107, 112, 113, 114, 115, 116, 133, 152, 157, 158, 195
class V (skilled manual) 63, 64, 65, 66, 68, 70, 72, 75, 76, 86, 133, 157, 158, 171, 195
class VI (semi-skilled manual) 63, 64, 65, 66, 67, 68, 72, 76, 86, 133, 157, 195
class VII (unskilled manual) 63, 64, 65, 66, 67, 72, 75, 76, 86, 133, 157, 182, 186, 195
clerks 47, 75, 82
closure 69, 78, 110, 122, 185, 192
  progressive closure 78, 89
clothing industry 25, 27, 198
Clyde 16
Clydebank 18, 24
coal industry 18, 19, 23, 111, 179
cohort 1, 93, 94, 101, 108, 110, 146, 149, 155–88

commerce 26, 27, 28, 198
communications industry 179, 198
competition, international 18
computer programmers 177, 194
construction industry 19, 113, 116, 198
consumer goods 18, 98
  demand 20
  control 82, 85
convergence thesis 5, 55, 57, 126
correlation 147
cosmetics industry 19
cotton industry 15, 18, 19
council housing 23
Courtaulds 22
credentialism 2, 5, 116, 122, 123, 126, 155, 190
  see also education, qualifications
crofter 194
crofts 12
CSE 134
culture, national 8, 9
Cumbernauld 24

defence *see* administration
degradation of labour 58, 180–1
demand 46, 93
density, population 12
  rural 12
  urban 12
department store 19
dependency theory 9
Depression 1, 19, 21, 22, 28, 31, 32, 50, 99, 116, 190, 194
deskilling 4, 46, 53, 93, 155, 171, 188
destinations, occupational 1, 2, 6, 60, 64, 144, 148, 154, 162
devolution 10
dilutees 178
directors 80, 82, 139
distribution industry 26, 27, 28, 54, 113, 173, 179, 198
doctors 35, 40, 41
domestic servants 53
drinks industry, 25, 27, 198
Dundee 12, 17, 24

economy, and change 42, 45, 90, 115, 118, 122, 123, 125
  market 35, 46
education 1, 11, 12, 16, 23, 29, 38, 47, 58, 83, 122–53, 169, 170, 190, 198
  Act 1944 125–6
  and the elite 138–43
  secondary 125, 131, 141

education – *continued*
  see also qualifications, credentialism, school
electric irons 19
  light 19
electrical engineering industry 98
electrical instrument manufacturing 198
electronics industry 24
elite 69, 78, 81, 138–43, 153, 192
  recruitment 80, 83, 87
emigration 30
employees 2, 38, 185, 186, 196
employers 38, 39, 40, 56, 140, 142, 186
employment 5, 18, 20, 21, 25, 35, 53, 81, 83, 98, 184, 186, 188, 189, 190
  status 63, 196
engineering industry 19, 20, 22, 24, 25, 26, 27, 28, 54, 198
engine, steam 16
engineers 35, 40, 41
England and Wales 2, 11, 12, 25, 26, 53, 54, 56, 60
England, regions of 19, 24, 25, 55
ESRC Data Archive 197
Exports 16, 10
Express, Daily 11

Fabianism 125, 126, 154
family 6, 63, 64, 69, 70, 71, 79, 84, 85, 95, 97, 122, 154, 187, 189
farm employees 50, 51, 56
farmers 42, 50, 67, 68, 82, 108
  'large' 51, 55, 56
  'small' 51, 56
fathers 19, 61, 63, 67, 68, 72, 84, 90, 93, 100, 101, 108, 124, 127, 158, 172
female *see* women
fertility, class differentials in 61
finance 198
fishing industry 11, 25, 26, 27, 108, 185
fluidity, social 89
  see also occupational fluidity
food industry 25, 27, 28, 98, 186, 198
Ford 22
foreman *see* supervisors
furniture industry 19

gender 6, 50
  see also women
GKN 22
Glasgow 12, 15, 16, 23, 197

glassware industry 186
Glenrothes 24
government, local 11
graduates, employment of 254
Grangemouth 24

HMSO 11, 198
  see also census
Highlands 12, 14, 15
health industry 29
higher grade exams 148
  see also qualifications
HND 148
  see also qualifications
Hope–Goldthorpe Scale 60, 94, 196
households, heads of 63
housing 18

ICI 22, 243
ILP 32
immobility 64, 65, 66, 97, 108, 144, 162
  see also mobility
Imperial Tobacco 22
income 79, 83, 172, 183
India 15, 17
industrialisation 4, 15, 17, 36, 58
industrialism, logic of 4, 40
industrial society 24
  change 30
  classification 29
  revolution 10, 16
  sectors 20, 29
  structures 55
  theories of 3–5, 9, 23, 35, 40, 45, 78, 111
  see also post-industrial society
industry 2, 29
  light manufacturing 112, 113, 114, 116, 117, 118, 119, 120, 144, 145, 149–51, 153, 165–9, 179, 180, 185
  old staples 18, 19, 21, 23, 29, 53, 54, 98, 111–14, 118, 119, 144, 145, 149, 150, 151, 165, 166, 167, 168, 169, 173, 179, 180, 185, 186, 187
  primary 22, 26, 50, 108, 165, 167–70, 179, 180, 185–7
  secondary 22, 110, 113, 151, 198
  service industry 5, 28, 29, 98, 109, 110, 146 (*see also* services)
  staple 116, 117, 198
  tertiary 111, 118, 198
  see also sectors *and named sectors of* industry

Subject Index

inflation 121
inheritance 67, 68, 79
innovations, technological 3
  see also technology
insurance industry 22
Internal combustion engine 19
investment, foreign 17, 25
Ireland 15
iron industry 16, 17, 18, 19, 23, 25, 27, 29
ITV 11

Jacobite rising 15
jobs 2, 26, 27, 28, 31, 33, 42, 55, 60, 68, 89
  title 63
  points 94, 98
  turnover 183, 185
  see also work, employment

knowledge 114, 123, 125, 128, 152, 185
industries 198

labour 3, 15, 18, 22, 32, 53, 67, 93, 111, 148, 171, 175, 178, 180, 181,189,190
  force 6, 18, 24, 25, 41, 46, 47, 50, 55, 56, 58, 91, 99, 108, 109, 177, 179, 182, 185, 191, 194
  craft 176
  division of 22
  process 4
  skilled 2
labourers 194
  manual 4
labour market 1, 2, 5, 6, 31, 53, 94, 95, 96, 97, 100, 107, 111, 155, 181, 182, 195
  dual 182, 184, 188
  internal 182, 186
  secondary 186
landowners 82
landward areas 196
lawyers 41
leather goods industry 19, 186
leisure industry 23
life-chances 25, 42, 100
life-styles 71
linen-making industry 15
LMS 23
LNER 23
log-linear analyses 198
Lowlands, Scottish 15

LSE 60, 124, 125, 126, 127, 154

manufacturing 5, 11, 20, 25, 27, 29, 93, 108, 110, 113, 146
  see also industry
market
  Empire 16,21
  local 29
  situation 68, 107, 113, 181
  see also labour market
mechanical engineering industry 198
metal trades and industry 21, 28. 53. 198
methodology 37, 88, 193-7
Midlands 19
migrants 32
migration 58
minimum school leaving age 60, 169, 170
mining industry 17, 21, 25, 276, 28, 108, 112
  see also coal
mobility
  absolute 62, 732, 74
  and class 3, 189-92 (*see also* class)
  counter 88, 156, 158, 171
  counter-balance theory of 127, 155-7, 169, 188
  and deskilling 122-53
  downward 58, 63-7, 71, 76, 85-7, 132, 134, 144, 171, 175, 190-1, 198
  gross 63, 159, 160, 162, 165-7
  inflow 1, 62, 70-2, 74, 80, 158-61, 165-6
  and labour markets 182-8
  long range 68, 74, 77, 83, 134, 190
  measures of 1, 6, 62
  occupational 2, 6, 7, 35, 60, 69-71
  outflow 159, 160, 166
  perfect 75, 147
  rates 7, 60-2, 78, 90-2, 101, 106, 109, 110, 114, 116, 120, 127, 136, 143, 171, 191, 192, 198
  relative 62
  short-range 89
  tables 61, 65, 69, 72, 111
  threshold 74-5, 89, 191
  trends 91-121
  upward 3, 6, 58, 60, 62, 64-6, 68, 81, 90, 95-103, 105-11, 114, 118, 120-1, 127, 134, 144, 152, 156, 165, 169, 171, 175, 190, 198
Mobility and Change in Modern Society xi

Mobility and Change in Modern Society
 – *continued*
  see also immobility, occupational change, recruitment
modernisation 5, 38, 118, 126
Monsanto 24
MPs 139

National Cash Register 24
National Health Service 23
national identity 9
nationalisation 23
nationalism 9
nation-state 12
new towns 23, 24
New Zealand 17
non-manual see class, work, workers
Nuffield (Oxford 1972) Mobility Study 94, 154
  see also Goldthorpe

occupational change 3, 4, 30, 45, 53–4, 67, 121
  and 'demand' 137
  and mobility 155, 194 (see also mobility)
  Marxist accounts of 3
occupational classifications 36, 60, 66, 75, 184, 193, 195–6
  distribution 66, 96, 106, 147
  fluidity 6, 7, 60–89, 191, 198
  hierarchy 82, 93, 155, 177, 191
  structure 3, 24, 29, 34, 35–59, 62, 70, 83, 126, 148
  transition 4, 5, 7, 35, 38–59, 61–3, 67, 90, 121, 126, 158, 181, 192, 194
occupations see work, jobs, employment
O-grades 134, 135
'O' levels 148
oil 186
OPCS 55, 94
'openness' 140
opportunity 96, 109, 121
opportunity structure 31
organisation 71, 82, 98, 114, 125, 187
  experts 35, 40, 41
  men 32
origin 2, 58, 60, 62, 64, 67, 68, 71, 72, 77, 80, 83, 90, 91, 92, 93, 103, 104, 106, 132, 134, 144, 154, 158, 159, 160, 162, 163, 164, 165, 166, 167, 168, 169
Orkney 196

Outer Isles 196
outflows 1, 72, 73, 75, 76, 80, 83, 133, 157, 159, 161
ownership 8, 36, 83, 84, 85, 108
  and control 22
  land 14
Oxford 31
  see also Nuffield Mobility Study

paper industry 198
participation rates 2
party political 12, 32
path analysis 136
periphery 9
planning 23
plastics industry 19
Plymouth Polytechnic xii
police and prisons 11
population 12, 13, 31, 36
positive percentage differences (PPDs) 20, 21, 28
post-industrial society 3, 114, 121, 192
  see also industrial society
power industry 3, 23, 81, 82, 83
power loom 15
Presbyterianism 11
press 19
primary industry see industry
printing industry 19, 98, 198
production 4, 8, 18, 22, 42, 46, 69, 98, 111, 112, 181
  factory 15
  primary 5
  productivity 22, 98
professional 2, 29, 35, 41, 54, 62, 63, 65, 73, 81, 82, 83, 85, 86, 112, 130, 140, 141, 190, 192, 195
professionalisation 125, 128, 143, 153
professions see under workers
profit 3, 4
proletarianisation 2, 4, 172
promotion 187
property 36, 67, 68, 84
proprietors 36, 84
public administration 8, 198
public health 11
public works 11
public services 12
public utilities 186

qualifications 5, 116, 122, 123, 124, 125, 126, 128, 131, 133, 134, 135, 136, 137, 143, 144, 146, 148, 151, 152, 153, 154, 169, 190

Subject Index

qualifications – *continued*
  see also education
qualified manpower 137, 148, 152, 190
quarrying industry 25, 27

recession 121
  see also Depression
recruitment 45, 67, 91, 92, 96, 101, 103, 106, 107, 114, 116, 120, 123, 143, 158, 165, 172, 173, 180, 190
  see also self-recruitment
Registrar-General 12
registration 11
religion 11
Research Centre for the Social Sciences xii
rivetter 193
Roman law 11

salesmen 75
sample 8, 36, 66, 74, 93, 108, 123, 124, 134, 135, 143, 144, 158, 172, 182, 196
school 125, 160
  comprehensive 128–30, 132
  grammar 129
  junior secondary 129, 130, 132
  private 128–30, 132
  public 138, 142
  secondary 129
  secondary modern 129
  selective 124, 128–30, 132
  teachers 47, 76, 82
  see also education
science 4
Scotland 2
  history of 7, 8–10, 14–34
  industrial base of 27
  as a unit of analysis 8–14, 33–4
  Lowlands 15
  West Central 16
Scotland: The Real Divide xii
Scottish (Aberdeen) Mobility Study xi, xii, 5, 36, 96, 124, 134, 142, 157, 172, 182, 183, 196, 198

Scottish Journal of Sociology xii, 11
Scottish Mental Survey 124
sectoral shift 5, 28, 176, 186, 188, 190
  see also sectors
sectors
  industrial 5, 50, 52, 101, 165
  primary 22, 26, 35, 50, 52, 107, 108, 165, 165–70, 179, 180, 185–7

quaternary 114
quinerary 114
  secondary 22, 52, 107–10, 113, 151, 198
  tertiary 35, 52, 107–11, 118, 150, 198
  see also industry
sectors of employment *see* employment
self-recruitment 68, 69, 73, 83, 84, 87, 88, 90, 141, 156
services 23
  basic 113, 114, 116, 117, 118, 119, 144, 145, 149, 150, 165, 166, 167, 168, 179, 180, 185, 198
  miscellaneous 26–8
  professional 26–7, 198
  new 114, 115, 117, 118, 119, 120, 144, 145, 146, 148, 149, 150, 151, 152, 153, 165, 166, 168, 169, 170, 180, 185, 187, 190
  scientific 198
share-owners 79
Shell 22, 24
Shetland 196
shift–share analysis 29, 53, 54
ship-building industry
  shipbuilding 16, 17, 18, 19, 21, 23, 25, 27, 28, 53, 112, 179. 198
shipping 19
Singer Sewing Machine Factory 18
Singer 24
SIP Occasional Papers xii
skills, occupation level 35, 40, 42
slump 18
  see also Depression
social change 35
social inequality 70
socialisation 71
Social Mobility in Britain 60, 127
Social Structure of Modern Scotland Project 10
social workers 82
socio-economic groups (SEGs) 20, 36, 37, 39, 40, 41, 42, 43, 44, 47, 48, 50, 51, 52, 53, 55, 56, 57, 66, 101, 171, 172, 193, 194
Sociological Review xii
sociologists 6, 11, 32, 42, 60, 78, 87, 122, 124
Sociology xi, 1, 8, 10, 61, 138
sons 19, 61, 62, 63, 67, 68, 69, 71, 73, 75, 84, 85, 86, 87, 88, 89, 90, 96, 101, 106, 108, 110, 112, 117, 120,

sons – *continued*
127, 158, 159, 160, 161, 163, 164, 165, 167, 169, 172, 187, 191, 192
South America 17
Special Areas Amendment Acts 23
SSRC xii
Standard Industrial Classification (SIC) 198
state 8, 23, 99, 114
steel industry 16, 17, 18, 23, 25, 27, 29, 112
see also iron
supervisors 42, 48, 49, 55, 56, 65, 68, 82, 112, 179, 193, 195, 196
supply 46, 93

taxation 11
technology 4, 15, 16, 17, 18, 19, 45, 58, 112, 179
and deskilling of labour 180, 189
technological innovation 29, 31, 54, 98, 100
television 11
textile industry 15, 18, 20, 21, 25, 27, 54, 112, 179, 186, 198
timber industry 198
time series 20, 35, 37, 53, 93, 98, 114, 117, 193
Timex 24
Titchfield 193
tobacco industry 15, 25, 27, 198
Toothill Report 24
tourism industry 14
trade, international 16, 17, 18
transport industry 11, 12, 20, 26, 27, 53, 54, 113, 173, 179, 198
trend analysis 93, 94
Turbine 18

unemployment 1, 2, 19, 23, 30, 58, 63, 67, 98, 121, 182, 183
Union of Crowns 14
University of Edinburgh 197
University of Essex 197
upgrading of skill levels 35, 37, 40
USA 24, 31, 32
utilities, public 198

vacuum cleaner 19
values 71, 76
vehicle manufacturing industry 98, 112, 198

Wales 10, 25
see also England and Wales
war 1, 2, 5, 16, 18, 19, 21, 22, 23, 30, 31, 32, 50, 86, 98, 99, 100, 106, 112, 113, 121, 143, 144, 161, 163, 170, 172, 175, 178, 189, 190
war effect 109, 116
wealth 79
welfare state/services 23, 100
white-southerner effect 33
women 1, 2, 5, 20, 38, 39, 40, 41, 43, 44, 46, 47, 48, 49, 50, 51, 52, 53, 66, 69, 99, 181, 182, 183, 194, 195, 196
woollen industry 15
work
manual work 38, 42–3, 63, 71, 73, 86, 91, 92, 117, 135, 145, 180
non-manual 2–4, 55, 61–4, 67, 74–5, 77, 91, 92, 96, 100–1, 108–9, 111, 114–16, 135, 146, 148, 151–2, 158–62, 165, 167–9, 179, 184, 188, 190
semi-skilled 45, 46, 57, 184
situation 181
skilled manual 45, 52, 56, 66, 68, 73, 184
unskilled manual 45–7, 56, 65, 71, 171, 184, 194
white collar 2, 3, 38, 42, 47–50, 56, 65, 68, 69
see also job, employment, labour, workers
workers 36, 37, 41, 42, 43, 44, 46, 47, 69, 73, 94, 171
agricultural 42, 57
highly skilled non-farm 38–41
intermediate non-farm 48–50
junior non-manual 55, 195
low skilled 41–7
manual 2, 30, 42, 47, 68, 69, 71, 110, 121, 158, 160–5, 191
non-manual 3, 72, 93, 112, 158, 163, 167–9
own account 48, 49, 56
personal service 42–5, 53, 56
professional, salaried 38–41, 55, 56, 76, 84
professionals, self-employed 41, 55, 84, 86
self-employed 65, 68, 116, 179, 195
semi-professional 38–41, 55, 56, 65, 68, 73, 82, 86, 112, 190, 195

workers – *continued*
  semi-skilled 43, 44, 56, 68, 71, 77, 171, 195
  skilled 70, 71, 195
  technical/technicians 68, 85, 112, 190, 195
  unskilled 35, 42–4, 57, 77, 195

  white-collar 22, 32, 82, 112, 172
    see also work, *and jobs by name*
workforce 49, 77
  see also labour force

yarns, artificial 19